D0193089

In
Search of
Burningbush

In
Search of
Burningbush

A STORY OF GOLF,

FRIENDSHIP,

AND THE

MEANING OF IRONS

Michael Konik

McGraw·Hill

New York   Chicago   San Francisco   Lisbon   London   Madrid   Mexico City
Milan   New Delhi   San Juan   Seoul   Singapore   Sydney   Toronto

1 2 3 4 5 6 7 8 9 0   AGM/AGM   3 2 1 0 9 8 7 6 5 4

ISBN 0-07-143521-2

Interior design by Steve Straus

McGraw-Hill books are available at special quantity discounts to use as premiums and sales promotions, or for use in corporate training programs. For more information, please write to the Director of Special Sales, Professional Publishing, McGraw-Hill, Two Penn Plaza, New York, NY 10121-2298. Or contact your local bookstore.

This book is printed on acid-free paper.

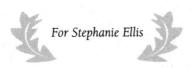

For Stephanie Ellis

Contents

1

Slowly but Surely

"Scyoose m' sar! A roond a gowf us s'posta tek thuree oohers! Nay sex!"

If I understand the shouting of this incensed Scottish fellow correctly—and there's always the outside chance I've completely mistaken his livid burr for an enthusiastically warm welcome—what he means to tell me is that a proper game of golf here in the land where the sport began is supposed to take only three hours to play. Not four. Not five. And for the love of Old Tom Morris, certainly not six!

"I'm very sorry," I say, truly very sorry. Like a guest in a stranger's home, I know two Americans playing golf in Scotland ought to be on their best behavior. Holding up the foursomes behind us hardly qualifies as impeccable manners, particularly since the club we are at, Royal Aberdeen, welcomes only a limited number of nonmember visitors. And besides, I myself know the frustration, the growing agony, of being stuck behind a group of sod-chunking snails weaned on the glacial pace of televised professional golf. Most Americans, emulating Tiger Woods and his highly sponsored colleagues, view a round of golf as an all-day affair best enjoyed at a crawl, as though the participants were coated with some sort of viscous fluid meant to lubricate their knees and elbows. The Scots, on the other hand, view a round of golf as a vigorous walk through the park—or along the sea, or upon the moors—best enjoyed as though the game were indeed a happy form of exercise, not merely an excuse to sit in a motorized cart and drink beer. The Scots leave slowness for their swings.

Gesturing with my head toward my companion, Don Naifeh, making his way toward the fourteenth tee, I tell the justifiably angry Scotsman that we're doing our best, but that, well, at a certain point there's only so fast Don can move.

The local fellow sighs hotly and harumphs back to his group on the thirteenth green.

"Like Casey Martin," I offer, weakly.

Fairly sprinting to the teeing ground of the fourteenth, the number one handicap hole, I join Don, who is breathing heavily and perspiring even more so.

"What was that all about?" he asks me.

"Just a little request that maybe we might pick up the pace a little," I say, as diplomatically as possible. "Don't worry about it. We'll just let them play through."

"Sure," Don says. "I could use a little rest, anyway."

We hit our tee shots. Don lays up with a 3 iron short of the ditch that gives the fourteenth, "Dyke," its name. I foolishly use my driver, partially in the hope I might fly my golf ball over all the trouble and leave myself a little wedge shot into the hard-as-an-industrial-diamond green. But the real reason for my poor club selection, I realize as we walk down the fairway, is to provide a physical release for the mild embarrassment I feel for holding up play at one of the oldest golf clubs (founded 1780!) on the planet. The satisfying crack of titanium meeting Surlyn somehow gives me the same kind of cathartic pleasure some patients derive from punching feather pillows in their weekly psychotherapy sessions.

Fueled by a growing frustration with my partner's unintentional breaches of etiquette—this will be the third group that has had to play through us today—I swing extra hard. Predictably, my drive flies forever and crooked somewhere over the dyke in the left rough. Don, on the other hand, huffing audibly, composes himself long enough to make his usual smooth pass at the ball, a replica of the simple rhythmic motion he makes every time he swings a golf club. Seventy yards short of where my wayward pellet has come to rest, Don plunks his tee shot into the short grass.

Trying vainly to banish thoughts of "The Tortoise and the Hare" metaphors from my mind, I march off into the high weeds.

I wave on the group behind us. While the charging foursome of Scotsmen play their tee shots, I stand in the rough looking backward toward the tee. Don, I notice with some chagrin, is *lying down* on the right side of the fairway, apparently staring at the flinty blue sky. Since each member of the quartet on the tee seems to have also selected a driver, he's probably not in any imminent danger of getting dinged. But I half suspect Don wouldn't mind if he were, anyway. He'd probably say if he was meant to go, it would be on a golf course where he'd like to perish.

One of the Scots hits short of the dyke into the left rough. Two of them fly directly into it. And the other clears it and rolls up near my black carry-bag.

I watch them stomping up the fairway, past my supine friend. Please, I pray, don't let this turn into something out of *Braveheart*. No war cries. No blood.

From my distant vantage, their brief conversation seems to contain nothing but the usual golf pleasantries—fine day, thanks very much, on you go, and so forth—though the Scotsmen don't seem particularly eager to stand around and chat with a sweaty American prone upon their ancient links.

While two of the gents fish their balls out of the dyke, a pernicious four-foot rut crossing the fairway, the big hitter approaches me and his ball. It's the same perturbed man from the previous green.

"Right here," I say, pointing toward his ball with as much sweetness and courtesy as a guy 3 down with five to play can muster.

The Scotsman waves at me. "Rrreight. Thunks."

I look into his blue eyes. "Again, sir," I say apologetically, "I regret the slow play."

"Nay, nay," he says, shaking his sandy-haired head. "I dinna knew aboot hum."

I could say more, and so could he. But we both understand.

The Scotsman plays on, and so do his companions, and I know as they trot off into the late afternoon light, Don Naifeh and I will likely never see them again. But I know they'll always remember the two American chaps they played through today, the talkative one with apologies at the ready and the odd fellow with a cigarette dangling from his mouth and a peculiar shoe on his right foot.

Royal Aberdeen—known locally as the Balgownie Links—is one of the most rugged golf courses in a country teeming with ruggedness. The elephantine sand dunes here, created by wind and sea, form natural amphitheaters through which the fairways scurry and off which the clever player is compelled to bounce all manner of golf shots. Royal Aberdeen is a cheering sight—and site—to anyone who cherishes primal golf, the kind of hardy challenge best enjoyed in an otherworldly landscape of mounds and craters, gullies and bluffs. Unless you are strong and fit, it is not, however, the kind of place one would choose for a pleasant afternoon stroll. Training for an Olympic steeplechase event, sure. But a little promenade along nicely manicured lawns? Not at Royal Aberdeen.

Which is why I'm mildly concerned. The caddies Don and I have requested haven't shown. (This happens occasionally—particularly, I've noticed over the years, when a big football match is on the telly.) Either we cancel our round—and there's less chance of that happening than of my breaking 70—or we sling our bags over our shoulders like the average Scotsman does and get ourselves (and our equipment) around the four-and-a-half-mile lunar loop.

"What do you think?" I ask Don, already knowing the answer.

"Oh, we're playing," he assures me. "If I can just get a—what do they call them here?"

"A trolley," I say.

"Yeah, a trolley. And a yardage book."

"Sure. No problem."

"Nah. No problem. I'll be fine, Michael," he says, in the way a first-time marathon runner tells himself there is no such thing as the mythical *wall*. "Really. No big deal."

Well, for my friend Don it is a big deal. But we're going to mutually pretend it isn't.

"Do you want to call off our bets?" I wonder.

"Hell, no!" Don says, scowling.

Though Don typically beats me like a drum in our $10 Nassau (with two-down automatic presses), I decide to even the playing field—if such a thing can be done on a place as rolling and bumpy as the Balgownie Links. Today I shall play without benefit of a yardage book. I figure I've got the physical advantage; I'll let him have the psychological advantage. With neither caddie nor "scoresaver," which Don consults religiously whether he has a caddie or not, I vow to play this round completely by eye, as have thousands of players before me on these storied grounds, which don't even bother with 150-yard stakes, not to mention labeled sprinkler heads. He'll have the discomfort of having to lug his own sticks up and down the giant dunes; I'll have the discomfort of not really knowing how far away my target is. This will be a classic matchup: Infirmity versus Insecurity.

The first tee at Royal Aberdeen Golf Club sits directly in front of a stately white clubhouse, whose large picture windows afford a splendid perspective of the Grampian coast. Members enjoying the otherwise unspoiled view of the North Sea may choose to inspect the swings of visiting hackers—or turn away in horror, if necessary. As I wave a few irons to warm up, I notice several of the club's older members looking toward me and Don, trying discreetly not to stare. It must be difficult. We are, admittedly, quite a sight: both wearing floppy bucket hats of the Gilligan-meets-Jim-Colbert variety; both toting identical Ping Mantis golf bags (at two pounds, four ounces, among the lightest made, and cleverly designed for the walking golfer); both playing Titleist DCI irons. Plus, I've got this all-red Tad Moore Skyrider driver, now a collector's item, that looks vaguely like a Porsche 911 painted with lurid nail polish. And Don—well, Don tends to draw looks no matter what color sticks he plays with.

Most clubs in Scotland don't have practice ranges of the American sort, where one blasts shag balls with impunity, certain that a sullen teenager driving a tractor and listening to Rage Against the Machine in his headphones will eventually sweep them all up and return them for future beatings. In Scotland, if you want to practice, you find an empty field and shag the balls yourself. On the one hand, this teaches you from an early age that golf is a game of accuracy, not distance. On the other hand, it discourages American visitors from littering empty Scottish fields with lost balls.

Before a round of golf, most Scots merely swing a few clubs, perform a few stretches, and fire away. (The really modern ones hit balls into a net.) They view the practice range as, well, a place to *practice*—unlike Americans, who often turn up at the range an hour before their scheduled tee time in hopes of locating their game somewhere amid the AstroTurf mats. On my first visit to Scotland, seven years prior, I found the dearth of practice ranges somewhat unsettling, just as some might find the dearth of lush green turf somewhat unsettling. Back then it was my stock excuse for not playing well the first few holes. But I've come to appreciate the simple wisdom of commencing a round of golf with the same swing you intend to end it with, and instead of hitting the expected dribblers, skullers, and poppers, I nowadays generally strike my opening tee-shots in Scotland with a purity I seem to lack back home.

Today, blessedly, is no different. Under the watchful eye of several Royal Aberdeen members who politely pretend not to look, I crush one down the left side of the first fairway, and it runs and runs on the baked brown turf. I resist the urge to tip my cap to the lads in the clubhouse and, instead, breathe in deeply the briny air, immensely glad to be just where I am.

Don steps to the tee. He studies his yardage book. He scans the hole, all 409 yards of it, through suddenly narrowed eyes. And he makes a few practice swings.

I peek toward the clubhouse. The members aren't even pretending not to look. *This* they want to see.

Don swings his driver just as he does his 3 iron or his 8 iron or his pitching wedge. Back-front. Tick-tock. In-out.

Where the clubhead speed comes from, I'm not smart enough to say. It doesn't look like he's trying. It doesn't look like he *could* try if he wanted to.

And yet . . .

There she goes: another one straight down the middle, with a gentle little draw on it, as graceful as the curl on a young lassie's forehead.

"Shot," I say robotically.

"Thanks," he replies, still staring at the ball, his hands frozen near his left ear and the slightest hint of a grin forming at the corners of his mouth.

We trundle down a gravel path toward the fairway below. Before we get to the forward tees I realize I'm already ten yards ahead of Don.

"You want me to carry something?" I suggest.

"No, no. I'm fine. I'm doing my best."

And he is. I can tell he is. From the moment Don steps onto a golf course until the time he departs, his eyes smolder with determination. Even when he's smiling he's determined.

Still, I can see this round is going to be a momentous struggle for Don Naifeh. After a couple of pars at the first—mine thanks to a standard 2-putt; Don's thanks to a beautifully judged chip-and-putt from the fringe—we ascend the second tee, where I can see that the twosome following us has already caught us.

"Let's let 'em through," Don says, wheezing slightly.

"Good idea," I reply, briefly considering if it's not too late to turn back and play on another day, when someone might carry Don's bag (and the virtual golf superstore contained therein) for him.

But before I can even suggest such an outrage, Don is directing my gaze toward the fairway. "Man, Michael," he says, shaking his head. "Will you look at this? I mean, this is just *made* for golf."

It is. It truly is—and I am so pleased to be sharing the vista with my favorite golf partner, even if it's under mildly unpleasant circumstances. For years, on each of my annual journeys to this magical world of roughly hewn playgrounds, I've imagined having Don standing by my side, seeing what I am seeing, feeling what stirs in my heart when a long fairway unfolds before me, leading to the sea. We both love the game of golf. Scotland, and in particular a place like Royal Aberdeen, which so insistently and eloquently highlights the game's charms, is, in our bedazzled eyes, something of a holy shrine. And today we are here accepting its blessed sacraments—beauty, ingenuity, honesty—standing upon the same closely mowed rectangle of ground. Together.

I drill another sweet drive down the right side of the fairway, probably long enough to get home in 2 on this 530-yard par-5. Don crushes his tee-shot beside mine. Together.

We both giggle involuntarily.

From a safe vantage in the rough, I watch the twosome behind us play through while Don fiddles with his trolley, which has a troubling tendency to fall over and disgorge its contents at least once per hole. Though they tee off from the forward markers, about twenty yards closer to the hole, their drives don't reach ours. Don and I say nothing, but our silent looks speak volumes. We're both secretly pleased, in an innocently smug way. A golf kind of way. There's a peculiarly male pleasure in being, um, longer than the other guys. Freudian explanations notwithstanding, almost every player I know takes some small delight in outhitting the competition, even if both guys, at the end of the day, are hopeless duffers. In Don's case, I imagine his length off the tee is especially cheering, mostly because no one expects him to be able to hit a golf ball out of his shadow.

The climb up the dunes to Royal Aberdeen's third tee is akin to something one might find in the Himalayas, albeit with less ice and more waist-high fescue. Don, a chain-smoker, is completely winded by the time he makes it to the top, where I am waiting, snapping scrapbook photos like a tourist at the Eiffel Tower. Though I hit first—getting my ball on the green 223 yards away thanks to a miraculous kick off an exceedingly friendly dune 15 yards to the right of the putting surface—Don is still wheezing as he puts his tee in the ground. He hits his iron shot weak and to the right, throws down his club in disgust, and proceeds to make an untidy bogey.

I can tell he's angry. Not at the golf course. Not at me. Not at the groups gaining ground behind us.

Don's angry because he's angry.

He's at the magnificent Royal Aberdeen, playing his favorite game with one of his favorite buddies. All should be right with the world, and with him. And he's angry that it's not.

He wants to be transported far from all his troubles, to a gentle place where the worries of real life fade away like a melting sunset. He wants golf to heal all his wounds. And it might, he suspects, if he will only let it. Right now, he's unable to let golf cast its salutary spell. And that's maybe more disappointing to him than hitting a poor tee-shot.

Still, Don's used to getting over (or around, or under) obstacles. He won't let himself beat himself for long.

Or, for that matter, me. His travails, both physical and mental, don't prevent him from shooting a stellar 1-over on the front nine, aided greatly by a putting touch on (and from just off) the greens that borders on immortal. I, on the other hand, suffering no handicaps other than my inexpert ability to guess distances and hit the ball in a direction resembling straight, do slightly worse. I'm 3 down to a man who, if you were to take an informal poll of the old boys in the clubhouse, might have been better off joining them for a wee nip at the bar while the stalwart lad with the funny red driver went off to lose golf balls on his own.

As we make the turn, both slightly stunned by the unrelenting goodness of the course we have just played, I can see that Don's wellness, his physical wellness, is deteriorating quickly. This is what I was frightened of. This is maybe why our journey together to the promised land has taken so long to have ever happened. Maybe we both knew this kind of hardship would inevitably befall him. And maybe neither of us ever wanted Don to feel anything but joy upon a golf course.

He's moving more slowly, taking more frequent breaks. Every other hole or so he requests a five-minute "breather," blissfully unaware of the ironic locution as he pauses to light another cigarette.

It's funny—well, actually it's weird and sort of spooky: I can see my friend Don Naifeh falling apart before my eyes, his body literally crumbling with each successive step. And yet his golf game—the quality of his shots and his ability to score—seems only to get better, as if the sport somehow sustains him through the visceral problem of getting himself and his accoutrements around the links. All the way in, "gettin' hoom" in the poetic local parlance, Don makes noises about having nothing left, of being totally exhausted, of being finished. Yet he still *scores*, the thieving bastard!

Royal Aberdeen is blanketed with gorse, that nefariously thorny plant species seemingly put on earth solely to consume misdirected golf balls. Everywhere you look: gorse. Doesn't matter where you miss your shot—left, right, long—the prickly stuff is waiting to devour your errors. The gorse on the Balgownie Links is a whale; we hackers are helpless plankton. Don, to my amazement—and gambler's chagrin—blithely swims past the intimidating threat like a jolly dolphin. Not every shot he hits is perfect. But even his prodigal balls never stray too far from home.

And when he's near the green, forget it. He 3-putts only once the entire round, and that occurs immediately after the disconcertment of having to let a third group play through. For a few fleeting moments the anger seizes him, confounding Don in a way, it seems, that wind and hillocks and physical frailty cannot. But then something else, something liberating and transporting, takes over.

After his putter hiccup on the fourteenth green, Don lights another cigarette. I gently propose that he might not be so winded, so utterly exhausted, if he eschewed the smokes. "That might even make you feel better than having a caddie," I joke.

"I've got no problem getting around without a caddie," he replies gravely. "But I don't think I could do it without the cigarettes."

"You're that addicted?" I ask, incredulous.

"Michael, they help dull the pain," Don tells me. "I know it seems sad to you. But these," he says, indicating the cigarettes, "are possibly the only way I can get myself from point A to point B without too much discomfort."

I shake my head, speechless.

"Well, now, at least I'm here," he says, chuckling. "Maybe without them I wouldn't even be able to come to Scotland." Don wipes the perspiration from his brow. "And you know I wouldn't miss this for anything."

Then he puts a peg in the ground and hits another gorgeous tee-shot. I'm 2 down now with four holes to play, and I know, I'm certain, I've got absolutely no shot of drawing even, despite Don's protestations of decrepitude.

As his body is allegedly getting worse, his legs weaker, and his hands shakier, Don finishes par, bogey, par, par.

As he holes his putt at the last, beside the same white clubhouse he commenced from nearly six hours earlier, Don Naifeh stands still for a moment and enjoys the silence. He's shot a 78.

Then he looks up at me and says, "I made it." He nods slowly and says hoarsely, "I made it."

"Yes, you did," I say, extending a congratulatory handshake.

"I didn't know if I could," he says, smiling, taking my hand.

"Yes you did," I say. "You knew."

He pulls his ball out of the cup and sighs heavily. "Yeah, I guess I did."

2

The First Time

Golf, I'm thinking when I see Don Naifeh limping toward the practice putting green at the Tournament Players Club (TPC) at The Canyons course in Las Vegas, is the last sport this poor fellow should be playing. Chess, maybe. Contract bridge. But not golf. The game of golf as I understand it requires flexibility and mobility, rhythm and grace, explosive power—attributes my pal Don sorely lacks. Fine motor skills and hand-eye coordination can often be cultivated, I realize, but usually on the condition that one is in possession of both a functional motor and a working hand.

Don, who is forty-five, suffers from osteogenesis imperfecta (known as OI, or "brittle-bone disease"), which puts him at risk of fractures from activities as putatively benign as shaking hands or walking down a flight of stairs. His pelvis is held together by several five-inch steel screws in his hips and a six-inch plate on his right femur, metallic reminders of a lifetime of broken ankles, cracked knees, shattered elbows, mangled hands, splintered fingers, and degenerating toes. His right leg is three inches shorter than his left. And his spine forms a slight hump.

The guy is a physical mess.

I feel foolish replying, "Well, partner, what's your handicap?" when he asks me how many strokes I'm going to give him on the front nine. Indeed, should I even be playing this guy for money? Sure, we're two grown men on a golf course (in Las Vegas no less). And he's the one who proposed playing for "a little something." But still. I'm financially well-off; he's not. I travel the world for an airline magazine and play the best golf courses on the planet; he usually digs up the sod at ratty municipal courses. I'm in training for the Los Angeles marathon; he's lucky to shuffle in and out of a golf cart without snapping a fibula.

Despite a natural predisposition to compassion and kindness instilled in me by a hippie mother who plastered my childhood home with "Make Love, Not War" posters, I have trained myself to feel as little pity as possible for those with physical disabilities—mostly because I know it's the last sentiment the object of my pity wishes I felt. (Friends in wheelchairs have told me how important it is to them to be treated like a "regular" person, albeit one who uses a chair to get around.) Yet that sense of egalitarianism, I tell myself, should not provide an easy excuse for taking this guy's hard-earned cash. On the other hand—well, we won't play for much, anyway. Besides, I rationalize, win or lose, it will be nice for Don to get to spend an afternoon on one of the PGA Tour's vaunted Players Club courses, where the game's best practitioners compete for millions of tournament dollars; where the fairways are manicured like a $1,000-a-fling call girl; where the greens are as fast and treacherous as a late-night crap table.

We've never before played together—and we probably never would have made today's date had Don's maniacal love of golf not radiated across the poker table we were sitting at a few nights earlier.

I was in town competing in the World Series of Poker, at Binion's Horseshoe in downtown Las Vegas. Don was there, too—dealing the cards, which is what he does for a living. He's a professional poker dealer.

Now, the general rule in casino poker games is that the dealers don't converse with the players, don't fraternize, don't do anything but distribute the cards and rake the pots. But Don couldn't help himself.

I was chatting with another player at the table, a guy nicknamed "Hollywood" (for reasons that have never been clear to me, since he is neither from Southern California nor a member of the entertainment industry), about some of our favorite European golf courses. Hollywood is seldom seen without a U.S. Open golf cap perched on his pate, and he likes to talk golf with anyone who will listen, no matter how tense the business at hand—in this case, high-limit poker. He and I were comparing notes about the traditional links courses that line Scotland's Ayrshire coast, places like Prestwick and Troon and Turnberry. It seems when two well-traveled golfers meet, whether over a pint of Guinness or a game of cards, the conversation takes on a subtle "can you top this?" tenor, as in "Oh, sure, I've been there. Nice track. But how about this other place? Now that's a golf course, my friend!" Hollywood and I, drunk with memories and growing ever more pompous, began dropping names as nonchalantly as a high roller doling out tips to the cocktail waitresses.

Gleneagles. Western Gailes. Barassie. The Postage Stamp. Yep. Been there. Played that. Good layout. Not bad. Cute little course. I bet. I raise. I fold. Yawn.

"You've played all those golf courses?" the dealer asked quietly.

I looked up at him. I'd seen the guy before—having competed in Las Vegas poker tournaments for nearly a decade, I'd seen *all* the career dealers before, hundreds of times. I even knew some of their names, particularly if they had a memorable style of shuffling the deck or pitching the cards. This guy, bald-headed except for a close-cropped dark fringe around his ears, looked familiar, though I hadn't recalled ever talking with him before. "Don," the name tag on his tuxedo shirt said, below his loosely knotted bow tie. Just "Don."

"Yeah, Don," I replied, "I have. Great place to play, Scotland. A fine place."

"I'll bet," he said, in an accent that sounded vaguely Texan to me. "St. Andrews? The Old Course? Have you played there?" he asked, attending to his dealer duties while he looked to me for an answer.

"I have," I said, shaking my head and sighing lightly. "Magic. Pure magic. I get chills thinking about it." Hollywood grunted his assent. "Mmm-hmm."

"Wow," Don said, his eyes widening. "Me, too! Chills."

"You've played there?" I asked, eager to relate to a fellow pilgrim the round of my life, the one where I shot 75 and had a putt at the last for even par on the back nine.

"Hell, no!" Don said, laughing heartily. "But I can imagine."

For the next thirty minutes, until another dealer came to take Don's place at our table, he and I talked golf. Well, to be more precise, *I* talked golf. Don mostly listened, occasionally asking questions and interjecting oaths of wonderment. You might have called his curiosity childlike, so wide-eyed and gleeful was he to hear of these far-off links, where the game of golf began. But a child could not have been so knowledgeable of terms like *stacked-sod bunkers* and *bump-and-run* and *knock-down shot*. The man clearly knew his golf, even if he had visited the grand shrines to the game only in his fantasies.

When the replacement dealer arrived, Don nodded toward me and said, "I sure have enjoyed talking with you. Love to chat some more some time if you're not busy."

"Sure," I said, watching him get up from our table and limp away.

As Don shuffled off, dragging one leg as though it weren't fully a part of him, Hollywood said, "I tell you what: That boy loves golf. Damn!"

I said nothing. But I knew what he meant.

"I'm a 7," I tell Don, extracting my official U.S. Golf Association (USGA) handicap card from my golf bag. "You?"

"Well, Michael, I'll be honest," Don says, shaking his head disconsolately. "These days? I'm probably an 8—but I'm playing more like a 12. Hell, the last two times I played, I'm lucky to break 85."

"So you want how many strokes?" I say, chuckling, prepared to give him anything he wants.

"Oh, I'll play you straight up," Don says, flashing a grin. "But I'm warning you, I might not give you much of a game."

"You sure? I'll give you a few on the front and we can adjust," I say.

"No, no, that's fine. Straight up. It's the only way I'm going to get better. I was down to a 4 some time ago, but I've really let my game deteriorate. I could use the challenge."

Having played several hundred matches against players with more money and ego than common sense, I am used to hearing otherwise trustworthy gentlemen assess their handicap with unwarranted optimism. Sandbaggers just flat-out lie. But the average American man, who would probably prefer to admit he is terrible in bed before copping to inadequacies on the golf course, tends to indiscriminately assign himself a lower handicap than his game deserves. Selective amnesia sets in—*oh, did I forget to count those two shots I hit out-of-bounds?; that two-footer I missed on fourteen, you gave me that one, didn't you?*—and a decent player mysteriously becomes a very good player. A very good one becomes great. And a great one is just *this far* from signing up for the Tour Q-school.

I know Don isn't a single-digit handicap. It's just not possible.

But I don't want to insult the guy; he's my guest, a late fill-in for a poker buddy of mine who likes to play for $100 a hole even though he's probably broken 100 twice in his life. Thanks to my golf journalist credentials, I had arranged a visit to this new TPC course prior to its official opening. When Mr. Poker canceled on short notice and I realized I had space for a playing partner, I fished Don Naifeh's number out of my wallet. He had given it to me a few nights previously, after our little Scotland reverie, and asked me to call any time I was looking for a game. So I did, and he accepted eagerly.

"The TPC, huh?" he had said, obviously excited. "What's the green fee over there, I wonder?"

"Don't worry, buddy, it's all taken care of," I assured him. "You're my guest."

He laughed quietly and said, "Well, that's awfully nice of you. Man! Thanks!"

And I could tell Don Naifeh wasn't just saying it. He meant it.

So here I am, one day later, standing on the practice putting green at the TPC at The Canyons golf course, confronted by the sight of a hunch-backed hacker insisting he wants to play me straight up.

"Whatever you want, Sport," I say. "We're just here to have fun, anyway."

"Hell, yeah," Don replies. "That's what it's all about. I mean, man, look at this," he says, gesturing around him. "It's gorgeous. The mountains. The sky. Where else you'd rather be, right?"

"Exactly."

"I'm just real glad to be here, Michael." He says my name like *Ma-kull*.

"Sure, out of the casino, away from the smoke. A little sunlight," I reply.

"I mean on a golf course," Don says, grinning like someone who has just unwrapped a surprise gift. "It just makes me . . . I don't know. *Happy*. Doesn't matter how I play. Doesn't matter the weather, or anything. Being here just makes me happy. You know what I mean?"

I reply, "Yeah, I think I do." But part of me thinks maybe I really don't.

How a man putts can tell you volumes about how he plays golf— if he's a weekend enthusiast or a Golf Channel–watching obsessive; a buy-the-latest-technology junkie or a late-night range rat; a slap-it-until-it's-in-the-hole joker or a *scorer*. I watch Don make a few practice putts on the TPC's emerald carpet: He's got a player's stroke, smooth and assured. His knobby hands, covered with hair, stay quiet as he makes a gently accelerating pendulum motion through the ball. The guy has clearly rolled the rock before.

"Man," he says, draining three eight-footers in a row, "this green is *nice*!" Don limps over to the now-filled cup to retrieve his balls. "You want to hit some on the range or just go get at it?"

"Whatever you'd like, Boss," I say, slamming a few practice putts well past the hole. "We're the only ones out here. No rush."

"Sweet!" Don says, surveying the waiting golf course. "I hear in Scotland they don't have driving ranges at most places. You gotta just bring your game to the first tee."

"True," I say, "which can be pretty intimidating when the first tee is directly beneath the clubhouse or in the middle of town."

"Oh, man!" Don says, shaking his head. "Talk about first-tee jitters."

"Oh, I've had them, I assure you," I tell him. "But on the other hand," I say, walking off the green, toward our cart, "there's nothing quite so sweet as standing on the first tee of some great course—

Carnoustie, St. Andrews, Dornoch—having all these grizzled Scotsmen sizing you up, looking at you like, I don't know, like you're a wee dram of whisky, and then just smokin' one down the middle. You just feel like, 'Yeah, I'm at the home of golf and I have some idea of how the game is played.'"

"Well, Michael, I'd love to experience that someday," Don says.

"Oh, you will," I say, trying to sound certain.

"Oh, I *know* I will," he says. "I've got to."

"I guess everyone who really loves golf has got to."

"Mmm," Don mumbles. "Yep." He's gone off somewhere far away—maybe to a land he knows intimately despite never having crossed the ocean.

As we drive to the practice range in our electric motor cart, I suppress the urge to tell Don about one of my favorite features of golf in the British Isles: it is a game played on foot. How wonderful, I want to tell him, to feel the good turf beneath your feet, the wind in your face, as you walk the land with a fine companion at your side. A salty caddie, a dear friend, the links spread before you—does golf get any sweeter?

I want to wax poetic about the purity of it all. But I glance at his misshapen limbs and say nothing.

When we arrive at the all-grass practice range, Don coos appreciatively. "No mats. Nice. And these balls!" he exclaims, inspecting the Titleist Professionals stacked into a tidy pyramid. "I'm tempted to stuff a few in my bag."

"You wouldn't be the first," I joke. "Well, actually, considering they haven't officially opened to the public yet, in this case you might."

I watch him as he prepares to hit the good-enough-to-steal range balls. Don looks like a golfer. He's clad in the standard-issue khakis-and-combed-cotton-collared-shirt outfit we've grown accustomed to seeing every Sunday afternoon on PGA Tour telecasts. His brimmed cap, which covers his head, round like a melon, says "Titleist" on it, as though he were a highly paid endorser of the company's balls and clubs. His white leather shoes, which would earn their owner immediate entry to a mental health facility were he to wear them any place other than a golf course, are freshly polished and newly shod with green-friendly alternative spikes. But the right shoe is unlike any I've ever seen in all my golfing travels: It has a platform sole four inches thick, an orthotic, custom-built design that allows Don's mismatched legs to work in something like harmony.

His bag looks like a golfer's bag, too. It contains good old Ping clubs—outfitted with superfat "arthritis" grips—and a flashy new-fangled putter and a titanium-headed driver with a graphite shaft. A small wire brush, for meticulously cleaning the grooves of Don's irons, hangs on the bag's side. So do commemorative bag tags—those trophies that say, "Yeah, I've been there," which most players accumulate like so many mounted antlers—from various courses in Arizona and California and Oklahoma. And there, beside the other tags, is a little white-and-green one with an illustration of what looks like a wizened old walking stick. It says, "The Shivas Irons Society."

Don notices me looking at this tag. "Michael," he says in his resonant drawl, rounded and smooth as a golf ball in your palm, "do you know about our group?"

"Yeah, I've heard of it," I say noncommittally. "*Golf in the Kingdom.* The hero of the book."

"That's right," Don says, smiling. "You're not a member, are you?"

"No," I say, wondering how I might gracefully change the subject. I have met other *Kingdom* freaks before, and they tend to exhibit the same evangelical zeal as the Jehovah's Witnesses who canvass my neighborhood, blithely ignoring the ferociously barking dogs and "No Soliciting!" signs meant to dissuade their entreaties. Shivas Irons, the book's Scottish yogi figure, plays golf with an ancient shillelagh and manages to do things like hit holes in one in the middle of the night (thanks not so much to physical skill but to transcendent mental powers). Shivas is the savior of this particular religion. He finds magic on a fictional links course called Burningbush. Zealots like Don quote him freely. Even more alarming, the "be the ball" woogie-woogie pronouncements they utter like so many parables from the Scriptures don't cause them even the slightest embarrassment. To them it is the gospel according to Michael Murphy. Frankly, the whole thing has often struck me as mildly pretentious and more than mildly silly, because no amount of spiritual enlightenment, I have found, will help cure a slice. But Don and his ilk consume the Shivas Irons epistemology with the same fervor that the average hacker buys into the latest metallurgical advancements in clubheads. It makes them feel better about a game that often makes its participants feel not very good at all.

"Well, it's a nice group of people," Don says, and mercifully leaves it at that.

I imagine a bunch of literary types weeping together as they attempt to identify the purple aura around their golf balls. "Sounds great."

"Yeah," Don replies, picking a ball off his pyramid with a pitching wedge, "that book taught me a lot. Man," he says, "Scotland . . ."

He lets the word hang in the desert air, like a talisman.

Scotland.

And then he hits the golf ball.

At first I think Don is making a practice swing, so effortless and unrushed is his motion. Unable to put much weight on his unstable right side, he takes the club back slowly, with a straight-but-not-rigid left arm. His head remains perfectly still as his shoulders rotate beneath his chin, which juts out slightly. His backswing stops just short of parallel, and without any discernible hitch or jerk his downswing begins, returning to the ball in the same easy, unhurried motion. His hands whip through the hitting area; the ball is gone; and he finishes in a perfect take-my-photo pose, facing his target with his interlocked fingers near his left ear.

"Wow," I hear myself whisper.

Don strikes another ball. This time I watch the orb sail into the air. It whistles slightly as it leaves the ground and gently turns from the right to the left, with the kind of pro-style draw most amateurs (including me) lust after.

Suddenly I feel nervous. Everything about Don Naifeh's golf swing is unlike mine. I *want* to have a classical swing built on Ben Hogan's "Five Lessons"; I *want* to resemble Ernie Els in my effortlessness; I *want* my golf swing to be akin to ballet with a stick. I would love that; I really would. But the truth is I have an ugly, too-fast, too-long, over-the-top, effortful golf swing that only gets worse when I try to hit the ball far. Oh, I can play. I can get the ball in the hole, and my short game often borders on satanic. But my swing? It is everything that Don's isn't. This gimpy fool standing beside me—the one with the fat grips and platform shoe and knobby hands—he's got one of the loveliest golf swings I've ever seen. And I'm suddenly jealous and confused and slightly frightened.

I watch him strike another ball. Where does the power come from? How does he make that damned Titleist Professional take off like a missile when there seems to be so little rocket fuel in the tank?

What I do know is this: Don Naifeh is someone who understands the mysteries of the golf swing. (He's probably one of those comical souls who lies in bed at night and reads about swing-plane and shoulder-hip ratios and everything else that reduces golf to an exercise in physics.) I know he will see my swing and instantly understand things about me that I may not want him to understand. I know he can't be bluffed.

Feeling his eyes on my back as I address the ball, I try mightily to keep my swing short and compact and efficient, though were I to see myself on videotape, I'm sure I would still resemble John Daly working himself into a corkscrew.

Don watches the ball sail off toward a flag 100 yards down the range. All he says is, "Man, you're strong."

I feel as if I've been found out.

I crush my first drive off the opening tee. It seems to fly forever in the hot dry air before turning gently to the right and tumbling back to earth. So much for style points, I'm thinking. There's no substitute for good ol' muscle power.

"Oh, nice shot, Michael," Don says, appreciatively. He chuckles and shakes his head. "Man!"

Then he makes one of his inscrutable "practice" swings and drives his ball about five yards past mine.

"Shot," I say, trying valiantly to hide my perturbation.

"Yeah, thanks. You know, I'm working on . . ." He tells me something or other about some sort of swing arcana involving elbow position or something, but I'm not listening. I'm seeing into the future, about four hours from now. And I'm seeing myself saying something gracious when I lose this golf match to Gimpy Don, a guy who shouldn't even be on a golf course in the first place—a guy who has no business whatsoever hitting a golf ball as far as I do (and in such an aesthetically pleasing fashion) and accomplishing it all with such good humor and grace. Damn.

We play the first nine holes almost even; Don leads the match 1 up. He strikes the ball better than I do, with a delicious low draw on most of his iron shots, but my short game is sharper than his. Strangely, every time I pull off a tricky little chip shot or a ticklish bunker blast or a clever pitch off a greenside mound, Don celebrates. He doesn't just say, "nice one." He doesn't simply nod his head and flash me a thumbs-up. He cheers, he relishes, he praises. "Man, Michael, that was a *golf* shot, beautiful," he'll say. "Just *beautiful*. That was fun to watch." I'm slightly unnerved by his enthusiasm, by his unrelenting sunny demeanor. What could this all mean? I sense some sort of conspiracy that is beyond my ken.

On the thirteenth, a visually arresting par-4 that plays over a cavernous arroyo, I make a long curling putt for an improbable par, a twenty-foot snake that finds the back of the cup. Don smiles widely and says, "I almost gave that one to you, Michael, before you putted it. I just knew you were gonna make it. I knew it. You had that look in your eyes, and I thought, 'Yes, sir, he's gonna drain this one. Good for him.' But I thought I'd let you putt it anyway, just so you could have the fun of seeing that baby take the ol' six-inch dive."

"Oh, come on," I say.

"No. Really. I knew it," he says, nodding. "Pretty spooky, I know."

No, I'm thinking what's spooky is how this hobbling train wreck of a man plays golf as though possessed by the ghosts of Jones and Hogan and Sarazen, with a classical elegance and calm I do not recognize in most of my peers, thirty-year-olds who have built their game on a foundation of virility and aggression. Don Naifeh makes few bad swings. When he does, what follows is not the expected string of juicy expletives and hail of clubs being thrown in disgust. The guy actually *smiles* after a poor shot, and following a moment of reflection he says something utterly annoying like, "Well, I learned something there."

I smirk outwardly. But inwardly I'm thinking I have never played golf with someone like Don Naifeh before.

Not once has he made mention of his "handicaps"—except for the moment he caught me staring at him limping from the putting green to the cart, and he said, "At least my dick works. Well, sometimes it does."

Not once has he urged me to feel sorry for him. Not once has he felt sorry for himself.

And no, despite whatever travails have afflicted his score upon the card, not once has he uttered a cross word during our happy round of golf.

A strange and unfamiliar sense of calm has enveloped me during our tour of the TPC course, a feeling of equanimity that I associate with long afternoons spent drinking wine and making love, not digging up sod on an emerald fairway. So therapeutic has Don's presence been to me that when our round ends I find I don't mind in the slightest that I have lost the match. I feel somehow honored to be digging dollars out of my pocket and handing them over to him with a sincerely said "well done." I don't know exactly what this hobbled, Shivas Irons–loving optimist has done to me today on the golf course, but I know I'm glad he has done it—whatever it is.

Don rests his hand on my shoulder as we leave the eighteenth green. "Michael," he says, looking me in my eyes, "I truly enjoyed it, and I hope we can do it again sometime."

"I do, too, Don," I say. I feel an impulse to make some sort of manly joke about getting my money back or giving him a good beating next time we tee it up. But instead I just tell him the truth.

"I would like that, Don," I tell him. "I would like that very much."

3

Gone but Not Forgotten

As soon as I was good enough to halfway enjoy spending a day on a golf course—which, in my late-blooming case, probably wasn't until my late twenties—I always wanted a friend to be there with me. Playing alone, I discovered, had its introspective charms, and teaming up with three strangers on the first tee often led to some memorable stories and hearty laughs. But golf, like most everything in life, I eventually learned, is best enjoyed in the company of some-one dear, someone who knows you fully, chaff and grain together.

I always wanted a best golf buddy.

For years my golf relationships often began passionately and ended badly. B, a Hollywood screenwriter, was smart and funny and immensely likable, the kind of golf partner that made afternoon death marches on Los Angeles Municipal Parks courses seem almost bearable. Whenever I had time for golf, B was the first person I called, because I thought of him not so much as a competitor but as a playmate. Then I caught him cheating, moving his ball with his foot in the rough. Twice. I was so heartbroken I didn't play for almost a month.

Then there was A. He was younger than I and way more talented with a wedge in his hands and marvelously inventive around the greens. His skill brought out my best game, for anything else was no match for A's wizardry. I liked his cockiness—he reminded me of my younger self—and he liked me for liking him. We met one afternoon by chance at a little nine-hole track in my neighborhood and enjoyed our round together so much we exchanged phone numbers, like two love-struck teenagers, and made a date for two days later, same time. Young A could have been a great golf buddy. But then, during our second round, mistaking me for Italian, he uttered a litany of anti-Semitic vitriol that made me realize I actually didn't like him much at all.

The most crushing of my golf buddy mishaps was the disintegration of my friendship with J, who, for nearly one year, met me on the local links at least once a week, and sometimes as many as thrice. J was tall and strong and could hit the ball with stunning power. He reminded me of Davis Love. Our matches typically hinged on the classic rivalry between immense length (J) versus scrambling short game (me), and, like most serious golf buddies, the money more or less got passed back and forth, so much so that we started keeping the same worn $20 bill at the ready in our golf bags. J was about a stroke or two better than I, and I liked that by playing only slightly better than I was typically capable of, I could bring this long-hitting Goliath down to my short and crooked level. My rounds with J were some of the happiest I've had; I felt, at last, that I really had a friend who loved the game as much as I loved it.

Then, as his knowledge of the game got deeper but his accomplishments did not, J began to throw clubs whenever he made a swing that was less than acceptable to him. Despite constant reminders that this behavior was not only ungentlemanly but dangerous—a hurled golf club can do unspeakable damage if it hits anything but turf—J persisted in his childish antics, which made golf with him increasingly less fun and more stressful. The day he whipped his 2 iron off a tree and the splintered shaft narrowly missed piercing my neck on the rebound was the last I saw of J for more than a year.

We reconciled nearly two years later after bumping into each other at our local club. He told me how bad he felt. I told him likewise. And he assured me he had thrown his last club. We started playing together again, and our matches were as good as ever, mainly because, in a poetic reversal, I hit it nearly as long as J did and his touch around the putting surfaces was just as sharp as mine. Still, our golf buddy relationship needed work. As with a couple trying to recover from a betrayal, old wounds are often difficult (if not impossible) to heal. Just as a once-cuckolded husband is constantly on the lookout for signs of his wife's infidelity, a golf buddy who's been disappointed once suspects he might suffer the loss of his favorite pal again. The relationship, it seems, can never be exactly what it once was, no matter how cheering the quality of golf.

Still, I try. I want that special golf buddy in my life, just as badly as I want a lover and a teacher and a friend. Golf is just *better* that way.

Maybe everything is. Except for the most misanthropic hermit, no one, I think, wants to be alone. Privacy and solitude are increasingly precious commodities to the overworked, overstimulated modern American, whose constant "connectivity" to the World Wide Web and officemates and popular culture is as much an umbilical cord as a restrictive tether. But having some quiet time to oneself and really being alone in the world are entirely different things. The former is a treat; the latter is purgatory.

How reassuring, how comforting to know that in one's quotidian duties and perambulations, he is not lost. How contenting, how inspiring to know that in one's lifelong ambitions and efforts, he is not struggling in a vacuum. How good it is to have a friend.

Human beings are social animals, and, therefore, like dogs and sea bass, inclined to gather in groups. Yet how many of us have at one time or another felt "alone in the crowd"? We are reminded at those moments how good it is to have a friend.

Failures seem unbearable sometimes without a sympathetic shoulder to weep upon, and triumphs seem somehow bland and denuded without an overjoyed face to gaze upon. Which is when we realize once more, yes, how good it is to have a friend.

On and off the golf course.

I am particularly appreciative of friends because, for much of my younger life, I didn't have many. Since this is a story about golf and not the script for a confessional daytime talk show—"Men with Sad Childhoods," on the next *Oprah*!—I will gloss over my often awkward youth, which, were it a nineteenth-century novel, might be entitled *Michael: The Misadventures of a Nerdy Lad*. It's not that I was the classic brainiac who got beat up and abused by the mean-spirited jocks. (In fact, I was a good athlete in elementary school, and pretty big for my age; no one bullied me.) It's that I was an intense weirdo who masked his shyness with braggadocio and who was shunned and disliked by most everyone.

My main problem—among several—was that I possessed a highly developed intellect and highly undeveloped social skills, a combustible combination that breeds obnoxiousness, eccentricity, and, eventually, profound introversion. My mother, a lifelong schoolteacher and lover of learning, taught me at home to read very early, when I was three, and by the time I arrived at first grade three years later, I was already well beyond my class's rudimentary spelling lessons and deep into the mystical world of books and stories, where dreams and adventures lived on a page, waiting expressly for my visits. This was in the early 1970s, before my suburban Milwaukee, Wisconsin, school district had programs for what are now known as "gifted" children, precocious boys and girls blessed with abnormally lofty intelligence quotients but cursed with a dearth of outlets for their abilities. Until I went away to college in New York City, most of my formal education seemed to me a waste of time. Despite hardly doing any homework and barely paying attention to the classes I bothered to attend, I scored well enough on final exams and standardized tests to float along in the top 10 percent of my school and earn National Merit Scholar honors—all of which served to reinforce the not entirely erroneous concept that succeeding in life meant doing well on tests, as opposed to actually learning anything.

Growing up in little Fox Point, Wisconsin, I was not popular. I was not well liked—not like Biff Loman and the classmates of mine whose charismatic behavior resembled his. Twain and Dickens and Stevenson and the imaginary worlds they created were my faithful pals. I was not someone who attracted many real friends.

The ones I had, though, were dear ones, and I cherished them like some kids coveted their baseball card collections.

My best and oldest friend—and maybe my only true one—was a towheaded neighbor boy named David Hanson, whose popularity and normality could be measured as an almost perfectly inverse ratio of mine. Dave was the kind of kid who, were he more venal and less scrupulous, could easily have ended up in national politics. He was what campaign consultants might call enormously "electable." Tall and blue-eyed, David was handsome in a non-threatening all-American WASP way, kind and courteous to everyone from the "brains" to the "burnouts," and a success at almost everything he tried, which was basically everything. Dave was the kind of young man fathers wished their daughters would date, athletic coaches wished would captain their teams, and quirky neighbor kids like me wished to call a friend.

We couldn't have been much more different: he was an Eagle Scout; I played in a punk rock band. Dave married his high school sweetheart and had three beautiful and brilliant children; I dated a menagerie of vixens you wouldn't want to bring home to Mom. Dave was a good and dedicated student; I was a sullen truant. He attracted admiration and approval; I seemed to repel it.

But we were like brothers.

Since the age of six, when we would play "Battling Tops" on his living room floor, construct Evel Knievel–inspired jumps in my driveway, or rehearse the patter for our amateur magic shows in someone's basement, Dave was my nearly constant playmate. Our houses were actually almost a block apart. But by running through my backyard, down a neighbor's driveway, and through "the Court" (a grassy patch of lawn in a cul-de-sac that to our children's eyes seemed as large and foreboding as Yankee Stadium), I could get to his house in fewer than forty-five seconds. Nearly thirty years later, I can hardly recall a weekday when, after school, Dave and I didn't meet at the Court—or the Creek (a trickling drainage viaduct perfect for conducting homemade-boat races and catching crayfish)—for some inventive diversion. On rainy days we made "crazy drinks" (mixing whatever inapposite fluids we could raid from the refrigerator) and played board games or Hot Wheels or toy soldiers. On every other day we exhausted ourselves outside with a variety of athletic challenges, playing not until there was a winner, because there almost never was one conclusively, but until my mom or dad rang "the bell" (literally a large cast-iron bell mounted on our house) to call their grimy son home to dinner.

The games we played generally mirrored the sport of the season, and they were comically specific. During football season we wouldn't merely toss around the ball; we would play "Punt Block," which involved one guy leaping at the other while the kicker tried to punt the pigskin over some distant line. The scoring system for this contest escapes my memory, but I do recall that the real victor seemed to be the boy who got fewer mouthfuls of leather. During baseball we wouldn't merely play pitch-and-catch; we created "Tag Out," an amalgam of cricket and war, which involved one guy running maniacally for home base while the other guy flung the hardball at an ill-defined target, whistling past the runner's head. And of course there were afternoons of H-O-R-S-E and one-on-one and makeshift boxing matches with clothesline ring ropes and squirt gun wars and cops-and-robbers (on bikes) and foot races and jumping contests and kick-the-can marathons.

And there was golf.

Well, sort of.

Mr. Vreeland, the Hanson family's neighbor, a gray and foreboding man, typically came home in the late afternoons, shortly before dinnertime. And as the sun started to set on our little patch of Wisconsin, Mr. Vreeland would chip golf balls in the Court. One after another, he hit his bag of balls to the same spot on the Court, in the same low parabola. Wiggle-*click*-watch. And do it again. When Dave and I and the other neighborhood rascals were using the thirty yards of turf between the semicircle of asphalt as our playing field, he never told us to move. Instead, Mr. Vreeland would shoot from his front yard across the street to a towering elm tree on the side of the Court—the same tree we used to delineate the end zone for our football games.

I was maybe nine or ten at the time, and I had never before seen someone hit golf balls. It looked ridiculously easy, yet I was utterly perplexed at how Mr. Vreeland actually made his dimpled white balls take off into the air like the miniature rockets Dave and I sometimes constructed. They just *did*.

I was also confused at the time as to why exactly Mr. Vreeland cared to do the same shot over and over, as if he were practicing free throws. And most vexing was this: why did he look so displeased after his nightly sessions? I thought golf was supposed to be fun.

Dave knew more about these things because his dad, Big Jack, a gregarious fellow with a famous grin and an even more legendary laugh, played the game. "Mr. V. is working on his 9 iron," Dave Hanson informed me. "I think you need it for short shots, when you're close to the green."

How golf was actually played was a mystery to me. I mean, I knew you tried to get your ball in a hole. But I wasn't aware of how exactly, or what made one guy good, like Bart Starr, my quarterback hero, or evil, like Dick Butkus, the villainous middle linebacker of the reviled Chicago Bears. The game seemed sort of like baseball, except the ball was smaller and didn't move until you hit it.

The one concept I firmly grasped was putting. Nearly two decades before the Tour 18 "tribute" concept became popular with golfers who will never get to play the original holes at Augusta National and Pine Valley, our little neighborhood putt-putt course originated the idea. (Well, probably not. But it was my first brush with Pebble Beach and Firestone Country Club in suburban Wisconsin.) The place was called Spring Green. It had, I recall, a ratty driving range and a tiny pro shop. But the main attraction was the "golf course," a not-to-scale replica of some of the most famous holes in golf, realized in concrete and all-weather green carpet. We kids would sometimes ride our bikes there and play for hours on the weekends, in preparation for the Majors—someone's birthday party.

Kevin Zarem, my Little League teammate, elementary school quarterback (I was his center), and frequent bowling companion, had one of his anniversary fetes there, with all sorts of magnificent prizes—like Wacky Pack stickers and glowing yo-yos—waiting to be claimed by the neighborhood's best putters. Neither Dave nor I won anything at Kevin's Spring Green Invitational, because both of us tended to frequently deposit our ball into many of the "water hazards," small birdbathlike indentations off the green "fairways," usually containing an inch or two of brownish rainwater. But we always thought guys like Kevin had an unfair advantage: they had their own putters!

Kevin, in fact, played golf. Or took lessons. Or something. (Actually, we learned later, he was coached by a guy named Steve, who Kevin nowadays likes to remind his golfing pals trained a whole generation of bright young Fox Point talents, including Mr. Kevin Zarem and the best athlete to ever come out of Fox Point, our classmate and current PGA Tour member Skip Kendall.) All we knew was that when Kevin Zarem stood on Spring Green's disheveled AstroTurf mats, he could really and truly hit the golf ball. He could make it fly. This inspired something like awe in my heart, because no matter how well I put my mighty .490 batting average baseball swing on the static orb, I couldn't make it do anything but feebly dribble into the grass, too short to be called a golf shot, too long to be able to retrieve it without being pelted by other players.

Since Kevin could actually play golf, he was allowed to sometimes accompany his mom on a *real* golf course, where they had grass instead of green carpet. Dave and I were made to understand that the difference between real golf, played on a 2,700-yard nine-hole monster, and the miniature version we knew was like the difference between spin-the-bottle escapades when Mom and Dad weren't looking and formal school dances under the watchful eye of proto-fascist chaperones. "You gotta try it sometime," Kevin urged his pals. "It's dy-no-mite!" (We were seventies kids, and we thought Jimmie "J. J." Walker was one of the funniest men on the planet.)

The news from our emissary on the links inspired David Hanson and me to canvass our neighborhood's weekly yard sales and cobble together some clubs and balls and all the other compulsory weaponry for an assault on Real Golf. I recall my mom having some old sticks that she probably used once or twice lying around in the basement, and I found a few old hickories in the attic, left behind by our home's previous owner. Dave, being a lefty, was granted the use of some of Big Jack's hand-me-downs. Never mind that we didn't own spiked shoes, or a sand wedge, or anything resembling a golf swing: We were playing!

I have little recollection of our first round, inflicted upon an innocent municipal course called Lincoln Park. All I know is that I managed to get exactly one ball off the ground that afternoon, a sixty-five-yard 7 iron shot that, to my amazement, went up and up before tumbling down somewhere near the green. I recall that one miraculous shot, the product of sheer randomness akin to a room-ful of monkeys dancing on a piano keyboard until one of them plays the overture to *Aida*, feeling splendid in my hands, solid and sweet and strangely pure. And I was hooked. I just didn't know then that the hook would take nearly twenty years to set in my heart.

Throughout our Fox Point youth, David, Kevin, and I played golf a few times every summer. Most of our free time was spent at the baseball diamond, where our squad, the White Sox, ruled the league. To our home-run-obsessed minds, golf was a pleasant enough diversion when there wasn't baseball practice, but it wasn't something you really paid attention to, unless you were one of those sniffy country club kids whose dad drove them to lessons three afternoons a week. We were scruffy, good-natured chops.

Now in our thirties, Dave and Kevin and I meet once a year, along with Mike Himmelfarb, another neighbor lad, for a weekend of golf and reminiscences. The winner of our two-day, match-play extravaganza earns custody of the Reunion Cup, a coveted travel-ing trophy inscribed with the dates and places of our annual get-togethers. Dave still can't play a lick. And Kevin still has had the most lessons. And, at the end of the day, golf is probably the least important reason we love our Cup weekends.

Back when our gang of hackers was growing up, Brown Deer Park, the course we eventually graduated to when we learned how to hit the golf ball out of our shadow, was merely the nearest place to fool around on the grass. I mean, we liked it fine. But it may as well have been some farmer's cow field. Back then you just showed up, asked the starter how long it would be before you could get out, and, usually within thirty minutes or so, you were on the first tee, playing your pals for grape sodas—despite the fact that anything under ten was considered a decent score. These days Brown Deer hosts the PGA Tour's Greater Milwaukee Open, is ranked as one of the better golf courses in America built before 1960, and is nearly impossible to get on unless you own an industrial-strength speed dialer programmed to work its magic at 12:01 A.M. Monday mornings.

Throughout my youth, I never got golf shoes or, for that matter, a swing. Kevin, who had both, eventually became too good for me to play with. We were pals and neighbors and playmates. But we weren't golf buddies.

Dave and I were best friends and neighbors and playmates. But since we never really mastered the game—OK, we never even had a lesson—we hardly devoted more than maybe a dozen hours a year to outings on the links. And thus, despite our closeness, we weren't golf buddies.

My mom and dad had clubs, but they didn't play. My younger brother, Eric, was far more interested in taking apart lawn mower engines and rigging his bedroom with enough switches and remote controls to fly a 747 than in mundane activities like individual sports. I didn't have an uncle or a neighbor or classmate who took me under his golfing wing.

For my whole life I never had a golf buddy.
Then I met Don Naifeh.

My first three trips to the British Isles were in the company of a woman I adored. This lassie—my ex-wife—did not play golf. Yet she seemed perfectly happy in Scotland, content to explore its myriad charms while her links-obsessed fool with balata on the brain spent most of his daylight hours depositing balls in the gorse. My memories of these journeys are almost all happy ones. I was young and in love and in Scotland.

The power of the place to heal broken hearts and set aglow contented ones should not be discounted. Scotland's misty hills and rugged coastlines have inspired romance for centuries. Writers as disparate as Robbie Burns and Walter Scott have sung the land's praises, and I concur with their lyrical odes, adding only that mere words can't adequately capture how lovely this verdant land of hills and sea truly is. Well, at least mine can't. I just know that every journey I've made to Scotland has been filled with profound joy.

Before my first visit, I read Michael Murphy's book, *Golf in the Kingdom*, thinking it would put me in the proper frame of mind to play where shepherds had once slapped around a rock while tending to their flocks. Much of the tale, steeped in metaphysics and Eastern philosophies, was far too confusing for my staunchly Western mind. But its essential message—that one could find one's center on the golf links—struck me as poetic and true. With Murphy's fantastical tale dancing through my newly expanded consciousness, I arrived in Scotland like a pilgrim at a holy shrine, expecting to be touched and transformed.

And I was. I was mesmerized.

At Gleneagles once, my wife and I found a tee marker on the Queen's course marked "Lover's Gait." We bent beside it and had our photo taken, beaming like newlyweds—which we almost were.

At Loch Ness once, my wife and I sat upon a bank, watching the sunset over the fabled waters. We picked a spot out on the opposite hillside and promised each other we would one day have a home there.

At Fort Augustus once, my wife and I met a dog at the boat lock, an impossibly cute mutt with brown eyes and white fur. We giggled at the thought we might one day have two mongrels just like him running around our house, responding to commands uttered with a thick burr.

Soaked in whisky, coated with deep-fried everything, and bathed in near–Arctic summer light, I was a happy lad. A terrifically happy lad.

And yet . . . whenever I stepped upon a golf course—and I did it at least once a day, and often twice—I felt lonely. In my wife I had a lover and a friend, a companion and a playmate, a temptress and a poet. But I didn't have a golf buddy.

Now, in the grand scheme of life, all those other fine things far outweigh the absence of a golf buddy. And I was thankful to be so blessed.

But I still longed for that rare friend who could share a day with me upon the salutary ground and experience with me the joy of seeing an ancient links unfolding before us, like a grand novel revealing its charms. I still wished for that rare friend who loved the game as passionately as I, and played it with as much enthusiasm, and felt as pleased to simply be out in the bracing air and warming sun, enjoying the challenges of an impossible game in the company of a pal whose very presence made the vicissitudes of a bad golf swing seem profoundly unimportant.

I wanted to be in Scotland with my best golf buddy.

Thanks to writing assignments from various travel magazines, I returned to bonnie Scotland annually, revisiting favorite haunts and discovering new ones. When I came back to America, laden with scorecards and commemorative pencils and snapshots, like a hunter returning from safari, I'd distribute the souvenir harvest among my pals. The Reunion Cup crew was always respectful and slightly befuddled, since none of them had actually heard of places like Cruden Bay or Brora, and since, in truth, none of them had any pressing plans to make a pilgrimage. The guys at my club in Los Angeles were likewise pleased but unimpressed. Scotland was too far off their radar to register. They would look at a photo of, say, the primordial dunes along the Ayrshire coast and grunt, "That's very nice," in the same way a sensitive mother might assess her teenaged son's disaster of a haircut.

Don Naifeh, on the other hand, was nearly breathless with glee to hear of my expeditions. I'd come back from the promised land with some small token of my journey—a ball marker, a cap—and he'd caress it like a sacred covenant. I'd tell him stories of the rounds I had played, and instead of doing the sensible thing and pointing out to me how boring it is to listen to an 86-shot play-by-play of an unexceptional effort on some distant links you've never seen and probably never will, he encouraged me. "Go on," "tell me more," "and then," Don would interject throughout my discursive narratives. It was like phone sex.

So palpable was his desire to be at the very places I described, to hit the shots I hit and be able to know forevermore that he had been there and felt it, I felt something akin to guilt each time I made another trip to Scotland and filled another notebook full of stories. Wasn't it unseemly—and wasn't it patently unfair—that I should visit this magnificent place again and again while Don never did? I felt like an overfed American transported to a famine-stricken part of Africa and confronted with the horror of starving children. Here I was tramping about on the Old Course and Carnoustie and all the rest, gleefully piling up the bogeys, while Don Naifeh, certified golf fanatic, had never—would never, it seemed—play even one hole in the Kingdom of Fife.

Yet my stories were not torture to Don. They were more like sweet lullabies that send a child off to a contented sleep, his head dancing with possibilities.

I never sensed jealousy or envy when I told my tales of golf in the Kingdom. I saw only wonderment in Don's eyes and fervent imaginations in his mind. And I knew he would—he should—be my golf buddy.

Just as a hot putter can "see" the invisible line on the green leading from his ball to the cup, I could envision us in Scotland. Forget the physical ailments. Forget the hardships. I knew in my heart Don Naifeh and I would play golf.

In Scotland.

Together.

4

Let's Go!

Every year, in May, the best poker players in the world congregate at Binion's Horseshoe, a dingy casino in downtown Las Vegas founded by an illiterate bootlegger with an ingenious talent for gambling. When he died a few years ago, Benny Binion, the patriarch of a warring clan of siblings (one of whom was murdered by his stripper girlfriend) left behind a simple formula for casino success: cheap food, fair odds, high limits. His offspring, whose exploits regularly produce tabloid fodder, failed to heed their dad's sage advice, and the Horseshoe is no longer the outlaw wonderland it once was.

It still, however, has one powerful thing going for it: the World Series of Poker. The winner of this event, the greatest spectacle in the otherwise depressing realm of hard-core gambling, receives $2 million. And each spring, players from every continent (except Antarctica, where the penguins have not yet mastered the art of making two pair) journey to Benny's place with wads of money in their pockets and dreams of triumph in their heads. Whether you are one of the 500 or so competitors or a keen observer hoping to get a glimpse of poker played at its highest level, a visit to the 'Shoe during the World Series of Poker is almost compulsory. Sort of like a devout Muslim's pilgrimage to Mecca. Or a devout hacker's to Scotland.

In May of 2000, Don Naifeh and I make our pilgrimage.

I am here to play; Don is here attempting to win a seat in one of the nightly "Super Satellite" tournaments, small buy-in events that award the winners a place in the big dance, similar to the long-odds Monday qualifying tournaments held in conjunction with most PGA Tour stops. He had done this before—we both had, actually, in 1999—and was hopeful of taking his place among the big shots, with a very real chance to turn a small investment into a life-changing prize. Since the time I first met Don Naifeh at the 1993 World Series of Poker, he had graduated from full-time poker dealer to poker room manager at an Indian casino in Phoenix, Arizona. Now he taught aspiring dealers the art of pitching cards and running a game, and his own poker skills had grown enormously. Instead of donning a tuxedo shirt and black bow tie, sitting mutely while others check, raise, and fold, Don is now a player himself, free to talk at the table about golf or any other subject dear to him.

Golf, of course, gets most of the airtime.

One morning, as a respite from the stale, cigarette-befouled air, I invite Don to join me for a round on the links. I tell him we'll have our usual fun. But this round, I suspect, will be a little different. This round we'll be playing in Scotland.

Well, sort of.

On January 15, 2000, I turn thirty-five.

It's supposedly a new millennium—though I'm of the school that believes January 1, 2001, deserves all the celebrating and journalistic hand-wringing over Where We've Come and Where We're Headed. Still, I do some accounting of my own.

The good: I am healthy. I have a magnificent dog and a delightful cat. I don't worry about money. My loved ones are well. I enjoy my work. The creations of Louis Armstrong and Mark Twain and Johann Sebastian Bach are extant in the world.

The bad: I'm single and still heartbroken from a long relationship that ended badly three months earlier. I mean, really heartbroken.

In conclusion: I am not a happy person.

I know I will be again soon, and I'm fairly certain it won't require the assistance of serotonin reuptake inhibitors or a conversion to an obscure religious cult to do the trick. Just time. Until then, though, I'm blue and low-down, like a Robert Johnson song about a no-good woman who done her man wrong.

Since, thankfully, I do not find comfort in alcohol or drugs—unless certain flavors of premium ice cream fall under that heading—I don't narcotize away my grief. Nor do I engage in reckless, potentially deadly activities—like leading the California Highway Patrol on a 120 mph tour of the Hollywood Freeway—simply because "nothing seems to matter." Nothing self-destructive.

But I *am* willing to take chances, to be impulsive, to find a way out of my sorrow. I'm willing to try.

A few weeks after my birthday, I get Don Naifeh on the phone.

"Howya doin', Michael?" he wonders.

"I'm all right," I lie. "Well, not really, but, well, you know . . . "

"Oh, yeah. I do," he says, chuckling softly.

"Hey, Don, I was looking at some of my scrapbooks the other night, looking back at some trips I made. You know, happy times, all that."

"Right."

"And I was thinking," I tell him, "don't you agree it's about time we went to Scotland?"

"Hell, I always think that!" Don replies.

"I'm serious. I mean, I think we should go. No more dreaming. We should just start living," I proclaim, probably more for my benefit than Don's. "This summer. Golf in Scotland. Me and you."

"Michael, you know I'd love to. I dream of it. I do. No, really, dreams and visions. I can see it. It's like scenes in my life that have already been written, and I'm supposed to act them out somehow."

Uh-oh. Here he goes. Off to a mystical realm that is way beyond my meager comprehension.

Don continues, "Ever since I started playing the game—I mean, way before I read *Kingdom* or anything—I felt I would have to be there one day. Because, in a way, I feel like part of me already lives there. Are you familiar with particle string theory?"

Oh, lord.

"Well, it wouldn't surprise me one bit to find myself playing golf in Scotland," Don declares. "I believe I'm *supposed* to be there."

"Great," I say. "So that means we're going?"

"I'm saying we will eventually. I'm sure of it."

I impress upon my pal the exigency of doing it *now*. The theme of my plea is that in the wake of my breakup I want to start living again. Not later. Now! "What are we waiting for?" I ask rhetorically.

"Well, the usual stuff," Don replies. "Jobs. Money. And . . ."

I cut him off. "I'll take care of all that. I'll get you over there. I'll take care of the golf. It won't cost you hardly anything."

"That's awfully generous, Michael," he says. "But what about? . . ." He let's his voice trail off. "You know I want to go. I just don't know if I *can*."

I've already thought of this. "I'll call and write, and we'll arrange a cart for you. They have them at some places for people with medical excuses. Not excuses—that's not what I meant," I say, feeling bad.

"I know what you mean," Don says, reassuringly.

"Anyway, you know what I mean. Now, some places I don't think have carts. But others do, and we could make arrangements and . . ."

Now Don interrupts me. "If I go, I'm not taking a cart."

"What do you mean?" I ask. Don *always* takes a cart. I've never seen him play without one.

"I mean I'm not going to Scotland and riding in a cart. I wouldn't desecrate the tradition of the game," Don says.

"Oh, come on. You're not going to go because you might need a cart?"

"If I had to ride a cart I'd rather not go. Michael, you say yourself how much you enjoy walking a great golf course. You should understand: that's how they do it there. Like Shivas says," Don recalls, quoting *Golf in the Kingdom* and attempting something akin to a Scottish accent that comes out sounding vaguely Pakistani, "'It's a game that's made for walkin',' that's all."

"True," I say.

"I'll go. I'm just going to have to walk."

"Good!" I reply enthusiastically, utterly perplexed as to how exactly Don intends to accomplish this feat. "Good for you!"

"I'm going to play golf in Scotland. And I'm going to walk," he promises. "I may have to take a few days off here and there, and, I don't know, I may discover I can't handle it more than once or twice. But I know I can do it at least once. That's not even a question in my mind."

"Sure," I say, unconvinced.

"There's only one question," Don says.

"What's that?"

"How many strokes you givin' me?"

In April of 2000 I go to Ireland to write a golf story for a travel magazine. My previous journey there, the summer before, was with my lover, shortly before we parted.

I walk the seaside dunes in a cloudy fugue state, sincerely glad to be playing golf in this gracious land but intensely lonely for my companion and my friend. The garrulous Irishmen—is there another type?—make me laugh, and the sheer wonderfulness of the Irish links makes me smile. But no matter how many pints of Guinness I drink nor how many deep-fried comestibles I ingest, the sting of being here on the right side of the Atlantic alone, terribly alone, has me flummoxed.

I want golf to rescue me. I want it to make all my pains go away. And it keeps telling me I'll have to manage that trick myself.

One Dublin afternoon, while playing at The Island Club at Donabate, I make a resolution. Passing through otherworldly mounds the size of a small New York City apartment building, I stop and sigh. And I vow to myself that the next time I trod upon one of the world's great golf courses, I shall do it with Don Naifeh.

Discussion of this matter has ended. It's time to live.

When I meet up with Don in Las Vegas, at the World Series of Poker, he's got a fancy new driver and a fancy new putter and a fancy new knee brace. Every few weeks, it seems, he's straining some tendon or cracking some bone or scraping some cartilage—just as he's been doing for the past forty-four years.

"You sure you can play?" I ask rhetorically, knowing about the only thing that will keep Don Naifeh from a round of golf is a nuclear holocaust.

"Hell, yeah," he says. "Today I'm going to finally get a crack at the Road Hole. And the Postage Stamp. And . . . what else?"

We're preparing for our Scotland sojourn with a visit to a peculiar, only-in-Vegas creation called the Royal Links. Just as the Strip is lined with a faux volcano and Arthurian castle and Eiffel Tower, the golf layout at this club, 8,000 miles from Edinburgh in the middle of the Mojave desert, is modeled after great holes from the British Open rota past and present. In one surreal, 100-degree Fahrenheit day, you can visit St. Andrews, Carnoustie, Royal Troon, Muirfield, and a bevy of other revered tracks without ever being more than ten minutes away from the nearest slot machine.

The greatest feature of Royal Links—aside from its ersatz Scottish castle clubhouse, which contains a remarkably authentic realization of a British pub—is that every foursome that goes back through golf history here must do so with a caddie. They wear white overalls with the names of past Open champions emblazoned across their back, and in addition to doing all the usual things caddies do—tend to clubs and clean balls and repair divots and rake bunkers—the caddies at Royal Links sometimes impart anecdotal morsels about the hole their man is playing, recalling how Seve got up and down from "this" spot, how Sarazen made an ace "here" at age sixty-four, how Jack reached "that" green in two. Caddies enrich the golf experience. (And they carry the bag.)

I love caddies, and I use them whenever they're available, regardless of cost. (I'd much rather pay $60 for the human services of a caddie than $20 for the inanimate grumblings of a motor buggy.) Since Don has not walked a golf course in decades, he doesn't generally employ caddies. But today, at Royal Links, although he avails himself of a cart, thanks to course policy he's basically compelled to hook up with a club-cleaning Sancho Panza, who will encourage his knight no matter how fanciful his delusions.

As we travel through history, imagining ourselves playing for the Claret Jug, I am gripped with apprehension. I watch Don interact with his caddie, a sweet guy named Jeff, and I fear my dreams of playing golf in Scotland with my friend are in serious jeopardy. There is no way we'll ever finish a round over there.

Don so loves the game of golf—and so loves having someone to talk about it with—that he stands over every shot, no matter how straightforward, and conducts a lengthy inquisition with his indulgent caddie. The wind, the ground conditions, the trajectory of the shot—you'd think he really *was* marching up the eighteenth at Royal Lytham, needing to make par to bring golf's oldest trophy back to the Phoenix suburbs. Don launches these Socratic investigations not because he needs a rest or doesn't understand where his target is or has any other good reason for taking three minutes to play a shot. He does it because he just loves talking about golf way too much.

Since I like to play with alacrity, his newly discovered fondness for preshot caddie dissertations is mildly irksome. But I find it endearing, too. My pal Don, I realize at Royal Links, is going to be in heaven when he hooks up with the loquacious loopers of Scotland. The only trouble is, the sun might set while Don and a fellow named Angus are jabbering on about the merits of bringing it in low versus high.

Walking off the eighteenth at Royal Links—a re-creation of the fourteenth at the Old Course, with the menacing Hell Bunker— Don turns to me and says, "Two more months and we'll be playing the real thing!"

"Yes, we will, pally boy," I chirp. And I almost believe it.

On the weekend of the 2000 U.S. Open, I fly to Phoenix to visit my brother and his family and to sneak in a round of golf with my favorite partner. Never mind that it's more than 100 degrees in the shade, Don wants me to join him for a tour of his home course, a municipal track called Papago, which, he swears, may be the best value in America. Though I've offered to get us booked at one of the finely manicured "daily fee" layouts for which Scottsdale has grown famous, Don insists we'll have more fun on his semiratty Parks Department course. "It's the real thing," he tells me. And I think I know what he means. No pewter bag tags, no freshly scrubbed bag boys scurrying to unload and polish your clubs, no fetching "cart girls" to sell you $4 sodas—just a good, honest place to hit some golf shots.

Papago is the kind of place where the local chops wear jeans and play shirtless and hit the beer cooler more frequently than the fairway. "Welcome to Ponky West!" Don says, beaming. He's referring to the fictional Ponkaquogue Municipal, generally acknowledged as the single worst golf course in America, from Rick Reilly's *Missing Links*, probably the greatest golf book ever written. Don and I love Reilly's tale of golf and love, set on the kind of trash heap of a golf course that tends to attract either the completely inept or the completely smitten. Like its fictional forebear, Papago is not an impeccably maintained facility replete with greens like emerald carpets and rich folks wearing nicely pressed khakis.

No, Papago is the kind of place where on the Sunday of the U.S. Open, when Tiger Woods is rewriting history at Pebble Beach and any sane person would be sipping a cool drink in air-conditioned comfort, golf-mad fools like Don Naifeh are out in the desert chasing balata. Sure, we sneak the occasional peak at NBC's coverage of Tiger's rout on a battery-powered portable television Don has smuggled into our cart. But the bulk of our day is spent discussing our upcoming pilgrimage. (And ogling a couple of delicious female chop-ettes, touring Papago in halter tops.)

On the tenth tee, while we wait for a couple of guys in tennis shoes and cowboy hats to hit their 120-yard drives, Don hands me a piece of paper with his handwriting on it. "I've been doing some thinking, Michael," he announces. "After some research and asking around and stuff, I drew up this list of places I feel I've got to visit. If this turns out to be my one and only trip to the Kingdom, these are the places I'd really like to see."

I unfold Don's list, scrawled on a piece of notebook paper torn along the holes on the left side. It says:

> For the most part, it doesn't matter when we play these courses, or even if we play all these particular courses. When we arrive I would like to find a course, preferably the Old Course, and just take a WALK. A course walk. Naturally, I want to play the Old Course, Carnoustie, and Royal Troon, because of the Open history. I'd also like to play Crail, Mull, Traigh, Lundin Links, Leven, Golf Club at Elie, and Ladybank—all in search of Burningbush. And if possible, Gleneagles, Royal Aberdeen, Royal Dornoch, Nairn. August 5 would be perfect to play Troon.
>
> These are some of the courses that have been brought to my awareness. I don't think I can be disappointed in any schedule changes. I want to connect to Scotland, golf, and the spirit of our pilgrimage.
>
> More to come, but go with this.
>
> Is Muirfield a must?

Many of the names are familiar to me; some I don't recognize. But I'm intrigued by Don's "dream list." I wonder what inspired him to select this eclectic group of courses. And why August 5 for Royal Troon?

"It's all about connections," Don explains. "That's why I play this game: connections. See, on August 5, I've got a good friend here in Scottsdale who's going to be playing Troon North, here at home, and I thought it would be pretty neat for both of us to be playing two different Troons at the same time. Maybe if the timing worked out we might both have a ball in the air at the same time, me in Scotland and him in Scottsdale."

I grin. "I see."

"Connections, Michael. That's what it's all about. All the courses in Fife—Leven and Elie and such—well, they're maybe somehow connected to Burningbush. Some of the guys in the Society,"—the Shivas Irons Society, he means—"have played there and had very memorable experiences. So, see, I'm looking to weave it all together."

"Connections. Got it." I say it before I believe it. I think I know what he means, but for my rational mind, the associations are tenuous.

"Nothing too mystical about that, is there?" Don asks.

We watch one of the chops take an eighteen-inch gash out of the tee with his 3 wood.

"No," I say, thinking about how we all find our place in the world, "Not at all."

Every time I play or think or write about golf, I start looking for connections. As I construct a potential itinerary for Don's maiden voyage to Scotland, I look for connections. Golf, life, the past, the present—I search for connections. And when I can't find them—or see them—I begin to suspect that a lot of my pal Don's pronouncements on mysticism and the unexplainable are possibly a bunch of highly refined hoo-ha.

But I'm not entirely opposed to the concept.

A few weeks after our Papago outing, I recount for Don a magical round I had going at my home course, Griffith Park, in Los Angeles. It was my first legitimate opportunity to shoot under par for eighteen holes on a golf course that didn't have windmills and dinosaurs on it. After fifteen holes I was 1 under, with three par-4s remaining. The sixteenth on the Wilson layout is probably the toughest hole on the course, a 440-yard gentle dogleg right that requires two mighty pokes to reach an elevated green in regulation. Par is a good—and rare—score here. The seventeenth plays downhill from a towering elevated tee, and if you can clear a fairway bunker 230 yards out, you're left with a short-iron approach to a generous green with a lot of back-to-front slope. It's your best chance for birdie of the closing trio. The eighteenth, about 400 yards, plays uphill to a well-protected green with out-of-bounds behind and around it. Par is not a rare score here.

"I'm thinking I go par-par-par, and I shoot 71. Or even bogey-birdie-par. And even if I go bogey-par-par, I'm still even for the day, which is my best score at Wilson by four strokes. Remember, we're talkin' a 7,000-yard course," I remind Don.

"Right," he says, imagining the scene. "You're thinking if you just play your usual game you've got a decent shot at 1 under. And who knows? You're obviously playing well enough that something wonderful could happen."

"Oh, yeah. I'm making everything I look at. One-putting everything."

"So, you walk off fifteen, . . ." Don says eagerly.

"So I walk off fifteen and get on the sixteenth tee. Gotta get a good drive here or it's a 3-shot hole."

"Right," Don says.

"Well, the key part, I forgot to tell you, is that I'm playing with Hal—you know Hal."

"Uh-huh."

"And we're a twosome. But on fifteen this other twosome comes up to the tee just after we're done hitting our tee-shots and asks if they can join us, make it a foursome. So we say, 'sure, of course,' and they hit their shots. Now, I'm watching them, and I've gotta tell you—it's a husband and wife—I gotta tell you, they play pretty slow. You know, lots of practice swings, lots of standing over the ball doing nothing."

"Paralysis through analysis," Don says, chortling.

"Right. But I'm sort of in the zone, or whatever, and I don't let it bother me."

"No, you're focused."

"I'm very centered. Very comfortable with my swing, like I have a pretty good idea where every shot is going," I joke.

"What's that like?" Don says, laughing.

"So, new players in the group, nice young couple, a little slow. No big deal. We all walk over to the sixteenth. Now, just as I'm getting set up for a little power fade around the corner, the foursome that had been following the other twosome, the couple, comes roaring up to the fifteenth green in their carts."

"In your backswing?" Don wonders.

"No, I haven't pulled the trigger yet. I'm still in my preshot routine."

"Oh. And then?"

"And then, this guy from the other foursome, the one that was behind the twosome that joined us, he comes marching over to our tee yelling like a mugging victim. Seems he's pissed at the young couple—the ones that just joined up with us—for holding up play, or not letting the foursome play through, or something like that related to courtesy. I mean yelling! And swearing like a truck driver," I report to Don.

"That's a little disconcerting," Don says.

"*That* I can handle. But this yelling and screaming between this guy and the woman who joined us almost erupts into a fistfight!"

"Between the girl and the yeller?"

"Yeah! They had to be separated before someone threw a punch. I mean, I really thought there were going to be blows. It was ugly, Don," I say. "And, as you can probably imagine, very upsetting."

"I'll bet."

"I'm having one of the best rounds of my life, feeling very centered and composed and all that, and then a fucking bar fight erupts on the sixteenth tee. Anyway, I probably don't have to tell you what happens next, but, of course, I will."

Don laughs. "Uh-oh!"

"I'm so shaken and disturbed by what I just witnessed, I promptly deposit my tee-shot into heavy rough on the left side and make a double bogey. I haven't missed a damn fairway all day, then, boom: jail. Double bogey. So now I'm 1 over. And, of course, I par the last two and fail to break par for the millionth time in my life. Don't get me wrong, 1 over is a great score for me, one of my best. But I had a very legitimate shot at going under! Then? This totally unforeseen and unnecessary brawl. Between two strangers I hadn't even seen up until five minutes previous! Outta nowhere. Like angels of death sent on some sort of cruel mission."

Don laughs softly. All he says is, "And you don't think this is a mystical game?"

When Don learns that his employers will let him out of the card room for two weeks (and only two weeks), I work in earnest to construct an itinerary that incorporates as much of Don's dream list as possible, while still leaving a day or two for some personal favorites that I know, I just *know*, he'll adore. These are courses where I recall in years past saying to myself as I walked the links, "I wish Don could be here now." And now, it seems, he will be.

We block out the first two weeks in August for our pilgrimage. Never has a fortnight seemed like such a ridiculously short amount of time.

Given the almost infinite number of golf courses we'd like to see together and the finite time we have to visit, I schedule one round per day. Normally, were I on my own, I would play thirty-six, with the possibility of taking advantage of Scotland's eighteen hours of summer sunlight and squeezing in fifty-four. But that can't happen with Don.

In fact, even one round per day, I realize, might be absurdly ambitious.

The truth is, I'm worried about him. What if he can't even make it through nine holes, let alone eighteen a day for two weeks? What if he snaps a femur the day after he steps off the plane? What if he just can't do it, no matter how much joy fills his heart? Then what? I envision Don sitting morosely in some Scottish clubhouse, peering longingly out at the links, urging his pal to go on without him while he wipes a tear of disappointment from his cheek.

Maybe this whole golf-in-Scotland fantasy is all a very nice but terribly bad idea after all. Sweet thought, but not possible. Potentially more damaging than uplifting. Depressing.

"Donnie," I confess to him, "I'm concerned."

After I pour out my apprehensions, Don replies calmly, "Worst comes to worse, I'll use a crutch, or a staff, or, what the hell, a shillelagh."

Knowing my friend Don Naifeh, I reckon he would quite like using a shillelagh, tramping around the course like his beloved Shivas Irons. If the thing had the right loft on it, he might even like to *play* with it.

"Don't worry, Michael," he says. "I'll get around. Might take me a while. But there's no way I go to Scotland and not play golf. Zero chance of that."

"And one round a day?"

"Well, if I have to sit out once in a while, get some recovery time, I'll do it. I won't *like* it," Don says, laughing. "But I've been dealing with my body for a pretty long time now. I know how to take care of it."

Relieved, if not entirely convinced, I urge Don to consult members of his "cult" (my affectionate nickname for the Shivas Irons Society) to get their insights on courses that an orthodox devotee like Mr. Naifeh should not miss. I figure that there must be some holy shrines on the Shivas trail that a *Kingdom* pilgrim would find exhilarating, similar to the inns and caves and riversides around Jerusalem and Nazareth that any self-respecting Pentecostal feels compelled to visit in the flesh.

"I don't know if Burningbush actually exists," Don tells me. "But if it does, I know I'll find it. Because, in a weird way—and I know you're gonna laugh, Michael—I've been looking for it most of my life."

I try not to laugh. "Even though you've never been to Scotland," I say flatly.

"Even though I've never been to Scotland," Don says.

For a brief, incandescent moment, I suddenly feel as though getting Don Naifeh to walk one round of golf a day in Scotland is going to be the least of my worries.

When I'm not writing letters to the secretaries of various esteemed Scottish golf clubs, requesting tee times for two enthusiastic duffers (one of whom has a medical condition that makes the presence of a caddie vitally important), I'm on the phone with Don, keeping him posted as the details of our trip come into focus. His naked enthusiasm for the results of my labors makes the logistical night-mare of booking flights, tee times, car rental, accommodations, and professional loopers seem almost easy, not a task worthy of a Her-culean air-traffic controller.

"I guess it's really going to happen," Don says one day. "Maybe I haven't allowed myself to really believe that it's true."

"Oh, it is," I assure him. "And you'd better get everything you need assembled sooner than later. Clothes, equipment, any medical necessities. You've got your passport, right? And make sure you bring plenty of warm clothes. But, on the other hand, don't bring too much, because, like the Buddhists say, material things are the root of all misery—especially when you're traveling. I mean, there's a lot to consider, Donnie. Don't leave it for the last minute." Catch-ing myself sounding like a badgering mother-in-law, I apologize to Don for micromanaging his pretrip preparations. I just want so badly for everything to go well. I want Don's introduction to golf in the Kingdom to be a dream fulfilled, not a nightmare.

"Did anyone ever tell you, Michael, you worry too much?" Don asks.

I know I do. My concern for my pal sometimes crosses over the fine line that separates compassion from coddling. But, still . . .

"We're going to Scotland," Don reminds me. "That's all that matters."

The week before we're scheduled to depart, Don watches the live telecast of Tiger Woods making some more history at the Old Course, and he calls me every thirty minutes or so to marvel at the golf course, which, he admits, looks like nothing he's ever played on. "I can't really tell where one hole ends and another begins."

I remind Don that soon he'll be playing this very course, the one Tiger's dismantling—albeit from tee boxes much closer to the greens—in ten days. "And the only other difference," I warn him, "is that instead of broiling in the sun, it's probably going to be raining buckets."

"Oh, man, I look forward to that!" Don exclaims.

"You do?"

"Oh, yeah! It wouldn't be right to play in Scotland without a good strong rain," he says.

"You're a sick guy," I tell him.

"It wouldn't be right!" he insists. "I don't even have a rain suit here in Phoenix. I guess I should get one, right?"

"Yes," I advise, "and bring plenty of golf balls. They cost like twice as much over there."

I discover Don cannot possibly suffer a shortage of ammunition: he's planning on bringing more than three dozen purely for ceremonial purposes—like driving commemorative balls into Loch Ness. "Always wanted to do that," he informs me.

As for a pellet to play with, Don claims he'll require only one ball.

"What do you mean?" I ask, utterly confused. "One ball per round?"

"No, one ball for Scotland."

"I don't get it," I say.

"Michael, I'm not going to lose a ball in Scotland. Won't happen," Don pledges.

"That's impossible, my friend. You're kidding."

He's not. Though Don hasn't ever been to the Land of Gorse, he's perfectly aware that Scotland is home to prickly plants that devour golf balls like an aardvark consumes ants. He knows, I assume, that some of the courses we'll be visiting aren't just near the sea—they're directly beside it. An untimely hook or slice can easily turn your shiny white orb into fish bait. And he's going to play fourteen rounds with one solitary ball?

"Yes, only one," Don repeats. "I promise."

I make a mental note: Should Don's One Ball Pledge hold true, even *I'll* join the Shivas Irons cult.

The night before we depart for Scotland, Don leaves work at his Phoenix casino and flies to Los Angeles, where I wait anxiously, certain that an unforeseen pilots' strike or hailstorm or something will doom our expedition at the last excruciating moment. So long have I been waiting to be there with him, I can't fully believe we really truly are less than twenty-four hours away from beginning our journey together. Lonely prisoners corresponding with infatuated pen pals, I imagine, couldn't be more eager to see the object of their affection in the flesh—or more tortured by lingering doubts that their fervent hope might somehow be dashed by forces beyond their control.

Like a concerned mama sending her boy off to summer camp for the first time, I make Don call me on his cell phone at each juncture of his travels. He humors me, mildly amused, I suppose, that a grown man could be so obsessively interested in the progress of a voyage of less than 300 miles: "OK, I'm at the airport"; "Just to let you know, I'm getting on the plane"; "All right, I'm waiting for a taxi."

When my friend Don finally arrives at my doorstep—*finally*, at the approximate time I've been expecting him—he's greeted with traditional Scots pipes and drums blaring from my living room loudspeakers. (Driving in Don's car once, on the way to the golf course, I learned that certain maladjusted golf fanatics listened to this obstreperous croaking and wheezing to get "in the mood" before a tour of the links. After I purchased a few CDs, I discovered that what I once considered the aural equivalent of a small mammal being stepped upon actually sounded quite beautiful when one knew a date with the short grass awaited.) We hug, and I take care not to squeeze him too tightly, fearful that an overzealous display of affection could dash our plans.

I briefly imagine the apologetic phone calls I'd have to make—"I'm so sorry, we won't be able to make our tee time since, well, I cracked Don's rib by accident"—and quickly move on to a small ceremony I've arranged in Don's honor.

From the hutch in my dining room, I extract a bottle of whisky, a rare and special blend made for the Loch Lomond Golf Club, and pour two glasses.

With bagpipes wailing in the background, I propose a toast. "To Scotland: where we will discover beauty in all its forms, in both the physical and spiritual realms."

We clink. Don says, "To the trip of a lifetime!"

That night, while Don sleeps, dreaming of birdies, I pack until 3:00 in the morning, repeatedly remembering one more essential item just before I attempt to shut my carry-case. Finally, after triple-checking my supplies, I get to bed. As the sun rises, after maybe two hours of fitful sleep, I stumble into Don's room and gently awaken him.

"Hey, Don," I say. "Let's go to Scotland."

5

Are We There Yet?

Thanks to turbulent weather in the Midwest of the United States, our flight from Los Angeles to New York City, where we connect to Europe, is delayed three hours. Parked on the tarmac at LAX, waiting for the masters of the skies to release us from our asphalt prison, I muse silently on the "connections" inherent in our present plight: it's summertime in the Midwest, but the weather is as stormy and violent as December on the Ayrshire Coast; I'm going to Scotland with my friend from Oklahoma, but my childhood was spent—ah ha!—in the Midwest; we're on a Delta Air Lines jumbo jet, and I write the golf column for their in-flight magazine, *Sky*, but no matter how well, um, *connected* I am to this company, they can't get me to my destination any quicker than Nature will allow, whether or not I'm writing about golf.

Which all means what?

"You know this connections concept you're always talking about?" I say to Don, who's fiddling with the electronic controls on his business-class seat.

"Yeah?"

"Well, if this plane doesn't take off in the next ten minutes, we're probably going to miss our connection to Scotland."

"Then what would we do?" Don wonders.

"I guess try to catch something else. Let's see: it's Friday morning now—well, Friday evening over there. If we don't get to Edinburgh by Saturday afternoon we'll miss our tee time at North Berwick." I frown and scrunch my forehead. "And that would suck, since I wanted our first round together in Scotland to be there, for reasons that will be apparent once we arrive."

"So worst-case scenario, we cancel our North Berwick round and start our trip with day two on the itinerary," Don replies, reasonably.

I sigh acidly. "I guess."

I look out the window morosely. Why can't anything ever just be *easy*? Based on a scheduled 8:00 A.M. arrival into Edinburgh, I figured a 4:00 P.M. tee time at North Berwick, which is maybe 45 minutes from the airport, would give us plenty of time to pack our rental car and orient ourselves on the map and remind ourselves once more to drive on the wrong side of the road—and still have hours to spare before we inaugurated the golf portion of our odyssey. Now, seven hours of "screw-up" time doesn't seem like enough to get us to the first tee on time.

Grrrr.

Don is too busy trying to decide between backgammon and trivia on his in-seat video console to be bothered.

More than six hours later, when we finally land at JFK, our flight to Scotland has long since departed. So has everything else to Europe on Delta, and the flights that haven't are already overbooked. "I've got you confirmed for tomorrow at six," a ticket agent tells me cheerfully.

"Six tomorrow morning?" I ask, incredulous.

"No, no. Six tomorrow night."

Don looks at me, pained. I look at him, devastated.

I want to cry and crumble into a useless heap right there at the Delta counter. But having been in these regrettable situations before, I know time is of the essence. There are probably 300 other passengers with similar missed connections tonight. All of them will be scrambling for hotel beds and transportation and meals. There's no time to waste on hot tears of disappointment.

While Don proposes a number of outlandish—and unworkable—schemes to somehow get us to North Berwick on time, I get us booked at a rotten hotel near the airport, where we spend the evening whining at each other while ESPN shows highlights of the Senior British Open, videotaped from the blessed side of the Atlantic we're supposed to be cruising toward at that very moment. As we chew glumly at room service pizza, I long for the inimitable taste of haggis.

"Are we really ever going to get to Scotland?" I wonder rhetorically.

Don laughs. But he doesn't answer.

In the morning—at about the time we're supposed to be passing through one impossibly cute fishing village after another as we get near the North Sea—I call North Berwick to cancel our afternoon tee time. When I get the starter on the line he asks me where I am. I tell him I'm stuck in New York, in a particularly god-forsaken region of Queens, to be exact.

Chuckling, he says, "Wull, tha' canbuh good! I assoom yull be mussing yer tee time."

To hear the simple music of his voice does my heart good—and the fact that he can accommodate us tomorrow, even more so. (I had scheduled our golf outings in an elegant counterclockwise loop, with no time-wasting backtracking or crazy detours.) After a few more long-distance calls, thanks to the kindness and flexibility of several Scottish booking secretaries, what initially seemed like a logistical disaster looks now like a respectable salvage job. I feel a little better.

So does Don. In fact, he confesses he's *glad* we got delayed one day. His mind and his heart, he tells me, have been completely preoccupied with, as he calls it, a "she-vixen," who has deliberately cast a shroud of misery over what ought to be his brightest fantasy.

"This relationship, Michael, has been like going birdie, double bogey. Birdie, double bogey. I'm elated and then I'm crushed," he says.

"Well, maybe this trip will help you get some perspective on the relationship," I suggest.

Don snickers. "This trip is exactly what's ruining the relationship."

He tells me that this woman he's been seeing for a few months, J, has something of a split personality: she's delightfully sweet some of the time and viciously mean the rest, with little in between. Though he should have seen the danger signs—she's sixty-two (seventeen years older than he) and divorced four times!—Don has willingly accepted her frequent emotional beatings. "She's particularly manipulative when I don't include her in my golf plans," Don explains. "Whether it's Phoenix or Vegas or this."

While Don is off in Scotland, realizing the golf adventure of his life, J has threatened to start seeing other men in his absence, including an old boyfriend she swore was out of her life once Don became her playmate. "I've told her how much that would upset me," he says, "and she seems to relish the fact that I'm upset."

I can feel powerful emotions churning in my chest, feelings I thought I had "processed," as the therapists like to say. The love I lost just nine months previous was destroyed by lies and deceit and, in the end, naked cruelty. What Don is experiencing I have known too well. And I ache for him.

I ache for me, too. Here I am, on the brink of a joyous return to a place I adore, and I am doing it without the magnificent (and ultimately malicious) woman who once accompanied me during my happiest Scotland sojourns. Instead, I'm in the company of a gimpy friend who's being twisted into knots by a horrible and hostile woman who claims she loves him. Ah, *connections*.

I take a deep breath. "Don, it's no good."

"I know. And you're gonna love this . . ." Then Don confesses that while we've been suffering the unforeseen weather delays he's been calling and leaving numerous messages for her, which she neglects to return, preoccupied, apparently, with her "alternative" social activities. Don's solution? Send her flowers. "Maybe she'll feel guilty," he explains.

I look at him incredulously. "What?"

"I know. I know." Then he shows me some e-mails she sent him in the past week. Why he's saved them I can't figure. They're dripping with vitriol and cruelty, claiming my gentle pal Don has "blackmailed" her into a suffocating relationship.

I'm sickened; I can feel a wave of nausea pass through me. "What are you thinking?" I say angrily. "Why haven't you gotten rid of this malicious monster by now? She doesn't love you; she doesn't respect you; she doesn't even seem to like you. Donnie," I say, placing my hand on his sloped shoulder, "you deserve far better than this. You deserve kindness and courtesy."

"Desperation makes you do stupid things," he says sheepishly.

I forcefully suggest he immediately cancel the flowers—and while he's at it, the unhealthy relationship. "Don, your lover ought to treat you with respect and compassion, not maliciousness."

He says he knows it. "But I keep kidding myself that she'll mend her ways." He sighs heavily and says, "I'm on the bogie train, Michael, and right now I can't get off!"

Talking the language I know Don understands, I say, "Don, I suggest you withdraw from this tournament immediately. Take a DQ and move on to the next stop."

He nods solemnly. "I will." Then he smiles ruefully. "Maybe I'll have some more spiritual revelations in Scotland. Hell, maybe I'll meet someone nice."

"I promise you, Don, you will definitely meet several nice people there—probably dozens of nice people. Now, most of them will be named Angus and Willie, but, hey, you never know."

Don says he feels better talking things over with me. The strange thing is, now *I'm* upset, reflecting on haunting memories that I mistakenly thought I had successfully consigned to the past, never to trouble me again. And here they are, reincarnated through Don and his "she-vixen."

Rather than wallow in our miseries, past and present, we decide to get out of our airport hotel, which has the unenviable effect of exacerbating whatever blueness a stranded guest might be battling. Don and I briefly consider renting a car and finding Garrison-on-the-Hudson, this wonderful little golf course he once played many years ago. But we come to our senses: we're about to attempt to play more golf on foot than Don has ever been able to handle in a motor cart. We can wait another day.

Instead, we take a cab into Manhattan, to Central Park, where I propose a match at a miniature putt-putt course near the skating rink. I played there years ago, when I was living in a five-floor walk-up in Soho and got to see a real golf course only when I traveled out of town for business. "It's a fun little layout," I promise Don. "All the New York landmarks: Chrysler Building, Statue of Liberty, that sort of thing."

Unfortunately, upon our arrival we discover the mini-golf course I remember was torn up years ago to make way for picnic space.

"Sorry," I say to Don.

"Nah. No problem. I've seen you putt. This probably saves me money," Don says.

With several hours at our disposal before returning to the concrete hell across the bridge, Don and I wander aimlessly through this most lovely realm of New York City, pausing to admire couples rowing small dinghies on the boat pond, and swans tending to their signets, and, to our connections-attuned delight, a life-size statue of Robbie Burns, bard of Ayrshire. We see a woman jogging somewhat awkwardly on the bike path, and Don says, "One leg shorter than the other. My dream girl." Between spirited discussions on the relative merits of *The Simpsons* versus *South Park* and *All in the Family* versus *The Andy Griffith Show*—I'm in favor of the two formers; Don supports the latters—we drift into Scotland reveries. We muse on where we ought to be at the moment—where we *want* to be— and where, in fact, we are. Instead of modest two-story B&Bs surrounding us and a moody sky above, skyscrapers loom on all sides, testifying to man's terrifying ability to both tame and defile his surroundings.

"Strange. Here we are in Central Park. Me and you. There's a lesson in all this," Don says in his characteristically philosophical way. "I just don't know what it is."

When we pause for a cappuccino at one of those peculiarly New York cafés where the outdoor tables occupy nearly as much of the sidewalk as the restaurant does, Don disappears inside for a few minutes while I watch an inexorable stream of humanity laden with shopping bags and dogs and children. When he returns, Don announces that he's canceled the flower delivery to J, left his last message on her machine, and completely exorcised the demons she placed in his heart. He proposes a photograph, right here, on Seventy-first Street and Madison Avenue. "Our trip to Scotland officially begins *now*," Don declares.

On the cab ride back to the airport, Don looks at me with a raised brow and says, "You know, all this talk of the she-vixen is well and good, and I appreciate your concern and everything. But we still haven't discussed the really important thing."

"Which is?"

"What kind of bets we got going once we actually get to a damn golf course!"

After a spirited negotiation, which we probably enjoy nearly as much as the actual playing, we settle on our usual $10 Nassau, with $5 birdies and $2 penalty for 3-putting. And instead of dollars, everything is converted to British sterling.

Don typically beats me, since I'm too proud (and stupid) to take strokes from a guy who ought to be in a wheelchair, not wielding a wedge. His handicap card presently says 5.5; mine is 8.8. But we agree to start off even, on the theory that I've seen most of the courses before and that, well, we're *walking*. Neither of us really knows what this will mean to Don's game. He might fall apart; he might be inspired. Therefore we leave room for an adjustment after the first round.

In addition to our usual wagering, Don insists—in a far too forceful way that makes me suspect I'm getting conned—I give him action on a crazy proposition bet: his "I won't lose a ball in Scotland" pledge. Surely there's got to be some trick involved that I'm too dense to see, because Don, I'm certain, isn't foolish enough to make such a promise without some sort of outlandish ace up his sleeve—like a trained ball-finding hound he's hired, or something.

"You're insane!" I tell him, refusing the bet.

"Well, if you think you're such a big favorite, lay me a price," he retorts.

I watch Archie Bunker's old neighborhood race past the taxicab windows. "Fine," I say. "I'll lay you 10-to-1."

"Done. I bet ten against your hundred I won't lose a ball in Scotland."

"Why are you so sure of this?" I ask him.

He looks me in the eye. "Because God told me so."

I catch the driver stealing glances at us in the rearview mirror, and I don't pursue the conversation. Because I'm afraid Don's serious.

As we sit on the tarmac at JFK, safely aboard the airplane that, barring any more capricious weather delays, will take us to Brussels, Belgium, and then onward to Scotland, Don turns on his cell phone.

"Hey, I think we're about to push back for the flight," I remind him. So *this*, I think, will be the next reason why Don and I never get to the promised land: We get hauled off the plane by burly New York cops for violating some FAA regulation involving Sprint nationwide calling plans.

He shakes his head and dials. "I gotta see if she'll pick up."

At first I'm dumbstruck. And then I feel something much worse: for the first time I can recall, I feel something like pity for my friend Don Naifeh.

I want to hug him. I want to tell him he'll be all right. I want him to know that Scotland will heal his heart, and maybe his soul. I want him to know that there is life beyond this one horrible woman. *Believe me*, I want to tell him, *I know*.

But even though he is sitting beside me, Don is far away, frowning coldly as he stares into a blackness I too have visited.

I think maybe I understand his irrational unwillingness to release himself from the grip of this hurtful woman, this J. Most women, I imagine, would find Don physically undesirable, if not repulsive. His shoulders and neck and back and arms are covered with hair; his pate is not. His belly is big and round; his ass and thighs are nearly undetectable. And almost any physical activity, including walking, leaves his shirt soaked with perspiration—"pitted," as he put it. I imagine when he finds a woman to sleep with him regularly, the rare phenomenon feels like such a welcome relief, a gift, that he's willing to endure whatever malfeasance she subjects him to. And I suppose I don't blame him for accepting such a brutal trade-off. Starved for affection, I've done the same hurtful thing myself.

It's a hateful state of affairs, and I hate myself for thinking this way about my friend, but I suspect it's true.

And I'm glad, I'm thrilled, to take him away from it, to the one place—a golf course!—where none of his physical oddities or gruesome appearances make the slightest difference. The one place where he can be beautiful.

May the golf course bring us both peace.

When we arrive in Brussels the next morning, after seven hours of way too much fine wine, dark chocolate, and in-seat blackjack, an airline agent informs us that the early connecting flight we expected to take to Scotland has been overbooked. We've been involuntarily put on an afternoon flight—which will cause us to miss another day of golf. (This doesn't sound particularly tragic in the grand scheme of things, but for Don and me it's like having to cut off a finger.) I try to explain to the agent some of the sorrowful details of our traveling travails, but she's in no mood for shaggy dog stories—or bleary-eyed Americans—and insists I must plead my case to a supervisor at the Delta ticket counter.

Fuming, I ask Don to hurry as fast as he can and meet me at the ticket counter, which I expect to arrive at ten minutes before he can. He tells me his plodding trundle is "as fast as it gets," but he'll try his best. I dash off in hopes of salvaging our day, not to mention our trip.

Twenty yards down the hallway, I spot two policemen, who speak enough English to direct me to this special fix-all-your-problems counter. Don limps over to where the three of us are standing just as I am getting my final instructions—"zet whey for ze Delta billet"—and I tell him to get pointed in the right direction while I tend to our rapidly disintegrating itinerary.

After a sprint worthy of an Olympian—an out-of-shape, desk-bound, 35-year-old Olympian—I am "helped" by Delta's head lady in Brussels. Despite her understanding frown and soothing voice, she is unable to get me and my friend to Scotland any sooner than 4:00 in the afternoon, except perhaps by renting a private helicopter, which she does not seem eager to do.

"Through London? Amsterdam? Frankfurt? Manchester? Nothing?" I ask, more than skeptical.

"I'm sorry, sir. Nothing."

This goes on for nearly an hour. I propose some outlandish series of connections that will buy us an hour or two of Scottish daylight; she summarily (and apologetically) vetoes it.

And just as I have exhausted my last and most ludicrous suggestion—something involving a train and a private car—Don arrives at the counter.

He tells me he's been wandering the Brussels airport, lost and confused, since I ran off. He's dripping with perspiration, as though he's just emerged from a shower and misplaced his towel. And he's not happy.

"The next time I get left behind," he tells me icily, "whether it's an airport or a golf course, or wherever, I park it. I won't—I can't—hurry. Michael, I'm not going to bust myself trying to keep up. You gotta adjust your pace of play or leave me behind, because I'm not going to run to stay up. I can't."

I apologize. And I explain I was trying to save our day, trying to be heroic when I should have just laid up and played the percentages.

I feel terrible. Seeing Don reduced to a bundle of saturated rags and seething eyes, nearly hyperventilating from his tour of the Brussels airport, I also fear for the viability of our trip. And I wonder why I ever thought this whole crazy idea could work.

Indeed, about an hour later, I'm nearly certain this journey together was a rancid idea.

We have nearly four hours until our flight to Edinburgh is allegedly departing—though, at this point, I wouldn't be surprised if it left three days later. In the interim, Don says he wants to buy a fresh shirt. We agree to meet at the Club lounge—which has showers and booze and more chocolate—in twenty minutes. This way we won't get separated; this way I'll never make him feel like he's being left behind. This way he won't have to run, and I won't have to worry.

Nearly ninety minutes later, during which time I've gone on several search-and-rescue missions and had the airline personnel page Mr. Don Naifeh about a dozen times, Don finally shows up at the lounge—and admits he never checked his watch once because, he says, "I don't like to be ordered around."

"But Don, you agreed to meet me here in twenty minutes," I remind him.

"Like I said, I don't take orders well."

Upon hearing this, the joy of this pilgrimage drains from my heart, like blood rushing from the brain of one who stands too quickly.

I suspect that while I've been frantically wondering what's happened to my golf buddy, making sure he never again feels he's been abandoned by his chaperone and friend, Don has been on the phone with J, allowing himself to be further poisoned. His blithe disregard for me, his traveling companion, I reason, is probably an "acting out" of the anger and frustration he doubtlessly feels toward his cruel lover. (Hey, even if years of therapy doesn't chase away all your woes, it sure helps you talk like an undergraduate psych major.)

Whatever his motivations, I hardly want to spend two weeks with someone who could be so thoughtless, let alone play golf with him every day.

We both seethe for two hours, both stricken with fatigue and disappointment, trading less than a handful of words between us until we board the plane to Edinburgh.

As we buckle our seat belts, Don asks me if I'm going to let twenty minutes of "bad communication" ruin our trip. "Is the whole two weeks going to be like this?" he wonders.

I tell him I don't see how we can possibly make it through two weeks together—not with this much disrespect infecting our relationship. Our pilgrimage, I tell him, was supposed to be based on trust and understanding and shared pleasure, like a good marriage. Now I have grave doubts.

As I tell Don this, I realize how much like a marriage our relationship has really become—for me at least. I've invested so much of my heart into being a friend to him, and I care for him so deeply, that I'm easily wounded by his transgressions. I know this is supposed to be only a *golf trip*, after all. But it has already started to mean so much more to me. And, like a good marriage, I want so badly for it to work. I have failed before, in a marriage and in other vital relationships, and this time I want very much not to. This time I want to succeed—even if my partner is being an insensitive prick.

Perhaps it's the relentless weight of what seems like two straight days of being on (or waiting for) airplanes pressing upon my heart, but I feel low and desperate, and tears start to sting in the corners of my eyes.

Don looks straight ahead, but he's talking directly to my soul. "Michael," he says, "I was scared. That's the plain truth. I was angry and all that. But mostly I was scared. I was scared of getting left behind. Of being abandoned. Here I am in Europe for the first time. I don't speak the language. And I don't know where I am. And I'm relying on you for everything, and then . . . well, you ran off. And, yeah, the truth is I was scared."

"Don, I know you were," I say, feeling the tears welling up, ready to soak the nice Sabena Airlines Belgian upholstery. "And that's why I never wanted to let such a thing happen to you again—getting lost and alone. So that's why I was so insistent on making a meeting place and a time, because I didn't want you to be scared again. I was trying to do something caring for you. And then . . ." I start getting sniffly, and the tears run hot down my dehydrated cheeks.

"And then I did something mean, I know," Don says, shaking his head. "Michael, I'm sorry," he says. "I've been complaining to you how J always treats me like shit. Then here you are trying to be kind to me and I throw it in your face. Well, that's not right. And I sincerely apologize."

Now I'm crying hard, like I'm watching the fourth act of *La Boheme*, when the reunited lovers remember their first kiss. "I'm sorry for making you feel abandoned," I say. "It won't happen again. I promise."

"No, I know. And I'm sorry, too."

I wipe the tears from my face and giggle. The flight attendant, trying not to stare, probably thinks we're having a mild lovers' spat. Which, in a way, I suppose we are.

I realize then I love Don Naifeh. He's not just some guy I play golf with. He's my friend and playmate and companion. He's gimpy and broken and eccentric, and I love him. He's helped me see golf—and life and the world—in ways I couldn't see before. Knowing him has been a gift of sorts. And I want our friendship to be bigger and more transcendent than all the hurts and failures that have come before it, bigger than petty squabbles and overblown pride. Bigger than the banal.

I want it to carry us through Scotland on a vapor of purple mist—or whatever color the aura surrounding a golfer is supposed to look like.

I sigh. "Can we get to Scotland already, for crissakes?" I say to Don, smiling for the first time in what seems like twenty-four hours. "This will all be behind us. We'll be playing golf and all our troubles will just, I don't know. They'll just all fly away."

"Brother," Don says as the plane's engines begin to rev, "I am so ready." He looks out the window to a far-off place, somewhere I reckon isn't on any map. He nods three times, very slowly. "I am so ready."

6

Treasure Island

Don does not drop to his knees in gratitude when he first sets foot
on Scottish soil. Which is just as well, since such a maneuver would
probably result in a shattered patella. He does smile and giggle and
nod a lot and even nudges me in the ribs when a Scotsman standing beside him at the baggage claim says something charming and
unintelligible. But Don Naifeh doesn't collapse or faint or suffer any
kind of ecstatic fit when he finally arrives in the promised land. He
doesn't have time to.

We land in Edinburgh shortly before 4:00 P.M. Our tee time at
North Berwick, about twenty miles away, is at 5:10. Gratuitous dis-
plays of overwhelming emotion will have to wait.

After packing two hard-shell golf carry-cases, three suitcases,
and two carry-on-size shoulder bags into our Avis rental—a sporty
silver Peugeot 306 that would qualify as a subcompact in America
but passes for fairly luxurious in Scotland—we cram in two full-
size adult hackers, a state-of-the-art radar detector, a plenitude of
maps of various degrees of uselessness, and a collection of compact
discs hand-selected by the Czar of the Radio (me). And then we—

all right, I—proceed to commit at least four egregious moving violations and several breaches of proper drive-on-the-left etiquette and speed (quite literally) toward one of my favorite golf courses on the planet.

While Don makes humorous but futile attempts to pronounce the village names on every one of the road signs we zoom past, I manically explain to him why I was so keen on North Berwick being the place we enjoy our inaugural round in Scotland. Strung out on a potent cocktail of airline chocolates and sleep deprivation, I'm afraid I don't make much sense babbling on about highfalutin qualities like "purity" and "aesthetics" and other easily felt but hard-to-express characteristics that supposedly make all the difference between a dog track and Elysium. "All I can say," I blurt out, "is that it's an amazing golf course that means a lot to me and, I guess, I don't know, you'll understand why when you're there, I'm hoping."

"Burr-wick-upon-tweed," Don mumbles, mesmerized by another road sign. "Fifty-five miles?"

"That's a different place," I tell him. "And it's pronounced 'bear-ick.' Silent *w* for some reason."

Don chuckles. "Heh-heh-heh. North bare-ick."

"Yup. Your first round in Scotland, my friend," I remind him, as though he might have forgotten why we've flown 8,000 miles and made a scenic tour of the Brussels airport.

"You think we'll make it?" Don asks.

"Let's put it this way," I say, glancing at the speedometer. "If I don't get held without bail, we'll just about be there on time." Since I've been to North Berwick—silent *w*—several times previously, I have a vague idea where the golf course is located. You pass a train station, and an old ruined castle, and a tree-lined boulevard, and you turn toward the sea, right near the Marine Hotel, and then, I think, you're there.

Of course, I could be getting it confused with some other wondrous links, since approximately half the great seaside courses in Scotland seem to have a Marine Hotel within a solid 3 wood of the first tee.

"Muirfield!" Don says, for the first time pronouncing one of the sign names perfectly.

"You've heard of that place?" I say, grinning. "Oh, I guess I forgot to mention: it's right up the road from where we're going. So is Gullane, where they hold qualifying for the Open when it's at Muirfield. We'll drive right past both of them."

"You want to check for cancellations?" Don proposes.

I remind him that when I made our request three months before, the nice people at Muirfield politely told me I was crazy to think a tee time at their esteemed club might be available with less than a year's notice. Spiritual pilgrimages be damned. If you want to play there, they sniffed, you either pay exorbitantly for a holiday package through a golf outfitter or get your request in early. "It's like season tickets for the Packers," I explain to Don. "There's a waiting list. But, unlike Packers games, you won't see any bare-chested overweight men wearing foam wedges of cheese on their head at Muirfield. Well, maybe at some naughty party I've never been invited to. They're pretty notorious for being one the stuffiest places in Scotland. A bunch of snooty doctors and lawyers. Not very Scottish in character at all. Great golf course, sure. One of the best. But attitude to go along with it." I'm trying to protect Don from feeling he's missing anything. I don't want this journey to be anything but glorious. I feel it's my duty—and Scotland's—to mesmerize him with revelations, to exceed all his expectations. To shine. "Now, North Berwick, on the other hand . . ." I raise my eyebrows conspiratorially and nod.

"No attitude?" Don asks.

"None. They'll even let a couple of chops like me and you play there."

"Well, I just hope I can make it," he says, absentmindedly rubbing the tops of his legs.

I check the odometer. "We should be there in the next fifteen minutes. Maybe—do you want to start stretching now, in the car? We're not going to have much time." I'm mildly concerned. Well, actually, that's not true. I'm terrified. Don typically requires fifteen minutes or so to "get ready" for a round, which involves a variety of stretching exercises and joint loosenings, not to mention stocking his bag with enough provisions to feed (and smoke) a family of four. Moreover, after our Brussels fiasco I'm painfully aware of how sensitive he is to getting rushed, being made to feel he's too slow to keep up with his "fully-abled" companions. The problem is, if my calculations are accurate, we should arrive at the first tee with, oh, about forty-nine seconds to spare. Which doesn't leave much time for anything but stuffing a commemorative scorecard in the back pocket and sticking a peg in the ground.

"I'll be all right," Don assures me. "I'll probably play horribly. But I feel fine. Not as tight as I expected after all the traveling." He shakes his head in wonder. "Scotland!" Don yells.

"Scotland!" I yell.

"Scotland!" we yell together.

After passing a train station and an old ruined castle and a tree-lined boulevard and the Marine Hotel, I turn down a thoroughfare helpfully named Links Road and find a parking spot beside the eighteenth fairway. "We're here!" I shout. "Our car is definitely in play from the eighteenth tee. But we're here!"

I jump out and breathe deeply the salty air. And I smile contentedly.

How I love this place. The golf is superb and the sights spectacular, and above all, it just *feels* so good. On my feet. On my face. In my fingers. It's a happy place.

At some point I know I'll have to explain to Don why I have such a Shivas moment every time I arrive at North Berwick. But, as Inspector Clouseau was fond of telling his valet Kato, now is not the time. Now is the time to fly. Despite the multitude of delays and misfortunes and relationship issues Don and I have endured these past two days, we are at North Berwick Golf Club—with exactly four minutes to spare before our scheduled tee time.

I sprint off toward the starter's shack while Don excavates his golf equipment from the disaster scene in the back of our car. Bounding over the dunes, perhaps 100 meters from our car to the first tee, I realize it's not just temperate or mild or even warm today. It's *hot*. Like eighty degrees. Sprinting like a lunatic in golf spikes must generate some of the heat I feel, I realize. But, it's true: the sun is blazing. I feel as though I'm in Palm Springs. Don, I think, will be mildly disappointed to not play his first round in an appropriately Scottish gale, with wind and rain blowing every shot sideways—but I'm not. I've had plenty of that weather. And I've always wondered what it must be like to play golf on these great courses when it was actually *nice* out. (I couldn't really picture it.) Now I'll find out.

I've also always wondered what it must be like to play golf on these great courses with Mr. Don Naifeh, certified fanatic and seeker of spiritual truths, by my side. (I couldn't really picture it.) Now I'll find that out, as well.

"Ah, Mr. Konik," the starter greets me. "We've bun expectin' ye."

"I am so very glad to be here," I tell him. And I'm not exaggerating at all.

"Isut jes' ye?"

I explain my partner should be coming along any minute now, though, when I peer back toward the car, I see no sign of Don. "He's a little slow. Gotta few physical ailments. But he'll be right along."

"Tha's fine."

Then the starter tells me that only one of the two requested caddies has turned up, since it was unclear if we were ever going to make it to Scotland, etc., ha-hah. He can carry both bags; will that be all right?

"Sure," I say, relieved that Don won't have to confront his first round without the indispensable assistance of a seasoned veteran, wise in the ways of these ancient links.

"Ah, heer he us new," the starter says. "George, heers yer mon."

I turn to meet George, whose weathered face and craggy hands and whisky-scented breath will no doubt tell stories all their own, stories that my buddy Don will slurp up like a thirsty puppy at his mother's teat.

"Oh," I say, taken aback. "Hello, George," I say, extending my hand to a lad of perhaps thirteen—a lad with sandy hair and fair skin and freckles, and a handsome silver ring pierced through his left eyebrow.

"Hullo, sir," he says quietly.

"George wull look afterya," the starter assures me. "Now if yer ready," he says, motioning toward the first tee. "Enjoy yer roond."

I mount the tee and look for Don. There he is, just leaving the car, a floppy bucket hat on his head and a mammoth shoe on his right foot, limping toward the clubhouse with his clubs slung over his shoulder.

Turning to the lad, I say, "George, see that guy over there? In the green shirt? With the funny hat and that big shoe? Could you run over there, please, and help him with his clubs. He's got some physical problems—sort of like Casey Martin—and I'm sure he'd appreciate your assistance."

"Yeah. Sure," George says, loping off in Don's direction at a leisurely jog, his eyebrow piercing glimmering in the late-afternoon sun.

While George retrieves my tardy friend, I swing a few irons to warm up. And as I do I survey the scene. It looks just as I remember it: the sea to the right, with fishing boats anchored in the low tide and Bass Rock, a huge hunk of stone protruding from the waves, sitting stolidly where it's always sat; straight down the first fairway there's a gigantic mound upon which the first green is situated; to the left and beyond is the eighteenth and the town, a perfect little postcard waiting to be photographed. From the second tee I know I'll be able to glimpse the beach, with dogs chasing driftwood sticks and lovers holding hands. To the left will be the Marine Hotel, where once I stayed with *my* lover, who looked out our window high above the links and waved to me as I passed on my way to the sixteenth green. She is not with me today, of course. And I will miss her beauty and vivacity—and the knowing that her kisses and embraces await me after I've holed my last putt. But I do have Don. Admittedly, he does not sport flowing auburn locks and the kind of figure that looks smashing in a little black dress, but he is beautiful and vivacious in his own peculiar way.

When he arrives with George, finally, at the first tee, I tell him, "I'm glad you're here, Don," and I mean it in more ways than he could presently understand.

While Don fishes around in his bag for tees and a golf ball and a coin and all the other accoutrements he needs for a proper round of golf, I tell him I'm going to hit. (It's already five minutes past our appointed time. I see the next group, a foursome, coming toward the tee, and I don't want to be later than we already are.) "I'm going to take the honor now, since I might never have it again," I joke.

"Sure. Sure. Go ahead," Don says, slightly frazzled. I know he's suffering from sensory overload at the moment, trying unsuccessfully to process a multitude of new sights and sounds and smells, a menagerie of images and feelings he's envisioned all his life but hasn't yet tasted.

I step to the markers, stick my tee in the sandy soil, and feel utterly liberated, free from all my quotidian cares. I'm here.

"Don, it's a real short hole. Maybe three-twenty. You don't want to hit more than 5 here. Right, George?"

"Five or sex," George says, nodding. "Thars a path oot thar. Ye wanna be shoort ovit."

The first at North Berwick is one of those quirky, thoroughly unembellished holes that makes golf in Scotland so fun. Depending on the wind—and the prevailing breeze is usually at the player's back—it's a tiny par-4 that requires nothing more than a midiron off the tee and a little wedge to an elevated green that's almost completely hidden. You aim at a marker post and hope. A public footpath—the one George counsels us to avoid—crosses the fairway, mounds shaped like Hershey's kisses dot the ground, and, I suspect, not a thimble of dirt was moved to construct the whole blessed thing. It's just a pleasant grassy strip of land beside the sea where fellows with sticks in their hands can take a nice walk.

I love it.

Instead of muddying my mind with "swing-thoughts," such as "left arm straight" and "keep your head still," and that sort of thing, my last thought before striking my tee-shot is, "You're back where you want to be, with the man you wanted to be with. Enjoy it!"

Effortlessly, magically, the golf ball flies high and far and pretty and lands more or less where young George has advised. I don't even try to mask my grin. "Something like that," I tell Don, reverting to golf talk. "Just a little bunt out there to the left."

"Got it," Don says, his eyes narrowing. He takes about seven practice swings, tees his ball, and hooks one out to nearly the same spot as mine. Safe.

"Here we go!" I say.

"Yup," Don replies. He's gone somewhere very far away from the North Berwick Golf Club. I can tell by the distant look in his eyes. He's someplace else.

George struggles to balance both our nylon quivers on his shoulders, and I help him get situated. Don, meanwhile, is walking toward his ball, using his 5 iron as a cane. I explain to George that Mr. Naifeh will often keep the club he's just hit for walking purposes and will give it back when he arrives at the ball.

George nods solemnly. "Ah," he says.

Catching up to Don, I lay my hand on his shoulder and say, "How 'bout it?"

"Nice," Don says, still occupying a space no one else can ever visit.

"All the times I've ever been to Scotland, I've never seen a day like this," I comment, perhaps a bit too enthusiastically. "We're, like, as far north as Vancouver, and we're wearing shirtsleeves. I mean, it's like they rolled out the chamber of commerce weather welcome for us."

"Yeah. Beautiful," Don replies.

We walk toward our waiting tee-shots. Even over a forty-yard distance I find myself pulling away from gimpy Don, trudging down the fairway with his makeshift cane. Somehow I've got to make myself walk more slowly—or get him to speed up a bit—or something in between. I remind myself that we are supposed to be taking this good long walk together, side by side. Golf buddies.

When we get to our golf balls, I see that Don has drawn his first quirky lie of the trip, less than five minutes after stepping onto his first Scottish golf course. His ball is just beyond the footpath, between two parabolic mounds, on a steep up-slope. If he has any prayer of hitting the green, he'll have to stand with one leg about a foot above the other, putting most of his weight on his back foot—the one that sports the prosthetic shoe. Even for someone that doesn't suffer from OI it would be a tough shot; for someone who has brittle-bone disease it's an invitation to a fracture.

I'm terrified. Our trip, our magical journey together in search of friendship and fulfillment and the spirit of Burningbush, could easily end right here, on the first hole of our first round. The simple solution, of course, would be for Don to take a drop. But there's about as much chance of that happening as me winning the British Open. I guess it will just be a case of "hit and hope"—him hitting, me hoping.

"Nice lie," Don says, sarcastically, surveying his options.

"Welcome to Scotland," I say cheerfully.

"Yeah. No kidding."

George directs Don toward a red-and-white marker pole, about 120 yards away, rising up from the back of the green. "Right there," George says, assuredly. "Jes a wee wedge."

Don looks about for some sort of yardage marker, to confirm his distance. He smiles wanly at me. "Nothing, right?"

"Nope. Not even a one-fifty stake. You just gotta trust your caddie," I say, winking at George.

"Uts jes a wee wedge," George reiterates.

"Like a hundred yards?" Don queries.

"Not even. Ye dinna wanna hut it more than ninety. Jes a wee wedge."

Don trades his walking-stick 5 iron for a fifty-five-degree sandy. He assumes his stance, teetering above the ball. He takes a few smooth practice swings, feeling the shot. Then he addresses the ball, checks his target, and swings.

I hear a tremendous explosion of steel meeting soil and see that there is a prodigious divot, the size of a porterhouse steak, where Don's ball previously lay.

He does not fall down. He does not stumble. He stands tall, with his wedge pointed in the direction of the green, like a lance.

We hear the unmistakable sound of ball meeting putting surface, a hundred yards in the distance.

"Purrfect," George says, nodding. "Shot."

"Shot!" I say with relief. "Golf shot."

"Thanks," Don says, evaluating his divot. "I guess when they say you can never expect a level lie in Scotland they weren't kidding." He limps off in search of the displaced sod, and I feel a warm wave of peacefulness run through my belly. The man hasn't come here to discover his shortcomings. He's come here to play.

After we trade pars at the first, Don asks if he might take a little rest on the second. "Sure," I say, noting the foursome behind approaching the first green. "You could hardly pick a lovelier view." Indeed, the vista is all sand and sea and sun, and it goes on forever.

"Pretty special," Don says, noncommittally. Even now, standing on one of the most blessed squares of turf in all of golf, I can feel Don Naifeh is somewhere else, where pars and birdies and doglegs skirting the surf don't exist.

Seeing the following foursome putting behind us, I suggest we ought to play on. After I crush one down the middle, Don hits a weak high hook away from the water and into the fescue on the left. "What was that!?" he exclaims bitterly.

We scurry down the fairway, with George hanging back with Don while I stride ahead to find his ball. I locate it promptly and wait nearly two minutes before Don and his pierced looper arrive with the equipment. The trailing foursome is now on the tee. Don sees them too and scowls. After getting his yardage from young George, he hits a poor approach shot, short and right, and stomps off like Quasimodo in search of Esmerelda.

When he's out of earshot, I instruct George to look after Don and not worry about me. "I think he could use some extra help," I tell the lad.

"Dya think ye might carry this bag," he says sheepishly. "I've never carried two bags, anna think I'll be completely knackered."

"No problem," I say, taking my kit from him. "You just look after Mr. Naifeh."

"Right," George says.

"Get to his ball as quickly as you can and have the yardage ready for him, and all that, so when he gets there he's ready to play," I say.

"Right."

"Don't worry about me. I've played here before."

"Right."

Somehow our round at North Berwick suddenly seems less about enjoying a splendid walk together and more about simply surviving. After only three holes, Don appears visibly winded, and noticeably cranky. Part of his sour mood, I reckon, is the absence of nicotine in his bloodstream, since he has pledged to play his first round of Scottish golf without cancer sticks. And part of it, I suppose is having his unavoidable slowness spotlighted by the fast-moving Scots behind us, who seem to play each hole as though there were a hot meal waiting for them on the next tee. I want badly to have the ability, the omniscience, to make all Don's pains and demons disappear, so that this glorious seaside links were more a playground and less a gauntlet. But all I can do is be insanely cheerful and positive and perky, like a morning talk-show host on amphetamines.

It doesn't seem to work.

After going bogey-bogey-bogey-double bogey, Don does something for the first time in my presence: he throws a club.

After snap-hooking his tee-shot on the short par-4 seventh, Don whips his driver into the ground. It bounces madly from side to side and comes to rest ten yards from the tee.

No one says anything. Don stands with his hands on his hips, shaking his head morosely. George looks at me, nervously rubbing his eyebrow ring. I look at George and shrug. We three stand there for a moment, frozen.

"So, George," I say, striding off the tee, "you got any girlfriends?" We head off toward the fairway, leaving Don to stew in his own bile.

"Sorry, lad," I say. "There's no call for that on a golf course."

George says, "Well, he's havin' trouble. Wuz wrong wuthim anyway?"

I briefly consider telling George about Don's disease and the attendant physical problems it produces. But, instead, I say, "His problem, I think, is that his body is here in Scotland, but the rest of him hasn't arrived yet."

"Oh," George says, nodding, allowing himself about four seconds of philosophizing. "Are American girls randy?"

We trade several closely guarded secrets about the women of our continent—George seems rather well educated on this subject for a lad of thirteen—until we come to the eighth tee. There before us is a scene out of a Constable landscape, too perfect and serene to be real.

"It's like God sendin' doon hus angels," George comments, looking at the sublime beams of sunlight streaming through high clouds, like threads of silver unspooling from the sky.

"It is, George," I agree. "And I don't even believe in God." I turn to Don, who has just saved par from an impossible lie in the left rough. "How 'bout that, pards?" I say, extending my arms like a game show model.

Don grunts something.

He barely acknowledges the magnificent sky. He doesn't hear the seabirds performing an atonal symphony of life. He doesn't notice the gorgeous bunkering, the clever green contours, the generous land. He misses everything that is wonderful about playing golf at North Berwick on the finest day of the century.

For about thirty minutes, my pal Spiritual Don behaves like the typical results-oriented American golfer, whose pleasure (or lack thereof) is derived solely from the score he shoots. I see this very clearly, because Don, during this ugly sojourn, has become me—the younger me, the one who was no fun at all because all that mattered was winning and proving I was good enough and strong enough and talented enough to be liked, to have a friend.

And then there's the current me—the one who plays like a man connected to the land, energized and enlightened by the power that rises up out of the ground, the one who plays very much like Don Naifeh has taught him is the true and finest way to play.

It's all very plain to me now, like a profound riddle whose answer comes to you in a dream. I'll be him and he can be me, and we'll see how it feels. And, I don't know, maybe we'll both learn something.

Connections. Connected. All that stuff.

I play like a connected man and beat Don 3 up, capping my front nine with a 2-putt birdie on the 510-yard closing par-5. And I feel like something—what? poetry?—has delivered me this tiny victory while the younger me, the ugly me—the one over there in the bucket hat, with the big shoe on his right foot—is still fretting over past wounds.

I'm done playing cheerleader and tour guide, drawing Don's attention away from his deteriorating golf game and toward the beauty of the day. My own spiritual quest has begun—even if I'm not sure what I'm supposed to be looking for.

After we exit the back of the ninth green and climb a short path to the tenth tee, Don finds a friendly bench and announces he'll be taking a ten-minute break. I couldn't think of a better spot for a midround daydream—and according to George, neither could Robert Louis Stevenson. The lad says it was here that the great author would sometimes sit, gazing toward the three big rocks in the sea, imagining fantastical stories of pirates and shipwrecks and secret maps. "Ye heard ova book culled *Treasure Island*?" George asks ingenuously.

I grin and nod. "One of my favorites."

"Wull, they say this is where Stevenson got his inspurration," George proclaims.

I feel a shiver run through my spine. When I was a lad, younger even than Pierced George, I read *Treasure Island* voraciously (and repeatedly), transporting myself from my jejune world of suburban ennui to a land of adventure and intrigue. Even if I had few friends and playmates, even if David Hanson was busy with some family function that didn't require his basketball-baseball-football-miniature-golf collaborator, my books were always at the ready, available for a fabulously liberating flight that never left the ground. I particularly liked the stories of Twain and Dickens and Mr. Robert Louis Stevenson; in them I sensed an omnipresent—and often explicit—indictment of injustice and cruelty, two notions I was acutely attuned to as a youngster. Years later, when preparing a biographical report on Stevenson, I learned he suffered from ill health—consumption or emphysema, I recall—and felt truly well only when he could retreat into the world of his narrative fantasies. I was too young then to fully appreciate the metaphorical bond between me and the esteemed Scottish author, but I wasn't too young to feel it in my lonely heart. And now, more than twenty years later, standing on the very swatch of turf Stevenson allegedly reclined upon as he concocted scenarios I (and millions of others) would later devour, I feel as if today the kinship between author and reader has somehow been fully consecrated on this blissful golf course.

Strange coincidence, I think, peering out to the sea, with young George standing beside me, looking very much as I once imagined Jim Hawkins might have, ruddy-cheeked and hale. Connections, I believe Don Naifeh calls them.

Fortified with Diet Coke and tobacco—Don's nicotine embargo lasts exactly nine holes—he's a changed man on North Berwick's scenic inward half. I note with some amusement that as Don's play improves—he strings together four pars in a row—his appreciation of the course's aesthetic charms grows in almost direct proportion. Don tells me that on the Treasure Island Spot, he took a few moments to find himself, to get comfortable with the new and unfamiliar strains on his body and his mind. "Michael," he declares, "I was feeling so tired I thought you might have to carry me in. But, you know, a good Cuban stogie seems to do wonders for my endurance."

What I'm thinking is, "No, hitting a few fairways and greens and making a putt here and there seems to do wonders for your endurance, not to mention your attitude." But I don't say it. I'm being carried along on a cloud of literary memories, happy remembrances of Long John (Silver, not Daly) and his cohorts, and I don't want to hop off just yet to the inadequacies of the here and now. I think of Robert Louis Stevenson, coughing into his fist, peering through rheumy eyes at the horizon, knowing there must be a world out there, beyond the waves, where all his pains and sorrows would drift away like flotsam in high tide. For Stevenson perhaps it was *Treasure Island*. For me it is his homeland. I realize as I walk the wonderful North Berwick links that Scotland has for many years been *my* Treasure Island, a gift-giving distant shore where hours spent chasing a little white ball beside the sea are filled with a peace and contentment quotidian life too often lacks.

Stevenson once wrote to a friend, "There is something in me worth saying, though I can't find what it is just yet."

Eventually he found it. And I hope I will too.

For now, I simply wish to bathe my face in the balmy light, listen to the melody of George's youthful voice, and watch my golf buddy Don play the game as though it were a blank canvas upon which he might paint in confident and inspired strokes. The sourness gone, joy rushing in to take its place, Don plays beautifully, despite the fatigue he clearly must battle. The exquisite control with which he authors his shots amazes me, particularly on the monstrous fifteenth, the "Redan," probably the most imitated par-3 design in the world, with a diagonal green that slopes away from the player, guarded by two gaping bunkers. It's 192 yards at North

Berwick and plays directly into a stout wind. The trick is to hit something long enough to carry the bunkers but soft enough to avoid running through the putting surface and down a steep slope. Don somehow manages to finesse a 3 iron to the front right of the green—which funnels directly toward the back-left pin position.

His ball stops seven feet from the hole. And he makes the birdie putt.

"Tha's rare," George assures him. "I've never seen a burrdie on thus hool."

"Birdie on the Redan!" I say, clapping Don on the back.

He nods happily. Don isn't a big course-architecture wonk, one of those slightly scary guys who can (and will) argue the merits of Ross versus MacKenzie until the sun rises. I'm not sure he's ever heard of the Redan. I'm certain he has no inkling of the hole's historical significance, of how everyone from C. B. MacDonald to Tillinghast to Stanley Thompson paid homage to the North Berwick original. But I do know this: he won't forget he made birdie on a beautiful golf hole at 8:00 P.M. on a Monday night in Scotland, doing it all on his own two feet.

I know something strange has happened to me here this day, with the ghost of Jim Hawkins walking beside me and the spirit of his author in the air. What's weird is I know in my heart I am more glad that Don birdied the Redan than I would have been if I had.

I want him to have something. Something bigger than birdies and two-pound notes and victories over his able-bodied competitor. I don't know what that something is exactly. But a birdie at the Redan is a good start.

On my favorite hole at North Berwick, I lose the first ball of our trip. The thirteenth here, the "Pit," is the kind of hole that were a brave course architect to design it today, he would be laughed out of the business. An ancient stone wall separates the fairway from the green, which sits in a huge depression—the eponymous pit—invisible from beyond the wall. All the player can see is the flag, which sits atop a stick that must be fifteen feet tall. It's a quirky, original, and utterly Scottish hole, and I love it. The last time I played number thirteen, I made eagle from the fairway, dropping in a sand wedge from 100 yards—and I never saw any of it.

With positive memories to draw upon, I promptly make the only mistake you can't make on this hole and deposit my drive in dune grass on the left that would frighten a lawn mower. The beach is perhaps ten yards from where my wayward orb lies hidden, and the water licks at the sand just a few yards farther out, beckoning me to forget this game of golf and come sail away with the pirates.

As George and I search in vain for my tee-shot, Don pulls a handful of golf balls from his bag and writes something on them with a pink Sharpie pen. I go back to digging through the vegetation, mystified at how easily an ostensibly solid object can seemingly evaporate when it comes in contact with native flora. When I next look up, Don has a ball teed up in the fairway, facing toward the sea.

"Michael, you don't mind, do you?" he asks. "I'm gonna hit a few balls into the ocean."

George and I trade quizzical looks. "No. Sure. Whatever you'd like," I stammer.

"Thanks," Don says.

No one says a word. Even the seagulls circling in the sky cease their cacophony. Don takes a deep breath through his nose, finds his balance on his two misshapen legs, and launches a drive into the water, flying forever, never coming down, it seems, until it gets to Treasure Island.

7

A House and a Home

Mr. A. Sneddon, the secretary of the Golf House Club, in the East Neuk of Fife, is justifiably proud of the grounds and membership he oversees. "Elie," as most of the locals call the place—after the town in which it sits—is one of the oldest golf clubs in the world, and it drips with tradition and history and all the other estimable values most players of the game seem to hold dear. Indeed, when compared to some other sports, in which thuggery and chicanery are not only accepted but extolled, golf floats on a rarefied plane of elevated virtue, and its adherents are keen to remind others (and often themselves) that it is this inherent *goodness* that makes golf different from almost every other athletic pursuit. We have on our side tradition. History. Gentlemanliness. The archetype golfer has a stout heart and firm chin, held high against gale winds, pounding rain, and the pernicious forces of radicalism.

Don Naifeh, I've noticed over the years, subscribes to all these fine ideals. But he's not as fully invested in them as others I've met, tweedy fellows who, it sometimes seems, would rather discuss the spirit of Bobby Jones than walk the links. Don knows his history, and he celebrates the game's traditions. But he's less excited by boozy late-night discussions of Vardon versus Braid than wide-eyed recollections of the strange-weird-unexplainable events that repeatedly occur on a golf course. He's the kind of guy who, even in the face of overwhelming evidence of a prankster's clever hand, doesn't discount the possibility that space aliens might be responsible for crop circles in rural Nebraska. In his search for connections—those damned connections—he is willing to dismiss reason and embrace the supernatural, or the spiritual, or whatever it is that makes golf such a spooky and wondrous passion.

So as Mr. A. Sneddon shows Don and me around the clubhouse at Elie, I can see Don's attention fading like an ill-tuned radio when the secretary points approvingly at faded portraits of past captains and various other esteemed members who once changed their socks in this very building. But when our gracious host points out the bay windows toward the links and tells us that holes four to seventeen occupy land where "golf has been played for more than 400 years," I see Don's eyes flash, like my dog's when she see a squirrel.

"Shepherds and such?" Don inquires.

"Yes. And probably the local fishermen and sea traders," the secretary says.

Don simply says, "Wow." Unsaid, I suspect, are fanciful theories about ancient spirits and ghosts and other unseen forces that I'm too dense to recognize.

"Mmm. Yes. Wow," Mr. Sneddon says, guiding us toward the first tee.

Like the eighteenth at Riviera Country Club, back home in California, the first at the Golf House Club requires a blind tee-shot—and has a periscope nearby to prevent overeager players (particularly visiting Americans hungry for a four-centuries-old links) from plunking the group ahead with premature "e-hack-ulations." Don peers through the device—which looks to me to be the real deal, salvaged from a decommissioned submarine—and coos appreciatively. "Oooh, this looks sweet," he declares.

We trade places, and I see what he means. Several hundred yards in the distance but clear as though they were right beside me, I can make out a plethora of stacked-sod bunkers, the kind that Americans often describe as "penal" and that Scots consider a regular part of the game. The turf is brownish and crusty, thanks to a recent spate of unexpected sun storms, and the greens look firm and fast, as though every living thing has been slow-baked. Most of my pals back home, weaned on Masters telecasts and overwatered real-estate-development golf courses that pass themselves off as "plush," would probably find the conditions here at Elie slightly ragged, if not objectionable. To me and Don it's heaven. Which is yet another reason I love playing with this Oklahoma hillbilly: Like the Scots, he knows the difference between a golf course that's been neglected and one that's the way nature meant it to be played. Damned be the fertilizers and irrigation sprinklers and the impossibly green carpets they produce—*this* is honest land for an honest game.

With a forebodingly gloomy sky boiling over the sea, which today looks angry and restless, Don and I wait our turn at the first tee. Two members of the Golf House Club, a husband and wife, play on. Though it is maybe fifty degrees and cooling rapidly, he sports knee-length shorts and knee-high blue stockings. She wears pants and a "jumper," as they charmingly call sweaters over here. Both of them smack the tar out of their golf balls.

Don murmurs to me, "My kind of woman. Man, did you see that swing?"

"Beautiful," I reply.

Mr. Sneddon says, "Let's hope you gentlemen can hit that nicely," and wishes us a good round and retreats into his office in the dignified white clubhouse.

Our caddies, two older club members named Phil (short, with a cute little Hogan cap) and Andrew (tall, with glasses thick as an airport paperback), nod approvingly at Mr. and Mrs. Slugger's pokes and withdraw our drivers from their sheaths. "Jes follow thoos two!" Andrew says.

Touched by the ancient spirits—or is it just the product of a good night's sleep?—we both hit crackers down the middle, over the blind bluff. The starter, spying through the periscope, gives us a thumbs-up. "Ye'll not be wanning thoos back!" he assures us.

Climbing the hill, using his driver as a cane, Don turns to me and says, "Well, Michael, I'm two-for-two."

"Two opening tee-shots, two fairways," I say.

"Well, yeah, that too," Don replies. "But I'm two-for-two. Two days in a row I can't find a single reason why I would ever want to leave this place!"

The night before, after our tour of North Berwick, Don and I scrambled to find a cash machine and something to eat and a place to sleep. Lacking reservations—with dozens of private homes hanging out "B&B" shingles in the front lawn, I've never needed them in Scotland before—we were forced to drive out of town to find accommodations, since, it seemed, there was some sort of annual regatta happening on North Berwick's picturesque shores. The next town and the next, and the next and the next, were all full up with boaters. Gullane, Luffness, Kilspindie—nothing. We stopped in Longniddry, at the local "chipper" (fish and chips and every other manner of deep-fried animal parts)/pizzeria/video store, for the first of what I expected would be many servings of grease-soaked, artery-clogging Scottish cuisine. I read somewhere that Scotland has the highest incidence of heart disease in the world—and I'd be willing to wager it's not because of stress or lack of exercise. They love to smoke and they love to eat unhealthy things, as though two decades of alarming news-magazine cover stories somehow slipped their collective attention.

While we waited for our battered delicacies to emerge from their bubbling brown bath, Don and I looked at the framed photos on the wall. Through a film of congealed chip oil, I could make out the shop's proprietor with his arm around various golf legends like Tom Watson and Greg Norman and Lee Trevino, posing, it appeared, when the Open was at various times in residence at Muirfield. A whimsical thought flashed through my jet-lagged mind: supposedly, Gary Player, during his initial trip to Scotland as a poor young pro, slept his first night in a bunker at St. Andrews; maybe I should propose to Don we do the same thing at nearby Muirfield, site of so many historic championships.

But then I realized Don would probably say yes, so I kept it to myself.

I asked the chip man if he knew of a B&B nearby. He said there was one old lady, next to the church, who had a spare room or two. But she doesn't take single males. "Ye can understand, right?"

Actually, I couldn't. But I was too tired, hungry, and coated with fry vapors to pursue this mystery.

"So I guess we'll just keep driving on," I said. "Next town."

"Aye. Ye can ask a' the inn. They might fix ya."

Toting our fried sausage (Don) and fried haddock (me), we squeezed into our overloaded Peugeot in search of a hot shower and a warm bed. It was nearly 10:00 P.M.

At the inn, a nice barmaid/psychiatrist/waitress/booking agent told me she might know a place with a spare room. She disappeared into a back room. I chatted about the weather with a quartet of congenial drunks. And two minutes later we had a room. Down the road. At the home of an elderly couple—Mr. and Mrs. Playfair.

Don, I knew, was going to love this. Who cares about the size of the room or the quality of the mattress or the selection of breakfast cereals? We were spending our first night in Scotland at the home of George and Aileen Playfair.

I was thinking this is like something out of one of Don's beloved Shivas Irons books, if not Dickens.

I went to the car, address in hand. "We got a place," I told him. "It's a private home. Our hosts are called the Playfairs."

Don smiled and said, "Perfect."

In the morning, after a meal that consists of virtually every imaginable part of a pig accompanied by fried eggs, Don announces that he has just eaten his first breakfast outside of America.

"Well, then it's fitting you had pork," I comment.

"Why's that?" Don wonders.

"Because I heard once that the pig is the only animal who can't look behind him. He's always looking forward, toward the future."

My pal the spiritual seeker nods appreciatively. "And I had sausage last night. My first dinner out of America."

"Thus, you will be looking straight ahead on this trip, never to the past. See?"

Don has got me on the lookout for these connections, these signs and symbols, that may or may not mean anything. On the other hand, they could mean everything, and, in a sort of a golfer's version of Pascal's Wager I figure there's no downside in keeping my eyes open for them.

So I wonder: is it merely an inspiring curiosity that my caddie at Elie, Andrew, who strides with the power and sure-footedness of a middle linebacker and looks to be about fifty-two, reveals to me on the fourth hole that he is seventy-seven years old? Or should I take it as some profoundly meaningful omen, a lesson perhaps, that days spent outdoors beside the eternal waters of the North Sea make a man seem twenty-five years younger than he really is? Or do I just dismiss this revelation as another example of good genes?

My default response before meeting Don Naifeh would have been incredulity. How could a man I mistook for early fifties actually be in his late seventies? But now, after only two days in Scotland, I'm prone to believe there's some sort of profound message I'm supposed to be getting—from where or whom I'm unsure.

This sort of epistemological distraction, I soon discover, is good for your golf game. Well, it is for mine, at least. At the Golf House Club I eagle the 316-yard par-4 sixth after driving my tee-shot downwind to just off the green, pin high. My putt-chip from fifteen yards away looks as if it's going twenty feet past the hole until it hits the flagstick and rattles in. Following this startling development, I turn back upwind and drive the 252-yard par-4 seventh and narrowly miss another eagle putt—and the chance to do something I've never done: write down two 2s in a row on my scorecard.

Andrew is a man of few words, a caddie who points the way, makes a gentle suggestion, and gets out of the way. He looks at putts for about three seconds, usually from but one perspective, and declares the perfect line. He does this neither imperiously nor insecurely, just very plainly, as if he is telling time. I admire his quiet certainty, his workmanlike efficiency, his lack of flash. He does not regale me with far-fetched tales of on-course miracles he has witnessed or famous people he has known or scores he has made in his younger days. He mentions only that he has a few children and several grandchildren and has lived almost all his seventy-seven years in the East Neuk of Fife—and that he has spent more time than he cares to admit walking the out-and-back loop from clubhouse to sea to home.

I trust Andrew. He is the kind of man I hope I will be when I am seventy-seven: healthy, vital, and profoundly comfortable with where I have been and what I have seen. He's wise in a wordless way. And he helps me putt well.

Very well. I make almost every putt of consequence I look at, rolling in clutch 6-footers, improbable 20-footers, even a 30-footer at the eighth. Don, his good humor restored, reacts to my comical flat-stick accuracy with his usual grace and cheerfulness. "Best I've ever seen!" he mock complains to his caddie. "The guy's made a hundred yards of putts on me today!" When I make a few more improbable bombs to eke out halves on holes Mr. Naifeh should have by all rights easily won, he amends the measurement to a "half a mile!"

"Aye, 'es a good putter," Don's caddie, Phil, agrees. "Kweet good."

Several years ago, back when I really *was* a good putter, if I was having a deadly day on the greens I would share a secret with my caddie: once, in 1996, I actually qualified for the World Putting Championship, where I made the cut and was paired with two-time U.S. Open champion Lee Janzen in the final round (where I promptly self-destructed as the ESPN cameras rolled). I still carry around an official contestant's money clip from that event, and I used to be proud to flash it around on the links, as though it were the Wanamaker Trophy. These days, when the vicissitudes in my putting ability seem to mirror the changeable Scottish weather, I keep this bit of personal history mostly to myself. It's too embarrassing to tell a grizzled old caddie (who's seen a thousand American golfers who think they know something about the game) that you were at one time a trained assassin with the blade, right up there with Crenshaw and Faxon and Mickelson, only then to putt as if the stick in your hand were about to sprout barbed thorns.

Today, though, every time I hear Don crow "best I've ever seen!" I feel the urge to reach in my pocket and start telling yarns about competing against Payne Stewart and Tom Kite and Beth Daniel. But I look at Andrew, taciturn and tough, and I decide I'd rather just play golf.

As we make the turn, far from the comforts of civilization, right beside the crashing sea, where marauding seals chase migrating salmon and where Andrew says the local lads (him included) wade into the low tide and snatch unsuspecting lobsters, the light mist that has been hanging over Elie all morning turns to a drizzle, and then a persistent rain. It's the kind of biblical downpour Don professes to love. (I hate it; I can't hold on to my clubs, no matter what trick someone suggests involving towels or socks or fancy gloves.) We cleverly packed an armory of umbrellas and rain pants and water-repellent bag covers before we came to Scotland. But since it was partly sunny—or was it partly cloudy?—when we commenced our round, Don and I neglected to actually bring any of our prophylactics to the prom.

It's not like I've never been to the British Isles before. I know it can rain viciously here with almost no advance warning. I know when in Scotland you must be prepared—always, like a Boy Scout—for showers. But I misread the signs. I figured the warming sun that greeted our arrival and heralded the start of our odyssey's second day was a symbol of something grandly spiritual, something connected to something else. And even if I couldn't identify exactly what those two things were—or, for that matter, even one of them—I shouldn't question the artistry of it all.

So now I'm soaked. And my kind caddie, peering through foggy glasses, is less interested in why I putt so well than how I could walk onto a seaside links in the Kingdom of Fife (on a partly cloudy, partly sunny morning) without an umbrella.

My ability to make pars and birdies—not to mention eagles—rapidly disappears. Forget about golf balls. Now I'm lucky to finish a hole with the same *club* I started with.

My grips feel as if they've been dipped in the deep fryer, I've got a pool of icy water collecting around my toes, and my competition, the gimpy fellow who wasn't even supposed to be able to make it around the course without some sort of intervention from the Gods of Golf, is smiling and laughing and behaving as though he were a geranium in Palm Springs. "Man, I love it!" Don squeals, turning his face upward toward the pelting clouds. "Paradise!"

While I'm vainly searching for a ball I've shanked, Don stands in the middle of the fairway, writing on golf balls with his Sharpie pen. His caddie, Phil, stands silently with his mouth agape, a trickle of drool running down his chin. Andrew notes this surreal tableau with a languid double take and resumes looking for my naughty orb.

We have our heads down, deep in the fescue, when we hear a crack, like the sound of small-artillery fire. Startled, we look up to see Don Naifeh facing the roiling sea, driving brand new Titleists into the water.

"Now wuz he doon?" Andrew asks me, utterly perplexed.

"It appears he's hitting tee-shots into the ocean," I say flatly.

"Now whydya suppoos he da tha?"

"I suppose he'd do that because there's some sort of weird symbolism involved. But, hell, I don't know. Maybe you should ask him?"

"He's kweet daft."

"Yes, Andrew, he is."

"Daft bugger," Andrew says, chuckling.

When Don has finished, after depositing half a dozen shots into the surf, he smiles slightly and limps on toward the green, radiating contentment. Phil and Andrew momentarily put their heads together and murmur quietly about what they've just witnessed. They're both laughing softly when I arrive.

"So? Did he say something to you?" I ask Phil.

"He wuz writin' neems," Phil reports. "Friends an' sooch. Why, I dinna ken." He shrugs and shakes his head in bewilderment.

The elderly caddies say nothing more about what they have witnessed. But I can see something like pain etched in their weathered faces: so many perfectly good golf balls—at three pounds sterling per!—sent to a watery grave! I envision Andrew waiting for low tide and wading out 200 yards to retrieve a few autographed Titleists along with his lobsters.

"You're killing those guys," I tell Don when I catch up with him, splashing puddles as I jog. "They can't bear to watch."

"Just a little something I like to do," Don tells me, looking far more peaceful than any soaking wet man has a right.

"What's the deal with the names, if you don't mind my asking?"

"Well, Michael, I believe when you're doing something wonderful—and, man, this is wonderful!—you should remember those who can't be there with you. So I write the names of friends and relatives on these balls. And I believe when I send them into the sea these people will feel a, um, like a . . ."

"Connection?" I say.

"Yeah. A connection. You understand, don't you?"

I nod. "I guess. Did you explain this to Phil?"

We look at our caddies huddled together, chatting and grinning. "Well, not in depth," Don says.

"Because you're killing these guys. You know that, right? You're killing them. All those nice golf balls."

"Oh, I think they understand," Don replies. "They're Scottish."

After his name-on-the-ball ritual, I make double bogey on the thirteenth; Don makes birdie. Do we have a patently dysfunctional relationship, in which one party can be happy only when the other is miserable? Or is Don merely insane?

As we slosh to the fourteenth tee, turning away from the churning ocean, I congratulate my saturated friend on his stellar play, lamenting the fact that my 1-up lead in our match has deteriorated into a 1-down deficit. We are on the oldest part of the golf course now, the land that Mr. A. Sneddon says has hosted golfers for more than four centuries. I am wet and miserable. Don is wet and delighted. There's a lesson here, but my brain is presently too squishy to comprehend it.

"Well, Donnie," I say, attempting vainly to be good-natured about the miserable circumstances, "you wanted weather. Welcome to Scotland."

"Yeah, it's great," Don says, apparently without the vaguest sense of irony. "I think if you really love playing golf—I mean *really* love it—then weather enhances it. Any kind of weather. Wind, sun, rain, hail. It's all good. It's all about being in nature. I mean, here's nature really letting us know we're in her house, you know?"

"So you like being soaked?" I ask, skeptical.

"Let's put it this way," Don says, wiping a rivulet of rainwater from his brow. "I'm carrying twenty or thirty pounds of wet clothes on this body of mine, yet I feel like this is one of the easiest walks I've ever had."

I know I should say something like, "That's beautiful, Don" or "I never looked at it that way, my friend." But instead I blurt, "You are seriously fucked up," and stick a tee in the soggy ground.

"Did you say I'm 1-up?" Don teases. "'Cause I'm about to go 2-up."

We all four laugh, a quartet of sopping fools, two gents with their faithful seconds, playing where countless other sopping fools once tended their sheep and slapped around a pellet, waiting for the storm to pass.

Beside the sixteenth green, after blasting out of a deep bunker to within inches of the cup, Don calls for his caddie to toss him an empty plastic bag he's got stored in the side pocket of his golf kit. To our collective amazement—well, I'm slightly less amazed than the caddies, since I've been privy to Don's eccentricities for some time now—he scoops up a handful of sand, deposits it in the baggie, and places it in his pocket. "For my collection!" Don announces.

"He likes to take samples," I explain to Andrew. "Like a geologist."

On previous visits to the Kingdom, golf acquaintances have asked me to bring back ball markers and hats and other souvenirs with official logos on them. Don, though, has always asked if I might retrieve sand from certain noteworthy bunkers. He says he wants his ashes to be mixed with these blessed granules so they might one day be scattered among his favorite golf courses. On one trip, I carried around Scotland a small chunk of Hell Bunker for two weeks, praying a zealous customs inspector wouldn't open my golf bag and wonder why I was toting home a piece of the Old Course. When I finally gave it to Don upon my return home, it was as though I had handed him a bag of golden ducats.

My eyes meet Andrew's. He's seen a lot in his seventy-seven years, I'm sure. But probably not this. "Completely daft," I tell him.

"Aye," Andrew says.

At the seventeenth tee, we pass three lady members toting carry-bags (and umbrellas), who, even in the downpour, crush their tee-shots like Laura Davies. Don moans appreciatively. "What a turn-on. A woman who plays golf in the rain. Now *that's* my kind of woman."

"And we're definitely their kind of men. They must have found it irresistibly attractive that we were clever enough to visit Elie without an umbrella," I tease.

"Man, I gotta move here."

I chuckle to myself. Only Don Naifeh could make such a pronouncement during the foulest conditions Scotland has to offer.

As we hole out at the eighteenth, where I graciously 3-putt for the first time all day, thereby saving my dear pal more than twenty pounds sterling, the rain stops, on cue, as if in a Buster Keaton film. Or a play Sam Beckett forgot to write. At almost the exact moment we shake hands with our caddies and depart the golf course, the sun begins to shine.

"Of course!" I exclaim, looking skyward. "Perfect timing." I turn to Don, who's wringing out his floppy bucket hat. "So, Mr. Shivas Irons Society? What's the message in this?"

"Hell, I don't know," Don says, shrugging. "That the weather changes a lot in Scotland?"

While I avail myself of the locker room shower stalls, Don explores the Golf House Club's pro shop. He returns with significantly fewer pounds in his pocket and significantly more shirts, caps, and commemorative geegaws than he left with.

And he's got something else: A rain suit.

"I thought you had one of those," I say, puzzled. "What is it? A gift for someone back home?"

"Well, no, I figured this was a good place to get a rain suit to wear during the rest of my time in Scotland. And you know I'll get my money's worth while I'm here," he says.

"So you're buying a rain suit at Elie *after* you get rained on at Elie. I see," I say, even though I don't see. Not really.

"Exactly."

"Hmm."

"And the next time I'm back home and I get to wear it—which is almost never in Phoenix, of course, but, you never know—I'll remember the day I played the Golf House Club at Elie in the rain with my buddy Michael."

"Connections," I say, smirking.

"Yeah. Connections."

After we are suitably cleaned and dried, Don and I go to Mr. Sneddon's office to thank him for his hospitality and to report our great joy in having toured his club's ancient links. The secretary introduces us to a friend named, intriguingly, Mr. Robert Burns. I almost blurt out the word *connections* to Don, but his look tells me he's already registered the significance. Mr. Burns (Sneddon's friend, not the immortal poet) is a member of the Royal & Ancient Golf Club of St. Andrews, and, we are made to understand, he was responsible for setting the pins at the 2000 Open Championship.

"Really!" Don exclaims. "I guess you couldn't have been too happy to see Tiger demolish the course," he says, perhaps a bit indelicately.

"Actually," Burns replies, with only the slightest whiff of defensiveness, "we felt the Auld Lady held up quite well at the Championship. It was only one player who made that remarkable score. And he putted like the devil."

"I guess it doesn't matter where you hide the pins when a guy plays like that," Don remarks. "He made the course look totally defenseless, like a pitch-and-putt."

"Not a single bunker all week," I interject, hoping Don doesn't pursue this line of questioning too thoroughly. "Tiger missed them all."

"Remarkable," Burns says.

I can sense that Mr. Burns, smartly clad in his blue blazer, is a decent and amiable fellow, with nothing the least bit mean-spirited about him. But I can also sense that he doesn't "get" Don Naifeh, that the slightly deformed man hunched before him is not what Mr. Burns pictures when he thinks "golfer." Don is not well schooled in politesse and country club banter; he's a chop, from Papago Municipal. (A highly talented chop, to be sure, but still a chop at heart.) Don will never be asked to join the R&A or, for that matter, any other stuffy organization. He'll never be consulted on Sunday pin positions for the Open Championship. But at that moment, standing in Mr. A. Sneddon's Golf House Club office, I feel as though Don Naifeh may more accurately represent what golf is all about than a whole roomful of proper old boys clinging to their rule books and snifters of brandy.

We shake hands and say our thanks and our good-byes, and we head for our silver jalopy. Don laughs and says, "Do you think we should have asked him if he could get us a tee time at the Old Course?"

"Unbelievable! Will you look at this sunshine?" I proclaim, taking a last look at a golf course I'll never forget.

In the interest of cost cutting, Don and I had initially considered sharing a room each night. But upon the revelation that Don snores like a drunken sailor with bronchitis, we decide on separate quarters, a restful sleep being worth far more than $30. The B&Bs we are interested in must have two available singles, preferably "en suite," and a place where Chimney Don can smoke. In Elie we find the Oak Tree Inn, less than five minutes from the golf course. While the proprietors, Lindsay and Linda, kindly put our drenched clothing "in the tumble," Don and I retire to the backyard garden, where the sun shines as if we were in Hawaii.

Don reclines on a lawn chair, takes a long drag on his cigarette, and declares, "You know I'm going to have to move here, right? It's pretty clear to me: I've gotta."

"And what are you going to do—I mean, besides play golf?" I ask.

"They don't have a poker game in this town, do they?"

"You could always meet a rich widow."

"With a membership at the Golf House Club!" Don fantasizes.

"Who wants a nice American lad to play golf with her every day."

"No, seriously. I've gotta figure something out," he says. "If only there weren't this issue of earning a living."

"Yeah, that old problem," I say. How many of us, I muse, would be doing something entirely different with our lives if earning a living weren't a concern? Would we be a planet overpopulated with poets and sculptors and avant-garde choreographers, a society utterly oblivious to commerce? A society composed of golf bums?

"You think we can find an Internet café around here?" Don asks. "I suddenly want to check my stocks."

"I don't think you'll find a business in this town that has either 'Internet' or 'café' in their name, let alone both words," I say. "This is like a little fishing village. A refuge from modernity. Slow. Hey, speaking of which," I motion toward Don's legs, "how are you holding up?"

He tells me he's fine, no problem, much easier than he expected, couldn't be better. But then Don remembers he wanted to take some Tylenol, "just as a precaution." He gets up gingerly from his chair, and I can see him suppress a grimace.

"You're sure you're fine?" I repeat. "We can always take tomorrow off if you need to."

He looks at me as though I've just used Shivas's name in vain. "No, we're playing, Michael."

"All right," I say, throwing up my hands. "Just making sure." I watch Don shuffle off to his room and try not to let myself acknowledge what I already suspect: there's no way he's going to make it through two weeks of this.

To distract myself from the inevitable, I go to the front of the house, where our car is parked, and systematically remove every item in the vehicle, covering the sidewalk with suitcases and golf bags and shoes and sport jackets and everything else we've crammed into our overburdened hatchback. At first blush, our Avis rental looks just about large enough to accommodate us and a sleeve of golf balls. But by employing the kind of penurious space-management techniques perfected by the airlines, wizards at cramming as many sweaty passengers into the coach cabin as FAA regulations allow, I manage to stow all our luggage, golf gear, *and* Billie Holiday compact discs into our noble chariot. Instead of a rolling toxic waste site, now we've got a mobile home—only about 1/100th as big.

For some strange reason—maybe because I'm an obsessive-compulsive, slightly autistic neat freak—repacking the car brings a calm to my heart, very much like the calm I've witnessed in Don's face after he's hit six factory-fresh Titleist Tour Balatas with names scribbled on them into the North Sea. Now at least I know where all our stuff is, even if I don't know exactly where we're going or what we'll find when we get there. If this is what people mean when they talk about "peace of mind," then I'm all for it.

Later, after another evening meal that covers all the key Scottish food groups—fat, tallow, cream, and sugar—Donnie and I take a wee walk around all of charming downtown Elie, a task that requires about three minutes, even at Don's shuffling pace. Following the sound of sea birds, we turn down a narrow stone lane and come to a precipice overlooking Elie Bay. It's around 9:00 P.M., and the dying light pours down like liquefied gold, coating all it touches with the kind of glow I associate with Tiepolo angels. The tide is out, and children play in the sand, their youthful voices (with the cutest accents) carry on the soft breeze to our waiting ears. A lighthouse winks in the distance, and a small fishing boat glides silently across the horizon.

Don looks as if he might laugh or cry.

"There's no use fighting it," he declares. "I've got to figure out some way to live here. I can't see why I would want to live anywhere else."

"It's magic," I agree.

"The only problem I can see is earning enough money to enjoy the life you've got here. Of course," Don says, waving his gnarled hand over the nautical scene, "getting to look at sights like this doesn't cost a penny."

We sit and breathe and listen, lost in private reveries. I recall perfect Scottish nights spent with my lover, gazing together on the sea, wishing time would never end. For me, those days have gone. Don, I suspect, imagines a happy future, filled with perfect Scottish nights spent with a lover who likes to play golf in the rain. His days are coming. He nods to himself almost imperceptibly. Yes, his days are coming.

A group of loud youngsters approaches and grows quiet as they walk past our bench. One of them, I can see, is fascinated by Don's enormous shoe. When they get twenty yards farther down the path, I can hear laughter.

"I guess we should be heading back," Don says. "I need to take some more Tylenol."

"Sure," I say. "But before we go, I want to take a photo of this gorgeous scene."

"Oh. Sure. All right," Don says, pushing himself to his feet.

"No, no. With you in the picture. Just sitting here on the bench, looking out there, toward Muirfield and North Berwick."

"Now why would you want to ruin a perfectly good picture like that?" Don jokes.

"For the scrapbook," I say. The light has turned orange-pink, and as I frame him in the heavenly glow, I think Don will like to have a memento from a peaceful time, when his dreams came rushing to the forefront and all his pains went far, far away.

8

Earth, Wind, and Fire

The gloomy gray Scotland of Don Naifeh's dreams, the one in which the clouds brood over the countryside and the winds blow with cold fury, seems to be on vacation in Greenland this week. One strong and bracing rain at Elie and the angry skies are gone, as though they just needed a good cathartic cry. Weep, rage, vent—and all is well again in bonnie Scotland.

This, of course, disappoints Don and delights me. (There's a metaphor in this, I know, but it's early, and I've had too much whisky the night before to decode it.) When we pile into our silver hatchback for a day at Lundin Links, an Open Championship–qualifying course fifteen minutes from our B&B, you could accurately call the day *hot*—which is not a word you generally connect with Scotland, unless you're talking about tea or fried potatoes. The sun shines so brightly, so insistently, I actually get burnt on my forehead and cheeks, as though while we slept this fair isle had broken off from England and drifted through the Straits of Magellan into the South China Sea.

Don's freshly purchased rain suit and fancy bag hood and Tour-style umbrella all go for naught. But the elements don't completely fail him: There's a steady fifteen to twenty mile per hour wind, gusting to thirty-five or forty, which does all sorts of wickedly entertaining things to imperfectly struck golf shots.

Before our round at Lundin Links, we visit next door at Leven, another Open-qualifying venue, where Don gently interrogates the starter about various *Golf in the Kingdom* references that may (or may not) have been veiled references to this splendid golf course. It becomes painfully clear—to me anyway—that the starter, a burly man with bushy eyebrows and cracked teeth, has not only not read this mystical book but hasn't even heard of it. It is also clear to me that the starter regards Don as slightly peculiar (which he is) and possibly demented (which he isn't).

My friend Don Naifeh's communication skills, it seems to me, haven't been honed in tea parlors and candlelit restaurants or, for that matter, by a mother who taught her boy to behave like a proper British prig, whether or not he grew up in Tulsa, Oklahoma. Forward and slightly loud, Don often sounds more like a New Yorker ordering a half pound of smoked fish in a delicatessen than a refined Southern gentleman. Instead of peppering his speech with copious "excuse me, Madam"s and "I'd like this, please"s, his standard locutions are more along the lines of "give me this" or "I want that." His abruptness and absence of social polish, I've noticed, occasionally alarms the Scots. When, for instance, we pull up beside a Scotsman in our car to ask for directions and Don's preamble to his otherwise polite question is "Hey!" most of the locals react as though someone is about to plant a cream pie in their face.

I gently explain to Don that this country, despite its historical difficulties with England, still retains an exquisite deference to British manners—specifically the good kind. I encourage Don to pretend he's in a Merchant Ivory production and say please and thank you way more than seems necessary.

Prior to our journey, Don had some sort of incident at work involving subordination to superiors (or something like that, typically corporate), which required numerous appeals and reviews to sort out before he could escape with an intact employment record. Knowing him well, I'd guess the whole nonsense was brought on by his poor communication skills—the same ones that so often give the locals here the mistaken impression that he's a gruff and inconsiderate oaf, the same ones that give his lover back home the mistaken impression that it's acceptable to treat him like an emotional punching bag.

Just as Don is trying to show me a new way of looking at the world, I'm trying to show him a new way to have the world look at him.

Sensing that Don's skepticism about the starter's ignorance of a fictional character is being misunderstood as a foreigner's indictment of his host's intelligence, I suggest to my buddy that we take a wee walk.

"Never heard of Shivas Irons," Don mumbles as I guide him away.

We stop on a public path beside the first hole, separated from the sea by a narrow asphalt road and a few yards of beach. "Let's get a visual feel for the links. Maybe you'll see something that rings a bell," I suggest.

"Sure," Don says, distracted and flummoxed that a local resident, a Man of The Game, a citizen of the Kingdom of Fife, hasn't even heard of the gospel according to Murphy.

"Come on," I say. "Let's have a look." I know this will be good for Don, because even if there isn't anything to see, he'll see something.

We watch a foursome of Leven Golf Club members tee off. None of them are particularly talented players, but it's obvious they all know something about the game, an insider's knowledge of its myriad secrets. Their shots fly low and hot, moving right to left with a classical draw, and though they don't stay in the air very long, they run forever when they hit the sun-baked turf, made harder still by a monthlong "drought" that started the week before the Open Championship. They play quickly and surely, if not expertly. And they all seem glad to be together.

I watch the golfers. Don watches the land. I'm noticing handsome checked trousers and funny caps; Don is looking at Leven's rolling sand dunes and parched grass. Seagulls squawk above us, and an amusement arcade across the road emits the squeals and buzzes of larcenous gambling machines. Don sways back and forth on his spindly legs, saying nothing. The landscape seems otherwise uninhabited. I feel as if I'm in a Fellini movie or one of those spooky plazas from a de Chirico painting, where solitude is tinged with terror.

"Let's go play golf," I say.

Don stares down the brown fairways for a few seconds, as if in a trance. Then he turns to me and nods. "Yeah. Let's go."

Lundin Links is the next village over from Leven, and the two golf courses, in fact, meet at their respective fifth holes, separated by a pretty stone wall. Many years ago, some holes on Leven were part of Lundin and some holes on Lundin were part of Leven—and once a year the members of both clubs have a competition in which they play out and back over the dividing wall, from clubhouse to clubhouse.

It doesn't take us long to drive from Leven to Lundin Links— which, in a fitting testament to the power of golf in this country, is the actual name of the town, "Lundin Links." Though I'm not sure exactly where the club is located, I figure it's somewhere near the beach, probably at the end of Golf Lane or the Old Links Road.

When I see a young lad walking through town with a golf bag on his shoulder, I know I'm headed in the right direction.

"Isn't that a great sight?" Don remarks, seeing the boy and his clubs. "It's like kids in America, walking home from the ballpark with a glove on the end of their baseball bat. Here you got kids walking around town with their golf clubs. Tremendous!"

Though the sun is at the moment turning all of Fife into a reasonable facsimile of Tahiti, we have learned our lessons well. We stuff all our rain-protection equipment into our bags. I do it to ward off the elements, since I know the surest way for the clouds to turn thunderous is for me to leave my Gore-Tex pants in the car. (This is the same theory that holds you should never wait to go for a par-5 green in 2, since the surest way to produce a pathetic mis-hit is to confidently allow the green to clear.) Don, on the other hand, packs his rain gear hopefully, wishing perhaps that the synthetic fibers stored in the pockets of his Ping quiver will have some extractive power, drawing precipitation from reluctant clouds.

What he doesn't have to pray for is wind. It continues to blow in great chewy gusts, whipping the rough fescues into a swaying troupe of modern dancers. Because Lundin Links, like almost all traditional seaside courses, has few (if any) trees on it, the only object tall enough to take the brunt of the unseen force is an erect human being. I feel the wind in my face, on my chest, on my thighs, and I'm reminded again how small and powerless I sometimes feel standing on an exposed swatch of the world, armed only with a puny golf club.

From the start of our round, Don handles the whirling winds exceptionally well, making the unseen forces work for him, like a jujitsu master. I, on the other hand, fight nature like a clumsy buffoon. It's a test, the wind is. He's passing; I'm failing.

The wind exacerbates everything that's wrong with my golf game: my tendencies to come "over the top," to employ power instead of fluidity, to get quick instead of languid. It also exacerbates everything that's "wrong" with today's round of golf: my fourteen-year-old caddie's ignorance of yardages; Don's incessant smoking; a left sock that doesn't fit well. Things I wouldn't otherwise notice become twenty-four-point-bold-type-ringed-in-neon catastrophes, thanks to the perfectly normal result of uneven heating of the earth's surface.

I hit a perfect 2 iron into the green on the fourth hole, a 452-yard brute named "Mile Dyke." (On the day we visit it seems to play more like two miles.) Though I strike the ball as pure as springwater, it comes up thirty yards short of the flag. "Damn wind," I mutter.

Now, I know I ought to be giggling, or at least grinning, at the comical absurdity of a mere hacker like me trying vainly to battle atmospheric forces that are bigger and stronger than any perimeter-weighted-graphite-shafted-titanium-headed implement of torture ever devised by the hand of man. It's not like I've never played in the wind before, in the Scottish wind moreover. The wind's ability to bend a flagstick and break a will is not unknown to me. Yet, armed with foreknowledge—and the equanimity such wisdom is supposed to bring you—I flail about helplessly, enslaved by my own demons.

Then there's Don, treating the enemy like a best friend. Which seems to make all the difference.

He wins the first four holes. I try mightily to enjoy the scenery.

On the fifth tee, beside the wall that separates Lundin from Leven, we take a photo together; I force a smile and try to banish from my mind all thoughts of clueless caddies, chain-smoking competitors, and badly constructed left socks. And I realize something: Don deserved to win the first four holes. Because, I come to understand, playing good golf is not always about making the best swings; it's about handling adversity (in all its forms) with grace and dignity and perspective. I did not grow up on the Great Plains; I don't like playing in ferocious wind. But by now, after multiple trips to a land where the wind tends to blow like Louis Armstrong on "Basin Street Blues," I ought to know at least how to deal with it.

So I do.

Golf is not a fight. It's a dance.

I vow to waltz and tango and sometimes even cha-cha-cha.

With my change in attitude comes a change in direction. We are now playing directly downwind. As unhelpful and disabling as the wind was going away from the clubhouse, it's now ridiculously assisting. Short par-4s are now potentially long par-3s. Approach shots that previously required fairway metals now demand a smooth sand wedge. I feel like a new man.

Strangely, as soon as we tack back toward the clubhouse, Don's spooky control of his game flies away with the breeze. On the sixth, "Spectacles," a wee par-4 of 330 yards that requires no more than a 4 iron off the tee, Don inexplicably hits driver and deposits his ball in waist-high rough on the right, where the old Leven train used to run. Though we search in earnest, his lost-ball promise comes to an ignoble end.

I'm pleased, of course, to win our silly bet (and mildly relieved to not have to pay him off at 10-to-1 odds). But I'm a little sad, too. I thought maybe God really had told Don Naifeh he, Don, wouldn't lose a ball during his entire trip to Scotland. I thought, sure, it's entirely possible (but improbable) that Don's spiritual connection with Scotland runs so deep that, yeah, sure, the land would agree to cough up any wayward shots and let him play on and on without pause or penalty. I thought maybe Don possessed some magic secret that would gradually be revealed as we made our way around Scotland in an overstuffed rental car. But, no, his tee-shot is definitely, unequivocally, undeniably lost.

Discovering that my pal is indeed human and not immune to the evil powers of prickly gorse is not exactly a Santa Claus or Tooth

Fairy moment, in which sacred childhood illusions are shattered by the blunt fist of reality. But still, I'm a little disappointed. I wanted to believe, even if I was too proud to admit it to him.

Walking off the sixth green, after winning the previous two holes with solid pars, I turn to Don and say, "I almost let you run away and hide. But I decided to grow up and enjoy myself."

"You think you won those holes because of you?" Don says, smirking.

"Well, yeah. I mean, I know you kindly hit your tee-shot out of bounds for me on this hole. But I started playing better when I quit fighting the wind and just enjoyed the day. See? I'm spiritual!"

"It's possible, sure," Don says, shuffling beside me to the seventh tee. "But I've got a different interpretation. I figure I'm just paying the price for being cocky. I had you 4-down after four, and I was feeling unbeatable. I even flashed four fingers in that picture we took on the fifth tee. Then, boom: bogey, double bogey. The golf course decided to punish me."

"I see," I say, chuckling. "So the moral is?"

"So the moral is if you get outta line on the golf course you'll eventually get spanked."

True enough, I think. Too high or too low, it makes no difference. You've always got to be searching for the center.

My daddy was fond of regaling me and my brother with what he called his "clichés," a collection of homey nuggets of wisdom whose profundity was masked by their simplicity. One of his favorites was, "Life is a series of peaks and valleys. The trick is to not get too dizzy when you're up on the peaks and not too demoralized when you're down in the valleys." I always knew what my dad meant. But today at Lundin Links, being blown around like a candy wrapper as I battle a gimpy competitor who refuses to lose his ball, I see how my dad's advice applies on a golf course. Which, as everyone knows, is a tidy little metaphor for life.

So now I'm feeling *really* enlightened.

Fearful that I might start making "be the ball" pronouncements straight out of the Shivas archives, I turn to the young lads carrying our bags and ask, "Do you boys have girlfriends?"

Michael, Don's caddie, the slightly older of the two, shakes his head disconsolately. "Nay. An' ut's soo depressin'."

He's a somber lad, Michael is, who barely ever smiles and takes his job quite seriously, as though Don were one of the potential Open Championship qualifiers he's been assigned to look after. (Michael's man this past month, a Frenchman named Pierre, actually made it through to St. Andrews but used his regular Tour caddie for the tournament.) He's also quite good looking and well-spoken. I wonder what's the problem.

"There's like five good-lookin' gurrls in these two toons," he reports.

"And so many lads. Yeah, that can be a problem," I say, nodding at Don.

"Depressin'," Michael repeats.

"Imagine growing up in a small town like this," I say to Don. "Pretty limited dating pool."

"You oughta come to America," Don suggests to the boys.

Without changing his dour expression, serious Michael says, "I hear the American gurrls are kweeet randy. Uzit true?"

I stifle a laugh. "Don?" I say. "Your thoughts."

"How old are you guys?" Don wonders, before answering.

"They're fourteen and thirteen," I remind him. "Actually, guys," I say, turning to our caddies, "everything you've heard is true."

"Really!?" Michael says, wide-eyed.

"Well, compared to Scottish girls, I would think so, yes," I say. "But you know what? When you get a little older, maybe by the time you're in university, you'll probably discover that all the girls who won't have anything to do with you now will eventually be even randier than you can imagine. Probably once they get away from home a bit, away from mum and dad."

"I can't wait," Michael says.

"Oh, it'll be worth it," I promise him. "Right, Don?"

"Yeah, that's basically true," Don says, nodding.

"Hhooooh," Michael moans. For the rest of the round, whenever he can sneak away from Don's side, he makes fervent inquires about the sexual habits of American girls, which I answer as best I can. His curiosity reminds me of me as a teenage boy, freshly inducted into the mysteries of romance and passion. It also reminds me of another day spent on a golf course—this one in Ireland, which is about the best substitute for Scotland I've yet to find—when my youthful caddie, about the same age as Michael, showed a healthy interest in the proclivities and appetites of American girls. This lad had never actually met one of these allegedly wild creatures, but he had snuck a look at programs like *Baywatch* on the telly, and he reckoned he had a pretty good idea of how liberated Yankee babes really were. Somewhere on the back nine, after feeling suitably familiar with me, he told me proudly that by the age of twelve he had already "shifted" ten girls.

I didn't know what this meant, but if it was something sexual, I was skeptical anyway. "Isn't this a Catholic country?" I asked my caddie.

"Aye, 'tis," he replied. But he insisted he had indeed "shifted" a large portion of the local female teenage populace.

"Do you believe that?" I asked my playing partner, a magazine photographer in his thirties.

"Hell, I don't think I've shifted ten girls in my whole life," he confessed.

I asked the young caddie, "When you say shifted, um, do you mean, like, well, see the word we use . . . What do you mean, exactly?"

"You know," he said, conspiratorially, sticking out his tongue.

"Oh, that!" I said. "Really? At your age? That's hard to believe. In a small town in Ireland?"

"No way," the photographer said.

"No. No way," I agreed.

The caddie protested vehemently, calling on his friend, the other caddie, to vouch for his prodigious "shifting" totals. His friend said it was true. The lad really had kissed all those girls. With his tongue in their mouth.

"See?!" the caddie said proudly.

The photographer and I traded a knowing look and congratulated this budding Casanova on what surely would be a life filled with many wet kisses.

Now, in Scotland, I look at the lads toting our bags, and I envy them all the girls they have yet to kiss. Am I really getting that old?

To my pal Don I say, "Randy American girls. God bless 'em! They're fun to play with and sometimes even more fun to talk about."

He nods, lost in smooch-filled reveries.

Was this the kind of repartee Shivas Irons enjoyed when he toured the links of Burningbush? Metaphysics, I realize, isn't half as fun as sexy chicks. "Ah, the golf course: where spiritual discussions never cease!" I then repeat a golf joke involving buttercups and pussy willows.

It's an altogether fun day, though neither Don nor I see any evidence that Lundin Links is the primeval source of spiritual enlightenment. I do, however, learn a couple of intriguing things about my friend Don Naifeh, and in turn about myself.

He plays much better *into* the wind; I play much better *with* the wind. I'm tempted to interpret this fact to mean that he hates being helped, by anyone or anything, since so much of his youth was probably spent fending off the well-wishes of those who would coddle or insulate him from the very real pains (physical and mental) of life. I, on the other hand, play like a champion with the wind at my back, which possibly means I don't mind at all when someone or something comes to my aid, generously augmenting my talents rather than attempting to minimize them.

On the other hand, it could just mean Don has better balance and feel with a breeze in his face, and I, conversely, play like a frantic maniac when my normal swing doesn't make the ball go as far as it usually does.

I don't know. I'm a little surprised (and mildly pleased) that I'm thinking about such things at all, instead of solely focusing on randy lassies and their soft warm lips.

Another curious thing I'm learning about myself is that whenever Don begins to play better than I, his eccentricities become dramatically less charming and exponentially more irritating.

He hates having conceded putts knocked away, even though it's a genteel gesture of good sportsmanship. "Hey!" he yells, when I slap his ball back to him after it has stopped within the leather. "Don't do that! Don't ever do that!" I look at him quizzically. "See, to me, Michael, the biggest thrill is hearing that ball fall into the hole. Why lose that thrill, even from four inches?" he tells me, scooping up his thrill-robbed golf ball. Don's insistence on putting out *everything*, even when we're struggling to keep pace with the foursome ahead of us, is quite mysterious to our Scottish caddies, who, understandably, want to get on with things, so they can get to the pub or their girlfriend, or wherever. To me, particularly when I'm playing poorly, this time-wasting quirk is less mysterious than vexing. It drives me crazy.

So does his cigarette smoking.

After I make a silly bogey after lying two greenside on the ninth, a 555-yard par-5 descriptively named "Long," I become acutely aware of how much Don smokes, how he addresses the ball with a burning fag in his mouth, how he stands over putts with the ash about to fall off, how there's an almost constant cloud of smoke wafting around him. When I'm beating him 3-up with two to play, I don't notice these things so much. But when he's got me pressing, they're about all I can see.

That my friend smokes more than a pack a day disturbs me for two reasons: the more important one is that he's killing himself. The less important one is that he smells like an ashtray. When we're on Lundin Links and I'm 3-down and the wind is blowing his exhalations into my nose, I become particularly intolerant of this nasty habit. It dismays me perhaps more than it ought to when I see him indiscriminately discarding butts on green fringes and fairways and sometimes even the putting surfaces. Anywhere, really. On the tenth, after he's beaten me on another hole, I pull him aside, away from the caddies, and ask him if, as a personal favor, he might use the rubbish bins provided on every tee.

Don says, yeah, sure he will. But not before invoking tradition. He says, "Even Old Tom Morris probably tossed his butts on the course!"

When I flash him a stern look, he quickly calls over our female-obsessed caddies and tells them, "Boys, you gotta promise me you'll never start smoking. It's a terrible thing to do."

They say yeah, sure, of course not. And then Michael asks Don if he can bum a smoke off him. They all roar.

Now I'm really pissy.

Regressing to an old childhood defense mechanism, in which I used to retaliate at my youthful tormentors by scoring higher on tests, running faster at races, being better at everything, I feel the impulse now to beat Don Naifeh in this match. Spiritualism and mysticism and searching for the meaning of it all suddenly seems like a flimsy excuse to come to Scotland. I'm here for one purpose: to extract a crumpled twenty pound sterling note from my opponent's chain-smoking, butt-tossing, slow-playing pocket.

This, of course, is exactly the opposite of what golf with a friend is supposed to be about, particularly when it's being enjoyed in a land where the very ground seems to ooze profound truths. I know this in my heart. But twenty-five-year-old demons churn in my gut, reminding me of past pains I don't really want to remember, especially now, at a moment in my life when I want desperately to know nothing but true camaraderie and fraternity.

Walking up the thirteenth fairway, a double-dogleg par-5 that features the only hardwood trees on the course, I see Don starting to labor as he limps toward his big tee-shot. This is three days in a row he's walked, and despite the copious Tylenols (and various other pain-killing drugs he won't tell me about) that he's been ingesting, I'm sure the pounding his brittle bones have endured must be taking a harsh toll. Suddenly I feel very foolish for worrying about my so-called pains. I'm sure I don't even know what that word means—not like Don Naifeh does.

Just then, as if to underscore my fleeting failure to see the big picture, Michael the caddie, perhaps noticing Don's growing motor difficulties, asks us, "D'ya ken Casey Martin."

"I don't know him, Michael," I reply. "But I interviewed him once at a press conference. Very brave guy."

"He rides a boogie, aye?" the lad asks.

"Yes, he does. And, I don't know if you've been following the whole story, but the PGA Tour doesn't want him using a cart in their competitions. Very controversial."

Don's eyes flash, and he inhales sharply. "I understand all the arguments," he says. "But, Jesus Christ, it's a no-brainer." Don stops walking, right there in the middle of the thirteenth fairway at Lundin Links, forcing us to really listen. I've never asked him previously where he stands on the Casey Martin issue. Today he lets me (and our slightly frightened caddies) know: Don supports the man unequivocally and believes he ought to be allowed to compete on the PGA Tour or wherever else golf tournaments are held. And he's furious at the PGA Tour for making Martin's life more difficult than it already is.

"Don't get me wrong, Michael," he says, his voice rising. "If I had been able to walk all these years—if I had been encouraged to walk instead of doing the easier thing, taking a cart—I'm sure I'd be a better golfer today. I mean, I agree with Shivas: the game *is* meant for walkin'. And the evidence is this trip. I'm playing better than I ever have, and I've played every hole on my own two feet. So, don't get me wrong, I'm all for walking. But when I was eighteen years old I was still learning *how* to walk. If it wasn't such a damn difficulty walking, if I wasn't always so discouraged, I might have considered playing this game competitively. And if there was a guy like Casey Martin around? Hell, I would have been *encouraged*. He's done for guys like me what Ellen DeGeneres has done for lesbos."

"She's a comedian," I tell the caddies. "Likes girls."

"I could have used a role model," Don says. "And the people who want to keep him out of the game because he needs to use a cart—well, they're crushing a lot of dreams."

When I was younger, approximately the age of our caddies, I read Lorraine Hansberry's play *A Raisin in the Sun*, a drama about a middle-class black family struggling to "make it" in America, which movingly answered the question: what happens to a dream deferred? The answer, I recall, feeling the midday heat sear my forehead as I stand beside my impassioned friend in the glare of a rare Fife afternoon, is that it shrivels. Like a raisin in the sun.

I feel an involuntary sigh escape my lips. "It's your shot, pards," I tell Don. "Go for it."

"Go for it?" Don asks.

"Yes."

He puts the 5 iron in his hand back in his bag and pulls out his driver.

Ten seconds later, after a perfect moment of harnessed rage, his ball is resting beside the green.

"Shot," I say, shaking my head in mock befuddlement.

"That one's for Casey," Don replies, shuffling off toward his future.

When we arrive at the putting surface, I've taken four shots to get there, thanks to an unfortunate pause to investigate the biological properties of the local flora. Don is bending over the result of his heroic effort. His ball has come to rest on some leaves, adjacent to a stand of trees that protects the left side of the green. Our match is all-square; I really need to salvage a half on this hole.

As I'm lining up my crucial twelve-footer, Don calls out for me.

"Michael, I need a ruling," he announces.

Seems he touched his ball while removing surrounding leaves. But the ball, he says, never moved. Touched but not moved. What's the rule?

I tell him I think it's a penalty, but I'm not certain. Regrettably, I discover as I sift through my golf bag that there's enough rain gear to outfit an expedition to the Amazon, but I've left my rule book in the car. "I don't know, Don," I confess. "I guess you should play your ball as it lies and we'll get it sorted out later."

After Don chips expertly to three feet and rolls in his birdie putt, negating my gutsy par effort, I wonder to myself how it is possible to know you have touched a golf ball with your (arthritic, frequently broken) finger yet not moved it. What I don't wonder is this: would Don fib about such a thing?

No. He wouldn't. End of story.

He has too much respect for himself and me and this funny old game to violate the rules. His integrity is unimpeachable.

Yet. But. However.

Touching a ball while clearing leaves without actually moving the damn thing? Is that physically possible?

I'm considering the distinct likelihood that this moment in our match, this little rules-based longueur, is an opportunity for me to explore a world beyond the physical realm and delve into uncharted metaphysical planes I've heretofore avoided. Is Don providing a forum for me to expand my consciousness? Or is his typically peculiar way of looking at golf (and by extension life) starting to seep into my brain through osmosis?

The answers, I'm finding, aren't always clear or obvious, and sometimes they never arrive. But simply thinking about them has pulled me out of my cigarette smoke/hard wind/adolescent trauma/bad left sock–inspired funk. Without realizing it until I walk off the eighteenth green, I shoot 1 over par on the last eight holes—most of which, not coincidentally, we play with a helping breeze.

The trouble is, so does Don. Despite his flagging strength, he scuffles around the back side of Lundin Links without ever golfing his ball into serious trouble, and we end up dead even.

But we still need to get a ruling. Maybe I didn't lose the thirteenth hole after all.

A nice fellow in the pro shop offers us a rule book, the Royal & Ancient version. Don goes directly to the relevant section, as though he's studied this document a hundred times previous. He scans. He finds. He reads.

"No penalty, Michael," he says, handing me the book. "See for yourself."

I do. He's right.

I make a big show of paying off our bet. "That damn ruling cost me twenty-five pounds!" I complain to the pro shop attendant.

"Oooh!" he exclaims, cringing. "Sorry, sir."

The truth is, I don't mind at all. Twenty-five pounds seems like a small price to pay for a mind-expanding tutorial. Even one I suspect I'll never truly understand.

After our round at Lundin Links, Don asks me to join him in the garden of the Oak Tree Inn for a big announcement. I figure he's somehow discovered the true identity of Shivas Irons. Or, even better, dumped that wicked witch J.

I find a spot in the shade to protect my sun-seared face. "So?" I ask. "You've had a revelation?"

"Well, yeah, maybe. Sort of." He opens a Diet Coke and a pack of cigarettes, some British brand they don't sell in the States, unfiltered and probably deep-fried for good measure. "Here's the thing, Michael: I noticed this today, at the tenth tee, right where you'd expect them to have refreshments. And I noticed it yesterday at Elie and the day before at North Berwick. They don't have snack bars here!" He raises his eyebrows at me, like a mad scientist.

"Right. They sell snacks in the pro shop. Candy and drinks, and so forth."

"Right, but they don't have a beverage cart out on the course, with cold beer and sandwiches and stuff like that," Don says, growing excited.

"Right, because they don't have any cart paths for a beverage cart to drive around on," I say, realizing anew one more thing I love about golf in Scotland.

"Right—but, now, here's my idea—you have some kind of refreshment stand, an outpost far away from the clubhouse, and you sell drinks and snacks, substantial things, maybe even fish-and-chips, or . . . what's that stuff they eat?"

"Haggis?"

"Haggis. And sandwiches, and, you know, whatever. And beer. I mean, hell, I would have been a customer today. You're miles from the clubhouse and you want a little something. See?" Don entreats me.

I think for a second. A snack cart at the turn. Hmm. This staple of the American golf experience is all but absent on the Scottish links, though I do recall there being one at Carnoustie, decorated with bag tags from around the world. Most local players here, I've noticed, sit down for a proper lunch in the clubhouse bar or dining room post-golf. And I've never heard a visitor wonder out loud where the friggin' beer girl was. "I guess it could work," I say, shrugging.

"It's irresistible!" Don corrects me. I neglect to remind him that he purchases more Diet Coke and cigarettes on a golf course than most people do at a Pick 'n Save. "I figure you make some sort of arrangement with the course," Don explains, "hire some local help, some pretty Scottish lassies, and give the people what they want. Very small capital investment. Cheap labor. Little risk. You find a strategic place to park your refreshment stand—like, today, maybe you have one where Lundin and Leven meet up, or maybe you put it behind the ninth green. Anyway, you figure out the best spots. And then, hopefully, you make a few hundred a day and play golf every afternoon and life's sweet."

The distant look in his gleaming eyes tells me he's serious.

I don't know if this is how Sam Walton got started. But I'm having trouble picturing Don Naifeh as the soda-and-sausage-sandwich king of Scottish golf. Then again, I'm discovering on this trip, my vision isn't always as clear as it ought to be.

9

Ghosts

"I don't think I'd be able to manage it without some emotional preparation. I'm afraid I'd faint." This is how Don convinces me we must visit the Old Course at St. Andrews the day before we actually play it. He's concerned the power of the place will overwhelm him, that he'll be struck dumb and paralyzed, as though a cross-country electrical line had fallen on his back. "Can we go there, Michael, and just let the place seep into my mind slowly?"

The truth is, I've been looking forward to Don's arrival at St. Andrews perhaps as much as he has, and possibly for a longer time. Ever since I first played in the Auld Grey Toon, several years back, I've fantasized of having Don Naifeh join me for a trip through time. I've known—I haven't supposed, I've *known*—this magical town, with its ancient golf links, would speak to Don Naifeh in a language that few people comprehend. And I knew he would hear it well. I did not create St. Andrews, and I certainly didn't discover it. But I am taking my friend there, as a gesture of shared love, and even being an informal tour guide makes me feel I am doing something good and lasting.

I know something wonderful will be happening inside Don's broken body, in a quiet, happy place untouched by disease, when the sights and sounds and smells of the Home of Golf bathe his senses. It did for me, and I don't even believe all this "True Gravity" hooey.

Early in the morning, a fine mist hangs over Fife, like the scrim curtain in a theatrical dream sequence. As we drive into St. Andrews from the east, on the old coast road out of Kingsbarn, Don is momentarily silent. He inhales as though he is about to begin a lengthy oratory—but nothing comes out. His speechlessness turns to nervous giggles. And then he loudly exclaims, "Fucking amazing!"

It's the first time I've heard Don employ this particular locution.

As we putter through the middle of town, past the university, alongside dozens of shops and hostelries and restaurants all connected, however tenuously, to the game of golf, Don repeatedly mumbles, "Why don't I live here? Why am I not living here?" And we haven't even gotten near a golf course yet. His darting eyes and open mouth remind me of my hound back home when we're in the car and getting close to our house. She gets all jumpy and excited. I understand why Don feels likewise: In a sense, he too is getting close to home.

When we turn right, toward the sea, the Royal & Ancient clubhouse comes into view. Don is momentarily speechless. Then he whispers, "Fuck." His oath, I'm sure, is uttered with supreme reverence.

I find a place to park on The Scores, yards from the first tee and eighteenth green, a mere wedge away from the very same place Don has witnessed a lifetime of indelible golf moments. The huge bleachers have not yet been disassembled, and we can feel the residual energy of 100,000 cheering fans urging on Tiger Woods, fans looking on from the same vantage point where hundreds of thousands previously urged on Jack Nicklaus and Tom Watson and Bobby Jones and all the rest. There's a low hum of excitement that is audible only if you let yourself hear it.

Don hears it. His usual shuffle, I notice, changes into an almost sprightly skip. It's like seeing one of those desperately ill religious zealots made "well" by an evangelical charlatan talking in tongues and bopping people on the forehead with his fist. Only this is no charade. Don Naifeh, I can tell, is being touched by the divine. Whatever is happening—and I don't know exactly what it is for sure—he's rubbing up against something real, no matter how invisible or irrational it initially seems to my jaundiced eyes.

"And there she is," I say, gesturing toward the place where many believe the game as we know it began. "The Old Course."

"Heh, heh. Wow. Heh, heh. Oh, man. Heh, heh. Heh, heh." Don is beaming.

"The Valley of Sin. The Swilcan Bridge. There's the Road Hole, right over there, on the other side of the burn. Pretty cool, eh?" I say nonchalantly.

"Oh, man," Don mumbles.

He's happy—and I'm happy that he's happy. Indeed, at the moment I'm feeling like a professional submissive whose greatest joy is gleaned from catering to the pleasure of his dom. St. Andrews is not new to me; its charms are not unfamiliar. But to see them brighten the heart of a dear friend—well, I might as well be discovering the place all over again. Maybe I've suspected all along that my capacity to be moved by the sight of the Old Course has always been slightly limited, that my sober outlook—some might call it skepticism or objectivism—has prevented me from completely giving in to the magic of this "holy" site. Faith is believing what cannot be seen. I've never been too good at that—which makes concepts like religion and mysticism and anything else requiring a suspension of critical thinking a supreme challenge for me. Don Naifeh, on the other hand, thrives on the intangible and ethereal. And, in that sense, maybe I want to be more like him.

Golf, being a tidy reflection of life, is an interminable series of frustrations, interrupted sometimes by moments of joy, little punctuation marks of success and contentment contained within baffling eighteen-hole-long run-on sentences. But magic does happen sometimes. And when it does, golf—and life—is sweet. There have been but a few times in my rational logical life that I have believed in unseen powers, omniscient energies that hide in the magnetic vibrations of the earth and the sky. One of those magical moments, I recall as Don and I step down the stairs from street level to the enormous first tee of the Old Course, was right here at St. Andrews. It was my first round at the Home of Golf.

Seven years ago, driving another tiny rental car, I rolled into town with a camera full of film, a "boot" full of golf equipment, and a head full of fanciful scenarios. I was keenly aware that St. Andrews was known for its excellent university and its superb seaside location in the Kingdom of Fife, but it was most famous for an expansive plot of land that appears to have once been an elephant burial ground but is now used as a place to chase around a dimpled white ball. I arrived at noon and found my hotel, near the clubhouse of the Royal & Ancient, which looms over the first and last holes of the Old Course like a caretaker fortress.

After dropping my luggage bags, I walked across the street to the links. Only a few hundred yards down the football-pitch-sized fairway, shared by the first and eighteenth holes, I could make out the Swilcan Bridge, that iconic landmark over which every golfer dreams of walking. And farther down a bit, I could see the seventeenth, the Road Hole, with its tiny green, about the size of a modest dining room, flanked by asphalt. And beyond, miles down the coast, there was all the rest of the fabled links: the Hell Bunker, the Beardies, the Spectacles, the Coffins, the acre-and-a-half double greens, the gloriously improbable and unpredictable mounds and dips and humps that make the Old Course impossible to play the same way twice.

Breathing in the scene—inhaling deeply, taking in the restorative tonic of this blessed place—I strolled over to the starter's box, below the Royal & Ancient clubhouse steps. "Would you have any space for a single this afternoon?" I inquired halfheartedly, knowing that players book times on the Old Course many months in advance, paying tour operators and travel agents prodigious sums to guarantee a starting time (and a hotel room) on the most famous and treasured golf course on the planet. "Anything at all?"

The starter looked down his sheet. "It's all four-balls until 1:15," he said. "But I might be able to accommodate you after that time. Why don't you come back then with your clubs and your handicap certificate."

I wandered around the neighborhood, never venturing far from the grass rectangle that begins and ends a round at the Old Course. The atmosphere surrounding this part of town—and it is *in* town, with shops and hotels and offices surrounding the links—is unmatched anywhere in the world of golf. Visitors, drawn by their love of the game, mill about the eighteenth green, which sits a few feet below street level, watching the players come home through the Valley of Sin and putt out on the same turf that has hosted the greatest players throughout history. Just a wee wooden fence separates the participants from the spectators, and polite applause and cheerful banter frequently greet a good chip or a well-holed putt. It's the kind of magnetic place, the area around the eighteenth is, that could keep you amused and happy all day. Surely, if you stood there long enough, everyone with a connection to golf, no matter how grand or humble, would eventually pass your way.

At 1:15 I returned to the first tee to watch a foursome of Americans, a quartet lucky enough to have landed a tee time, play away toward the Swilcan burn. As I was dreamily watching their drives, the starter, clipboard in hand, approached me.

"Are you looking for a game?" he said politely.

I told him I was, yes! Anytime. I'd be ready.

"These two gentlemen," he said, pointing toward a young man with a mop of hair and an old man with none, "would be happy to have you join them. You're on the tee at 1:30."

I paid my fee and was introduced by the starter to young Ian, a 2-handicap Englishman studying at the university, and old Arvid, a 24-handicap Swedish retiree making his first pilgrimage to St. Andrews. And exactly an hour after first stepping outside the hotel's front door, I was playing the Old Course.

Yes, magic does happen.

Without time to torture myself with swing thoughts, without time to imagine what my first shot might be like in front of the crowd that congregates around the first tee, without time to do much of anything but grab some tees and fish a ball out of my bag, I played like a man without a care in his head.

I made par on the first. And the fourth and fifth and sixth. I birdied the fourteenth, the "Long Hole," home of Hell. I made par on the Road Hole, getting up and down from beside the nefarious pot bunker that guards the green. And on the eighteenth, as rain poured down in Scottish sheets, I had a putt to shoot even par on the inward nine, a putt to shoot "straight 4s" (a score of 4 on every hole) on the back side.

I missed the putt, eliciting audible groans from the few hearty souls still hanging over the fence. The tap-in bogey gave me a

1-over total of 37. Paired with a 2-over total on the front, my score for this breeze-into-town-and-jump-on-the-first-tee round at the Old Course was 75. One of my three best scores ever.

Was it dumb luck? Was it the deliriously liberated product of a mind unencumbered? Was it centuries of history and tradition and knowledge seeping into my feet, as if by osmosis?

I don't know. The very next day, again jumping straight onto the course after almost no waiting, at approximately the same time of day, in perfectly calm, sunny conditions, I shot an 83.

So what happened that first day at the Old Course? Skill, chance, kismet?

I'd like to think it was magic.

Oddly, I don't say so to Don. I just clap my hand on his shoulder and tell him I shot 75 my first time on the course—and I leave out all the mystical stuff. Maybe I'm a reluctant convert. Or maybe I'm too frightened to look at the world through Don's eyes, preferring to let him do the looking for me and report on the results.

What he's seeing now, I know, is profoundly pleasing. "Michael, I know it's a cliché," he tells me. "But this truly is a dream come true. Now would you remind me again why I don't live here?"

"Come on," I say, "let's get our names on the ballot."

I lead Don to the caddie shack, where my friend Rick MacKenzie, the St. Andrews Links Trust caddie master, works. He's the author of a popular golf book, *A Wee Nip at the 19th Hole*, about the history of caddies at St. Andrews, and a talented raconteur, whose dry humor and wry language have always struck me as delightfully Scottish, a clear-eyed realist with a touch of the poet. We once almost worked together on a publishing project, but although the deal fell through, Rick and I have remained friends. I keep him apprised of the nefarious goings-on in the American book industry, and he keeps me supplied with memorable anecdotes about the game we both love. He is a golf friend; I want him to know Don, the golf friend I hold most dear.

"I've been lookin' for ye!" Rick announces as Don and I amble up to Mr. MacKenzie's open caddie counter.

"You got my message!" I say, extending my hand. "You heard I was coming."

"Aye, eventually I did," Rick says. Rick MacKenzie is the kind of happy Luddite who has a computer in his home but doesn't really know how to send or get e-mail. Phone or fax messages sometimes get answered, and sometimes they don't. But he always seems to know when I'm harking back to his hallowed city. And every time I do return, he has a fresh—and slightly crazy—story to tell me.

This time it's about his quest to rediscover his American Indian ancestral roots. His great-great-grandfather, Rick tells us, traveled around Wyoming and Montana, and after exhaustive research, Rick has turned up ample evidence that there is Indian blood running through his clan's veins. It's all a bit surreal: here I am standing with my golf buddy Don Naifeh, right beside the first tee of the Old Course, and the St. Andrews caddie manager is regaling us with a tale of long-lost relatives who may or may not have done battle in the company of Sioux warriors.

Don's eyes flash. What a strange coincidence, Don tells Rick. "I work with Native Americans, in a casino, on tribal land. And I've been thinking for a long time about starting some sort of golf program, you know, to build self-esteem and discipline and perseverance. I never knew the Scottish clans and the Indian tribes had so much in common. And I never met a Scotsman with such strong ties to American Indians."

Never mind that before our journey I don't think Don had ever met *any* Scotsmen, except maybe for a gentleman named Johnnie Walker, he of black-and-red fame.

Within minutes of meeting, Don is thinking out loud, trying to figure out how he can get his new friend Rick MacKenzie—whom I've failed to actually formally introduce—to come speak at the Indian casino in Arizona. "Man," Don marvels, "what a connection!"

Strangely, it seems Don and Rick have an even eerier connection. When I explain to Rick the purpose of our visit—that Don and I are on a golf pilgrimage that has long been postponed or forgotten because of Don's disability—Rick nods knowingly and reveals that he has a cousin who also suffers from OI. "I know what yer fightin'," he says to Don. "And it's all been goon all reet?"

Don modestly says, yes, sure, no problems. I proudly say how brave and strong and determined he's been. Don shrugs and says, "Rick, I've been inspired by your country."

"Why are you so fond of the golf here?" Mr. MacKenzie wonders.

"I think it's the ground," Don says thoughtfully. "It's very receptive. And, I don't know if this makes sense—it's very expressive in a way. Like it talks to me. It takes me and it talks to me. It feels good when I walk and it feels good when I take a divot. It's very comforting, I've found."

"I understand," Rick says, nodding sagely. I can tell he likes Don as much as I do.

Dozens of eager visitors want to hire caddies and buy commemorative pencils and scorecards, so Rick has to get back to his work. In the meantime, he encourages us to check the ballot later in the afternoon to see if we've made it on the list for a precious Old Course tee time. "Have a walk around," Rick encourages Don. "I think you'll like what you feel, sir. It's truly a magic and inspired place."

"Thank you, I will," Don replies. "I'm sensing what you're talking about already. It's like an electricity, a vibration."

"Don's a member of the Shivas Irons Society, and he's into all that metaphysical stuff," I needlessly comment, as though Rick MacKenzie wouldn't immediately comprehend how and why a first-time pilgrim would say such a thing upon beholding the Home of Golf for the first time.

Rick merely smiles. "Enjoy, lads."

Seven hours later, after golf and lunch and sightseeing, we return to the caddie shack to see if we've made it through the ballot. The odds, I've heard, are approximately one out of four, depending on the time of year and the number of players in your group. We've indicated on our ballot that we'd be happy to play at any hour, with any number of people, including a six-some at 4:00 A.M. if need be. I've told Don that I won't let him come to Scotland without playing the Old Course, even if I have to pay some tour packager a usurious fee for one of his reserved-a-year-in-advance tee times. Don has told me, hey, no big deal, he'd love to play it and all, but if we can't get on it's all right.

I appreciate his cooperative and high-minded sentiment, but I know it's really not all right. An Elvis fanatic does not make a holiday in Tennessee without visiting Graceland. A baseball devotee does not travel to New York City without enjoying a game at Yankee Stadium. Certain marriages of man and place are somehow blessed, almost preordained. And Don, I have vowed, will not leave Scotland without having his nuptials with St. Andrews consummated.

So it is with some trepidation that I approach the bulletin board containing the next day's tee times for the Old Course. As a seasoned gambler, I know the odds are against us. But still, magic and all that.

Rick MacKenzie pops out of his office. "Checking the ballot?" he says, deadpan.

"Yeah," I say tersely, catching myself sounding very much like a high school senior about to open an official-looking envelope from his first-choice college.

"Well, let's see," MacKenzie says gravely, escorting me and Don to the board. He stands aside with his arms furled over his dark green St. Andrews tartan sweater.

I scan from the top: No. No. R and A. No. Konik!

"Haaah!" I yell, slapping Don on the back, nearly breaking one of his brittle ribs. "We're in!"

"Heyyy!" he yells. "All right!"

"Seven-twenty. Third time of the day. We're playing the Old Course, buddy," I say to Don, who flinches involuntarily as I raise my hand for a high five.

"Oh, baby!" he says, chortling.

I look at Rick MacKenzie. He's smiling devilishly, as if he knows a secret. "Great luck," he says, raising his eyebrows and disappearing back into his office.

Don and I clasp hands, like a couple of musketeers arm wrestling in the air. We hop up and down, like girls at their first pop concert. (Well, I do. Don sort of rocks back and forth while I jiggle.) "Don Naifeh, on the Old Course!"

"Wow. Imagine that," he says.

A portly American fellow approaches the board. "Didja guys make it in?" he asks, noting my effervescence.

"Yes! Third time of the day."

"Wow. Great." He looks in vain for his name. "Damn. Oh, well. Next time." He shrugs and says, "Hey, have fun."

"Thanks. Thanks. We will. We will," I say nervously. I feel as if Don and I have been somehow anointed, that ours were the lucky names to show up on The List—the one that saves us from extermination at the hands of a ruthless tyrant or gets us on the last plane out of the Third World capital before it's overrun by anti-American terrorists. I know it's only golf we're talking about here, nothing more. But at the moment, seeing the faintest hint of tears in Don Naifeh's eyes, it seems like immeasurably more.

My gimpy friend, tottering on sore legs and aching feet, asks if we might do a course walk this evening in the fading light. He wants to get acquainted. I tell him to walk the course would mean another five miles or so of wear and tear on his already beaten body. "I want you to be fresh for tomorrow," I say, proposing we do a miniloop, going from numbers one and two to numbers seventeen and eighteen—just like the past champions did at this year's Open, in their four-hole exhibition tournament. Don agrees that would be sensible. Slightly excruciating—but sensible.

It's nearly 7:00 P.M. The last paying golfers teed off nearly an hour ago. The starter is closing up his hut and hanging a "Course Closed" sign on the first tee. But this ancient playground remains a public park, even after the golf has ended. Dozens of residents stroll beside the coast with their happy dogs, and several more bicycle across the public path that traverses the soccer field of a fairway that comprises the first and eighteenth holes. Aside from the early morning, when the mist has not fully burned off and the place has a spectral and haunted quality that gives me shivers, this dusky time is my favorite at St. Andrews. People are hurrying to and fro, going home to their loved ones, rushing to the market, communing with their hounds, and all the while the golf course sits placidly and permanently, providing a vast stage upon which visitors and residents alike may play out their individual dramas.

With an official yardage book in hand, Don and I "play" the Old Course with imaginary clubs and balls, much like Jim Dodson and his dad did in the author's *Final Rounds*. Don picks out his targets and decides on favorable approach angles and all that—despite the fact that neither of us has the faintest idea of how the wind will blow tomorrow, whether it will rain tonight, or what our caddies will sagely recommend. (Well, I have a vague idea of what they'll recommend, since there are a couple of distinct schools of thought on how to best play certain holes, and the boys like to argue these points over a few pints of lager until they agree to disagree.) Watching Don reminds me of seeing touring professionals playing a practice round, marching off yardages and making notes in their little orange books. It's very endearing, Don's earnestness. He cares so deeply about how best to get his ball from here to there. In the grand scheme of things, this oughtn't be the most pressing issue on the table. But when he sets his mind to playing golf as well as he is able, nothing else seems to matter.

The crazy hillocks and surprise bunkers that lurk in every corner of the Old Course delight and confound Don Naifeh. This is not a straightforward golf course, just as almost nothing about life, it seems, is ever as straightforward as we'd like to imagine it, and Don revels in the challenge of making sense out of a seemingly random minefield of obstacles. "Where are you supposed to hit here?" he asks, gazing over a wall of gorse bushes at the second tee. "I can't see the line."

I consider telling him what my caddies have told me in the past, about aiming for the middle gorse bush. But instead, I say, "You will, my friend. You will." And I feel very metaphorical about it.

When we get to the green, I can't get Don to turn back and head for home down the Road Hole. He wants to keep going—more, more, more, like a child at the state fair, high on cotton candy and corn dogs. More roller coasters. More Tilt-A-Whirls. More treats.

We march on, down the third, noting the incoming traffic on our left, playing the sixteenth. Nearly everyone with a golf club in his hand has a smile on his face. Things like score and swing plane and hip rotation don't seem to matter to anyone anymore. They're at St. Andrews, and all is right with the world.

We say it at almost the same instant: "I can't wait to play here with you!" Then we giggle like schoolgirls and pat each other on the back.

When we reach the fourth tee, I convince Don that if he wants to fully enjoy his tour of the Old Course tomorrow, we ought to head back so he can conserve his legs.

"I feel like I'm flying," Don says. "Like I could walk forever."

"That's very inspirational," I say sarcastically. "But I don't want to have to carry you on my back."

We turn toward the R&A clubhouse, and I notice a bank of phones left over from Open Championship week just off the sixteenth fairway, just beyond the out-of-bounds fence on the right. "You wanna?" I ask, pointing toward the booths.

"Oh, yeah. Definitely!"

And so, as the sun sets on another blessed day at this blissful place, Don Naifeh and I call our loved ones back home in the States from the Old Course at St. Andrews. We tell our dads and brothers and coworkers and girlfriends that we "just wanted to say hello." But we both seem to consistently preface each conversation with the impossibly cool phrase, "I'm calling you from the Old Course in St. Andrews."

To my dismay—and chagrin—one of the calls Don makes is to J, who he mistakenly imagines will be moved and thrilled to hear his tremulous voice all the way from St. Andrews, Scotland. I have seen a disturbing pattern emerging on our trip: Don gets happy playing the great links of this magnificent country; then he calls J and gets inconsolably sad; then he is no longer happy playing golf, or anything else for that matter, until he cleanses her from his short-term memory. I've never met the woman. But I instinctively hate her for doing this to Don, and for doing this to *us*. We're on a search for truth and wisdom and joy, and she's punctuating every other day with lies and cruelty and pain.

I see Don's face begin to fall. I see the confusion and hurt spread across his forehead and into his eyes. And I want to hang up the phone for him, liberate him from his demons. But I know I shouldn't. I know I can't.

He'll have to make his own discoveries. He'll have to find his authentic swing.

Eventually, we all do.

Golf course yardage books do not ordinarily make for the most scintillating reading, unless, like Don Naifeh, you find a map of a golf hole, with numbers and arrows drawn on it, akin to the Dead Sea Scrolls. Rather than absorb buckets of local color—and slightly less local ale—in our hotel pub, Don studies his Old Course yardage guide all night, until he falls asleep. His bag is prepacked for an absurdly early morning departure (he wants to get there an hour before our tee time), filled with clothing and disposable cameras, and, most important, eighteen different golf balls, each numbered in sequence.

"What are you doing?" I ask, seeing him hunched over his hotel room bed, scribbling on the brilliant white Titleists. "I don't think there's anywhere on the Old Course where you'll be able to hit balls into the sea, unless you can uncork one about 700 yards. It's not situated that close to the water. Well, there's an estuary behind the twelfth tee, but it usually seems to be empty and muddy during the day."

"Actually," Don explains, "I plan on playing a different ball on each hole and then giving each ball away to the right person. I play it once, it goes in the bag, and it comes home to America with me."

"Souvenirs?"

"Well, yeah, sort of."

"And who's the 'right person' in each case?" I wonder aloud.

"I don't know," Don admits. "But I figure I'll know after I play. The connections will sorta clarify themselves, like they usually do."

I feel the impulse to pet Don's bald head, as if he is a lovable chimp. But instead I go to bed and dream of shooting even par at the Old Course.

The morning can't come quickly enough. When it does, Don is already up and active, milling about our car in the parking lot, packing and unpacking his golf bag for the third time. And he's looking for signs, like a degenerate gambler at the horse track. Everything, no matter how seemingly innocent to my untrained eyes, has import and symbolism; everything foreshadows something wonderful or horrible, depending on how you interpret it. This morning everything matters.

The selection of breakfast cereals the innkeeper has left at our door (since we're departing too early for a proper Scottish gorging of pork entrails) is promising, since it was this very same brand of wheat flakes that Don ate the morning before he made his first birdie in Scotland. The cool—almost cold—breeze in the just-starting-to-brighten sky is disturbing, since it was blowing this way two years ago on the day Don suffered his last hand fracture while playing golf. But wait! Actually, it may be a good thing after all, since, he just now realizes, it's been two years to the day—like the actual anniversary—since he had his last bone breakage. Now there's gotta be something in that, surely! Two-year anniversary of his last major physical pain—and what is he doing? Playing golf! And where is he doing it? At St. Andrews, home of the game. See? Ah-hah!

"What does it mean that there was no hot water this morning in the shower?" I ask him.

"Hell, I don't know," he says. "But let's go. Let's go!"

"All right, junior, we'll get there. Don't you worry."

Of course, Don does worry the whole way there. Is there time to stop for cigarettes and Diet Coke? (Unfortunately, yes.) Have I forgotten where the turnoff is? (Fortunately, no.) Will we be able to park near the course? (Unknown.)

To heighten the mood even further, which is about as unnecessary as turning up the speaker volume at a Metallica concert, as Czar of the Radio I decree that we shall listen to a CD I've brought along for inspirational purposes.

"What is it? More Billie Holiday?" Don asks, already braced for disappointment.

"No, my friend," I say, pushing Play on the console, "this." The unmistakable sound of a cat being stepped upon comes blaring from the speakers. "Bagpipes!"

We roll down the windows, stamp the accelerator to the floor, and utter various Scottish oaths in utterly indecipherable accents: "Laddie!" "Aye, sir. Right doon tha muddle!" "Freedom!" "Haggis!"

When we pull into St. Andrews at 6:30 A.M., the town is still quiet. But the golf courses are already buzzing with activity. A small mob has formed around the starter's hut, looking for cancellations and prime spots on the walk-up waiting list. Caddies mill about the caddie shack, eager to be one of the first loopers out so they might get in two tours of the links with plenty of time to spare for dinner and a wee dram. And there's even the odd shutterbug or two, who merely want to get a shot of the Old Course in the ineffably lovely morning light. Seeing all the people congregated near the first tee, I feel a sudden pang of nervousness shoot through my bowels, a flutter of anxiety. Most of these people want to be doing what Don and I will be doing in exactly thirty minutes. We best not let them down.

While Don performs his peculiar stretching exercises against a wooden fence that separates the teeing ground from the viewing ground, another golfer—an American it looks like—walks past and places his black carry-bag on the tee. Seems he's first off today. Don immediately notices the bag tag on this gentleman's equipment: The Shivas Irons Society.

"Now that's gotta be a good sign," I say enthusiastically. "Your first round at St. Andrews and you run into another Shivas freak!"

The two acolytes shake hands and ooh and aah together for a few minutes while I linger in the background, letting them trade stories of mystical golf courses touched by the spirit of their hero. They chat of sheep and ghosts and the like while I busy myself with the mundane task of rounding up caddies and making sure I employ the appropriate ball marker from my vast collection of foreign coins. See, Don and his *Kingdom*-loving ilk might think what really matters in a round of golf is connecting with unseen realms and becoming one with your golf ball. I know the truth: the key to a fulfilling round is matching the right lucky talisman with the locale. Today I must decide between a stout one pound coin and a shiny twopence. I go with the cheaper denomination on somewhat flimsy but poetically compelling blue-collar, democratic-principles grounds.

It is this kind of nonsense that I occupy myself with in the minutes leading up to our tee-off. I feel as if I'm about to make my entrance at an important function, like a graduation speech or the acceptance of a distinguished-service award, with those I care about most dearly in the audience, and I desperately want only not to trip and fall before I get to the dais. Don, meanwhile, finished with his woozy discussion with his fellow weirdo of all things Shivian, wants me to understand a troubling recollection he's just had at this most inopportune moment: every time he's played an "important" golf course—Pebble Beach, Southern Hills, places where they have Tour events—he invariably makes a rotten score. "I'm lucky to shoot bogey golf at a famous course," he confesses, pained to have realized his track record just now.

"Well, they're usually tough courses," I say, consoling him. "If the wind stays down, I think you'll find that the Old Course can actually be quite gentle."

"Yep. Yep. True. See, but, the thing is, I just discovered something I've been doing wrong all those times before. I was talking to Scott there," he says, gesturing toward his Shivas brother, getting ready to start his round, "and I realized a crazy thing."

"Yes?" I ask, taking care not to cringe.

"If you evaluate your golf—or your life or your daily interactions, or whatever—on a performance basis rather than a results basis, you'll get a better picture of how you're actually doing. See, for me, the key to maintaining some perspective on my golf game is recognizing when I'm performing well, when I'm finding my balance and my rhythm and thinking clearly, and not worrying about the numbers I'm writing down." Don smiles. "So, see, every time I've played a great famous course, I've been all wrapped up in what score I was making, instead of being happy at how well I was playing. You see?"

"I do," I reply. "I really do." And I really do.

We're next up. Our caddies greet us on the tee. Colin, a big man with distinguished gray hair and thick eyeglasses, takes Don's bag, and, as far as I can tell, makes no protestations about the presence of a dozen and a half spare pellets in the pockets, having previously carried the overladen Tour-style bags of foreign visitors who, except for their stop at St. Andrews, never play golf without a motor cart. David, a slight bantam of a man, takes my quiver, nodding approvingly at its lightness.

"Only two pounds four ounces," I say for approximately the seventh time this trip. "Lightest made." Somehow I've convinced myself that this piece of information will make caddies like me more, so I repeat it stupidly whenever the chance arrives.

We're joined by two American guys, Rob and Bob, from Indiana and New York, respectively, both singletons drawn off the waiting list, who showed up slightly before 5:00 A.M. to be first in line. Like virtually everyone who stands upon this sacred swatch of turf, we pose for a few snapshots, holding a golf club (as if to document that we were really once here playing golf of all things), with the R&A behind us.

The starter calls out on his loudspeaker, "The seven-twenty group, off you go."

Everyone is momentarily paralyzed, so I, the seasoned veteran at these sorts of things, volunteer to take the psychological bullet. "I'll go," I say, noting with only a smidgen of chagrin that Don, as usual, is nowhere near ready to play, preoccupied with rummaging through the pockets of his golf bag, possibly arranging his numbered balls into odds and evens or fronts nines and back nines.

I pull a 3 metal from my bag and stride to the box. David stands beside me and asks, "First time didya sea?"

"No, sixth, actually. It's my buddy Don's first time."

"Ach. Aye, right. Then ye ken—a'tha flags oot thar."

The tee-shot at the Old Course's first is possibly the most comforting opener in all of golf. Hook, slice, pop up—it doesn't really matter. Except for the most egregiously horrible attempts, virtually anything off the tee will end up somewhere in play out in the vast awaiting openness. The only mistake is to hit a drive too far and trundle on the hard ground into the Swilcan burn fronting the first green. Knowing all that's required is an efficient bunt to get the round started, I make an utterly effortless pass at my ball, striking it with a purity and goodness one typically associates with various Biblical saints. It flies straight and strong, turning ever so slightly to the left, and runs and runs like it stole something when it finally returns to earth, stopping in the grassy Eden near the Swilcan Bridge. For a transcendent, blessed moment, I'm not a jerky writer-hacker, with a swing only a mother could love. I'm Ernie Els. I'm Fred Couples. I'm butter.

And I'm happy.

If this is my authentic swing, my authentic self, I want it.

"Shot," David says, nodding appreciatively.

"Thanks," I say, trying mightily to behave as though I always swing so pretty and true.

"Shot, Michael," Don says, looking up from his bag. Perhaps he knows I would never forgive him if he didn't see that one, off the friggin' FIRST TEE AT THE OLD COURSE!

The other fellows go next and, to be honest, I don't even see what they do. I'm sucking in joy through my nostrils and exhaling pain through my mouth, just like they teach you at the better aerobics establishments. I'm here. Playing golf with Don Naifeh. On the Old Course.

Did I ever want anything else?

After what seems like an interminable wait while Don makes warm-up swings behind his ball, visualizing I don't know what—his entire life up to this point?—Don limps up to his ball, sets himself (and his determined jaw), and makes the same swing he always makes.

The ball—the one marked #1 in red, indelible ink—comes off sort of low and hot, and when it lands, just beyond the public footpath bisecting the fairway, it runs forever.

"Tha's fine," Colin says, and he's right.

And we're off.

I want to throw my arms around Don's shoulder and walk down the first fairway with him, as an expression of fraternity and shared vision. But even more I want *him* to throw his arm around me, to say something understated and moving, like, "Yes. Oh, yes," and carry me off into his world of invisible force fields and hidden meanings.

He doesn't. But I silently vow to get there on my own.

As if the "golf gods"—whomever these oft-invoked but seldom-seen deities may be—mean to test me, as if "they" wish to gauge whether my convictions are as solid as my pretensions, something very unpleasant happens right there on the first fairway of the Old Course. Just as I am at the top of my backswing, sand wedge in hand, ready to gently plunk my perfect tee-shot onto the capacious green, so close I can read the break of a putt from where I stand— just as I'm swinging, Rob (or is it Bob?) let's out a giggle that's alarmingly reminiscent of Woody Woodpecker's unlovely trademark.

Now, a giggle or a laugh is different from a camera click or a murmured question, or even an ill-timed shout of congratulations. A giggle feels like and indictment of one's laughable golf swing, of one's physical idiosyncrasies, of one's transparent attempts to pretend he is Els or Couples or butter when he is, in fact, merely some writer visiting Scotland with his gimpy voodoo pal.

Swing. Giggle. Chunk.

I deposit my beautiful perfect delicious tee-shot into the water— the only water on the entire course, except for that which comes out of drinking fountains. Where once my splendid white ball sat, there is an ugly gash in the hallowed turf, roughly the size of a twenty-four-ounce porterhouse.

I look toward Rob—or Bob, I'm not sure—and shoot him a glare that could melt the ice off of the summit of Ben Nevis.

Everyone is silent.

"Whoops. Sorry," he says meekly.

Now I know what I ought to do—what the good and evolved and spiritually enlightened me ought to do. What I ought to do is smile warmly and say, "I understand." (And I do. I mean, rationally I do. The guy is nervous, he's excited, and he's trying to make friends with the guy carrying his bag whose English he may or may not fully comprehend. So he laughs a bit too forcefully, too effortfully, at something vaguely funny his caddie has told him. And that laugh, that obnoxious *giggle*, just happens to emerge from his lips at the indelicate moment when some other American dude who acts like he's played this course every day for the past twenty years is making his transition from backswing to downswing. Whoops, indeed.) I should embrace my fellow golfer with overwhelming kindness; I should lead by example; I should look not in the past but always, always to the future, realizing in my heart and soul and very consciousness that the only shot that truly matters in the game of golf is the next one.

But the Mr. Hyde of my personality chooses to make a cameo appearance this fine morning—another creation of my Scottish pal Mr. Stevenson, incidentally (a connection! a connection!)—and instead of being sweet and forgiving and utterly civilized, I shake my head in disgust and say out loud to no one in particular, "On the first hole at St. Andrews! Unbelievable!"

I instantly hate myself for not being a bigger and better man. And though I'm not able to admit it at this hot moment, I wish a certain member of the Shivas Irons Society would give me a huge hug and tell me everything is fine, and that it's still a perfect day, and that we're still here together, and that no matter how many times I gouge the ground because someone unthinkingly giggles at a very unfortunate time to giggle we are still playing golf on the oldest links extant, with fine local caddies and a clear sky above and the promise of unlimited discoveries ahead of us.

Sitting down right upon the evidence of my misfortune and having a good long cry does not seem like such a bad idea, either.

David, my looper, shakes his head and chuckles. "Ach. Snow big deel," he says loudly, putting everyone at ease. "Tha' stoopid fecker!" he says under his breath, for my benefit.

Were I the golfer I dream of being, I would put this debacle behind me where it belongs and go on to make a sterling up-and-down for bogey. Instead, I overshoot the green with my fourth, chip to twelve feet with my fifth, and make the putt with my sixth for a double bogey. And I'm smoldering like an active volcano.

Meanwhile, on his debut hole at the Home of Golf, Don Naifeh also makes double bogey, managing his short game as awkwardly as I've seen the entire trip. But he doesn't seem nearly as upset as he does bemused. "That was strange," he says, walking beside me toward the second tee.

"Yeah, strange that someone could come to St. Andrews without having the slightest idea about golf etiquette. Man! Right in the middle of my backswing!" I whine.

"Hey, that was a hell of a putt you made, Michael," Don reminds me. "In fact, that's one of the best putts I've seen in a long time."

"What do you mean?" I ask, confused. "It was only ten, twelve feet, hardly any break. I make those all the time."

"I think the putts that show a man's true character are the ones he makes for double bogey. Really, that may be one of my favorite things to do—1-putt for a 6 or 7. I *love* doing that. No matter how bad I butchered a hole, I like to stand up there and grind over a putt and knock it in the jar, like it was for the U.S. Open," he says. "You showed me something there. A lot of heart."

I muse on Don's lesson for about ten seconds as he exchanges his #1 ball for #2—and then I promptly begin obsessing once more about Mr. Giggle.

This is the difference, I understand later, between me and Don Naifeh, between most of us able-bodied golfers and this gimpy, epigram-spouting creature: while I fume for three additional holes about the injustice of it all, Don has relegated his unplanned travails to history and gotten on with the business at hand, enjoying the rest of his day on the links. While I fight the golf course, he melts into it, as though it were a lover whose welcoming arms provide a sanctuary from the cold, callous world. While I pout inside, he smiles.

Now, Don is not always this paragon of golf course demeanor. I've seen for myself already once on this journey to Scotland an ugly side of him, and it repulses me because it reminds me of me at my worst. But he is largely and consistently a man whose goodness shines through, a man whose appreciation for the simple act of walking upon a golf course with a good friend inspires me, and reminds me of me at my best.

Which is why I am thankful and pleased and gladdened to the core to see Don Naifeh follow his opening double bogey with pars at the second, third, and fourth, a birdie at the par-5 fifth, and another par at the sixth. The morning gloom is burning off rapidly, and by the time we reach the gargantuan (and strangely attractive) "shell" bunker at the seventh, the sun beats down so persistently as to inspire the shedding of wind shirts and jumpers, leaving us golfers in shirtsleeves. Here in the corner of the links, at the beginning of the "loop" that encompasses the Old Course's easiest holes (and where Tiger Woods finally left David Duval—and all the rest of the 2000 Open field), I silently resolve to play with joy and courage, to never look backward at all that did not go as I would have liked. I vow to play like Don.

Which, even without all the attendant good-for-the-soul benefits, would be nice. He is 4-up in our match, and only 1 over par, despite his double bogey at the first. And he's happy.

I mean, I suppose he's happy. During our tour of the Old Course, Don doesn't talk very much. I half expected a running commentary from him about feeling ghosts tapping him on the shoulder. But he's surprisingly terse, content to golf his ball, breathe the air, and walk the ground.

He does, however, joke good-naturedly when I drive the green at the short, downwind par-4 ninth and 1-putt for an eagle. "What's the world coming to?" Don wonders aloud, complaining to Colin and the rest of our merry band. "I make birdie on a par-4 and *still* lose the hole? Outrageous!" And I can tell he couldn't be happier— really and truly. The state of our match means nothing to him; that both he and his golfing pal both played the ninth hole under par is all that presently matters.

That eagle at nine is, regrettably, the extent of my heroics for the day. Don, meanwhile, has enough memorable moments to fill a highlight reel. He 2-putts from 100 feet twice: on the brutal thirteenth, a 398-yard par-4 that typically plays into the teeth of the wind, and on the sixteenth, yards away from the phone booths where yesterday we called home, up and over the kinds of humps and bumps one ordinarily sees only on golf courses of the miniature variety. On seventeen, possibly the most famous par-4 in the world, Don makes the kind of alchemical up-and-down from beside the Road Bunker for which 9/10ths of the Open field would give up their club sponsorship.

Walking up the eighteenth fairway—actually, limping is the more accurate description—he turns to me and finally says something Donlike. "Michael," he says, biting his lower lip, "I belong here."

I start to say something sarcastic, something about how one more slow-play reprimand (he's gotten two already) from the course marshals will earn him permanent banishment from this place he loves. But instead I put aside my inchoate jealousy—he's slow, I'm not; he's making a great score, I'm not—and take a deep breath. If it is possible to inhale goodness, to feel something wonderful fill your lungs and then your veins and your very cells, then I have done it. I breathe in. I breathe out. Ahhh. This moment, this little moment in endless banal unextraordinary time, is why I wanted to come to Scotland with Don Naifeh in the first place—to hear him say such words, and to know exactly what he means. Screw the slow play. Damn the injustices of those malicious golf gods. Be here, in the now, alive.

"It's a special place, my friend," I say, genuinely wishing we were only beginning our round, not finishing. I could play eighteen more. Or thirty-six. Or forever.

"I feel like I'm playing a dream. Words can't express how much I've enjoyed this," Don says. "I guess you could say this is the round of a life."

Before getting bogged down in a swamp of apposite metaphors, I remind Don that it's not quite over yet. "You've still got to finish," I say, tilting my head toward the waiting eighteenth green and the modest gallery of onlookers surrounding it. "Come on, pal. Show 'em how it's done."

Don plunks his 8 iron approach into the heart of the putting surface. And he laughs and laughs.

Before he can totter off to the conclusion of today's story, I tell him I've got a surprise, something I know he'll like. From the bowels of my bag I produce a "feathery," a hand-stitched, not-quite-round golf ball our athletic ancestors once used on this very course—before gutta-percha and balata and Surlyn became all the rage. A reader of my *Sky* magazine golf column, a fellow from Iowa who makes featheries as a hobby, had sent me the ball in appreciation of an essay I had written about the charms of the "old" way of golf. Fearful of losing this kind present—I envisioned wasting hours (days?) of handiwork by sending the helpless orb to a thorny death in some inaccessible patch of gorse—I've waited until an appropriate venue to have a go at the bumpy and slightly beige pellet. Where better than the last at the Old Course?

To my great delight—and shock—the feathery flies low and strong off my 7 iron and settles softly on the green just beyond the Valley of Sin. Don and I trade smiles and don't say a word. We're connected.

Everything is connected. We to the golf course, and the golf course to the world, and St. Andrews to history, and history to home sweet home, where we're all eventually headed, whether we know it or not.

After Don taps in for his par, I guide him gently from the green. He doesn't want to leave. Not ever.

Beside the Royal & Ancient stairs, I take a photo of Don with his faithful caddie, Colin, and the eighteen numbered balls laid out in a row before them. The onlookers viewing the tableaux see a peculiar-looking man in a peculiar pose. I see that thing we call joy.

We are sitting in the dining room of the esteemed St. Andrews Golf Club, whose historic clubhouse sits beside the eighteenth fairway, on the right side, just over the road that gives the "Road Hole" its name. Don's caddie, Colin, is a member here, and he's invited us to join him for a postround beer and to avail ourselves of a superb lunch while he goes back to work on the golf course. While we wait for Rick MacKenzie to join us—he's been promised a full report—I tell Don what a rare gesture it is for a caddie to invite a player back to his club. "You must have made quite an impression on old Colin," I say.

"The score, the surroundings—wonderful. I mean, the greatest. But you know what, Michael?" Don says. "Colin asking us here, you know, making an invitation for people who were strangers just five hours ago—that makes me feel better than anything."

"I guess Colin didn't mind carrying all those extra balls for you," I joke.

"No, he didn't. He was great. Best caddie I ever had. Told me where to hit it, and I did, and, well, it went where it was supposed to." Don nods. Then he nods faster. "I've got it!" he says, pumping his fist as though he's just made a crucial putt. "I'm going to send Colin the #1 ball. And I'm going to send a note saying something like, 'If I knew I would have a round like the one we experienced

together, I'd take double bogey on the opening hole every time!'"
or something like that."

"Nice," I say, gazing out the clubhouse windows, which over-look the eighteenth green. I want to go back. I want to try again. I want to start over. You can't get a mulligan on your life, I know. But sometimes I wish I could.

Rick MacKenzie comes bounding in then. "Sew, lads?"

Don makes little one-word ejaculations. "Great." "Wow." "Amazing."

I do the bragging for him. "This guy," I say to Rick, "his very first time around the Old Course, shoots 76. And that's with a double bogey on the first! Guy doubles the first and shoots 70 over the next seventeen holes. Makes par on the Road Hole. Only 3-putts once all day. Plays like he's been here a thousand times. And he does it all on his own two feet."

"You were touched, aye?" Rick asks.

"Yeah, yeah, I was. I mean, Colin was a huge help. But, yeah, I was touched. There were a couple times today that I definitely got some assistance from someone or something. A ghost, probably."

"Really?" Rick asks credulously.

"Oh, yeah. Especially near the end. At the seventeenth? I could feel something, or someone, guiding me to get up-and-down. I'm serious. Like some sort of force coming out of the bunker. And on the eighteenth, it was really strange. I'm standing there in the middle of the fairway, knowing if I don't shank this 8 iron, I make 75, 76, or, worst case, 77 on the most revered golf course in the world. And you know what? I couldn't remember how to swing a golf club. I didn't have the faintest idea how to pull the club back. And then someone, or something, did it for me."

"Aye, thars lotsa ghoosts on the course," Rick says, as though Don had just reported seeing a rabbit or a wren.

"And they found me," Don says, nodding. "They found me."

Just then, our waitress pauses beside Rick MacKenzie and says, "I'm sorry, sir, fer interooptin'. But I hadda tell ye how tooched I was by yer book." The waitress, Alice, who appears to be in her sixties, tells us that her husband, John, was a longtime caddie at St. Andrews. Rick wrote about him, evocatively and truly, in *Wee Nip*. John, she tells us, died not long ago, after a sudden illness. "An' I jes' wanna see thanks to ye, sir."

Rick rises from his chair and embraces her, there in the dining room of the St. Andrews Club. "He was a good man," he says.

"I miss 'em soo," she says, wiping a solitary tear from her eye. "But every day I see the links," Alice says, looking out the window, "and I can feel he's still aroond."

At this moment, I have no idea that in a few weeks, when we return home, Don will develop the film from our round at St. Andrews and notice something peculiar and maybe inexplicable. He'll see that in every image the air is clear and sharp, the day bright and warm, as it was when we toured the Old Course. But in one photo—the one in which he is poised over his short putt to make par on the Road Hole—the air is hazy and white, as though a cloud had descended over the green. Don is in sharp focus, concentrated and determined. But everything around him is blurred and indistinct, as though in a dream or a fugue state. When he shows me the snapshot, I will confidently offer a million explanations for the foggy picture. I'll talk about processing chemicals and dirt on the lens and flawed photographic paper. And I'll be pretty sure there's some good reason for this anomalous image.

But if someone were to ask me now, at this very moment, sharing lunch with two great golf friends beside the grounds where the game began, I wouldn't be ashamed to admit the limits of my frail intelligence. I would shrug and smile and tell him the truth:

I would tell them that, for the time being, I believe in ghosts.

10

Talking with the Oracle

I first played the Balcomie Links at the Crail Golfing Society two years previous, in the company of my lover and companion. She did not play the game of golf (too frustrating!), but she occasionally liked to walk a golf course with me, veering off from the normal down-the-fairway path to search for wildflowers in the rough. Crail, I recall her telling me the day we visited, was a blessedly special place, and not just because it was one of the oldest golf clubs in the world (established 1786). She said there was something serene about the land, something restful and easy. She couldn't explain it exactly, but she knew there was some sort of magic coursing through the air at Crail. (She also believed in witches and numerology and psychics, so these kinds of pronouncements seemed at the time like random selections from her usual vernacular.) I agreed that it was a very nice golf course, with some memorable views of the sea and of grazing cattle. But I generally paid no mind to the transcendental aspects so readily apparent to clairvoyant types like my lover.

Now, over lunch in St. Andrews, Rick MacKenzie is telling me that Crail is "a little slice of heaven" and, he suspects, the real-life inspiration for Michael Murphy's fictional Burningbush.

I have heard such theories. Indeed, the professional at Crail once told me that members of "that daft society"—Don's Shivas Irons cult—would often show up at his gentle links and remove chunks of turf and handfuls of sand. Why they were so mad about the place he wasn't sure—something about inspiring a book he thought—but neither he nor any of the members could recall a man named Shivas Irons playing on the course, in daylight or moonlight.

I have also heard rumors (confirmed by several reliable sources) that Clint Eastwood, who owns the movie rights to *Golf in the Kingdom*, has been to Crail several times to scout for potential filming locations. He too seems to think that the Balcomie Links at Crail was where the legend of Burningbush began.

Most people, including my friend Don Naifeh, have always thought Burningbush was a slightly fictionalized version of the Old Course and that Shivas Irons was an amalgamation of Old Tom Morris and, I don't know, Kahlil Gibran. Though Murphy provides no explicit clues in the style of a roman à clef to guide readers to this conclusion, the general consensus among casual readers of spiritualism-soaked golf books is that the author *must* have intended his Burningbush to be a stand-in for the place where it all started and his main character to be a stand-in for all that is good and pure about the game. My research has turned up nothing to either dispel or confirm the truth; on the record, at least, Mr. Murphy has heretofore been charmingly coy (if not downright evasive) about the source of his literary inspiration.

Hearing whispers in the golf community (which these days is like saying "in the world") that St. Andrews and the Old Course weren't, in fact, Murphy's muse—and having been to the Balcomie Links myself—I decided that Don and I ought to investigate in person. Prior to leaving for Scotland on our golf pilgrimage, I told him I wanted to take him to an old links not far from St. Andrews, a place where, I had reason to believe, the "real" Burningbush existed. I told Don we would play the course and he would be my human divining rod, acutely tuned to vibrations and magnetic forces and all that other silly stuff. If he got some of the same feelings that my ex had—and she hadn't even read the book—then maybe, I suggested, we were on to something.

Don, naturally, liked the idea. And though he promised objectivity, I could tell he badly wanted his search for Burningbush to conclude successfully, at the proverbial pot of gold at the end of his golf rainbow.

Now, months later, less than an hour from Crail, Rick MacKenzie is telling me and Don that, yes, indeed, he wouldn't be at all surprised if the Balcomie Links were in fact the Burningbush of Murphy's imagination and Don Naifeh's dreams. "Some remarkable similarities," Rick comments.

"Especially the thirteenth," I say.

"Oh, aye," Rick concurs.

In *Golf in the Kingdom*, Shivas, playing in the middle of the night with a wooden shillelagh, as he is wont to do, makes a hole in one on a par-3 called "Lucifer's Rug," an impossibly difficult monster of a hole set aside a clifftop, framed by two gnarled cypress trees, flanked by a steep ravine on the left, and separated from the teeing area by 200 yards of clotted gorse. In the book, this climactic par-3 is number thirteen at Burningbush.

The thirteenth hole at Balcomie Links is a par-3 called "Craighead," an impossibly difficult monster of a hole set aside a clifftop, flanked by a steep ravine on the left, and separated from the teeing area by 200 yards of clotted gorse. There aren't any twisted cypress trees framing the green—which is about the only "evidence" that might plant reasonable doubt in the mind of a fair juror that the thirteenth at Balcomie is not, indeed, the thirteenth at Burningbush. In every other regard, they are virtual tintypes. Moreover, the Old Course doesn't have a single hole, par-3 or otherwise, that remotely fits the description of Lucifer's Rug. Nor, for that matter, does any golf course in the entire Kingdom of Fife.

Your honor, I move for summary judgment!

"Anuts not jes tha'," Rick remarks.

No, indeed. In the book, Shivas's teacher, the old master called Seamus MacDuff, lives (for reasons that have never been altogether clear to me) on the golf course in a hidden cave. Tucked into the steep hillside below the fourteenth tee on the Balcomie Links, there's a small cave, one of the few of its kind in the region.

Very interesting.

"And, if I'm not mistaken," I announce to the table, "Murphy has a minor character in the book named Seymour Crail."

Rick and I trade knowing smiles.

Don Naifeh puts down his fork, takes a sip of Diet Coke, and says, "Well, have you asked Michael Murphy?"

"Hello, Mr. Murphy?"

I am sitting in the lobby of the Balcomie Links Hotel, an unlovely three-story cinder block that sits beside a trailer park—they call them "caravan parks" over here—on an otherwise desolate stretch of land that separates the golf courses of the Crail Golfing Society from the postcard-worthy fishing village of Crail. Don and I have taken rooms at this modest hostelry because they had two singles available at a good price and, more important, because they have the only phone in the area that accepts international phone cards. I am presently using mine to chat with the author of *Golf in the Kingdom*.

"Yes, it's me," he says, both firmly and kindly, just as I had imagined Shivas Irons might speak.

I explain to him that a friend of mine is friends with a friend of *his* and, thanks to this web of, um, connections, I've ended up with his home telephone number. I tell him further that I'm sorry for the intrusion, but I'm doing something wonderful with a dear friend of mine who is about the biggest Michael Murphy fan on the planet and, well, if the esteemed writer wouldn't mind, I'd like very much to ask him just a few questions.

Oh, and by the way, I'm five minutes from the first tee of Crail.

Murphy seems tickled that two golfing pilgrims would seek out the source of his inspiration, particularly since he thinks he knows one of them. "What is your friend's name, again?" Murphy asks me. "Your golf partner?"

"Don Naifeh," I tell him and add a brief physical description.

Yes, Murphy says, he's fairly sure he met the man at a Shivas Irons Society function. "Wonderful guy," he recalls. "Very passionate. So how can I help you?"

I can't wait to tell Don that Michael Murphy remembers him—so, hissing, I turn to Don, who is sitting in a chair beside me, "He knows you!" Don grins and returns to analyzing his scorecard from the Old Course.

Then I ask Michael Murphy the Question.

Trying to sound neither too blunt nor too timid, I say to him, "Both Don and I—and lots of other readers—have always wondered, where did Burningbush come from? Some very smart people say it had to be Crail, the Balcomie Links at Crail. And that Lucifer's Rug, the thirteenth, has got to be the thirteenth at Crail. And then there's the caves, and—well, anyway, we're sitting here late at night right near the golf course. And in the morning we're going to play Crail. And it would mean a lot to us, to Don in particular, if you could confirm that we're about to play the real Burningbush."

This is what Michael Murphy tells me:

The truth is quite complex. Much of it appeared to me as I was writing. It just appeared in my mind. I had played St. Andrews in 1956. That was the only links golf course I visited on my visit. Yet the thirteenth, the one you mention, appeared to me with the utmost vividness, like I had played it a hundred times. Now, remember, I had never tried to write a book before. But I had played golf since I was fourteen and practiced meditation since I was twenty. When I sat down to write—and I think it took me seven months in all—things started to appear. The eighteenth should be built on a gravesite. I knew this. What I didn't know was that—well, I learned this years later—the eighteenth at the Old Course is a former grave. You could call them coincidences. You could call them clairvoyances.

I'm looking at my friend Don and wishing the Balcomie Links Hotel had one of those fancy telecommunications setups where two people can listen to the same call. (They don't, of course. But they make a pretty mean black pudding for breakfast.)

In my ear I hear Murphy saying, "These experiences came up in 1970. They appeared. You know, Robert Louis Stevenson said that Brownies—I think that's what he called them—gave him his books."

"Like the birds gave Richard Bach *Jonathan Livingston Seagull*," I interject, almost involuntarily.

"Perhaps, yes," Michael Murphy says. He has a very comforting voice. Very kind and musical.

"So you're telling me Burningbush was *not* inspired by Crail? That the course just came to you in a vision? Like Robert Louis Stevenson?" I'm skeptical.

"I think it would be fair to say that Burningbush is St. Andrews and Crail at one remove. The fact is, the first time I even heard of Crail was in '93. Clint Eastwood, who wanted to make a movie of the book, asked me then if I had modeled Burningbush on Crail. Well, I had to admit I had never heard of it, let alone seen it!" Murphy chuckles warmly.

"That seems impossible," I say. Don has looked up from reliving his magical string of pars and birdies at the Old Course. "The similarities are almost exact."

"The truth is I never even visited Crail until 1996," Murphy reveals.

"Surely, I'm not the first person to tell you about the startling similarities between your fictional golf course and Crail?"

"No, no. I've heard. For the past, oh, twenty-eight years, I've been hearing stories about this, and all sorts of other unexplainable phenomena. By now I must be the leading expert on occult and magic on the golf course," he says.

Since I've never personally been blessed with any sort of unseen muse—be it a bird or a leprechaun or a ghost—to bring me stories from another realm, tales that I merely have to transcribe onto paper, I'm, shall we say, *skeptical* when Michael Murphy tells me he conceived Burningbush without ever seeing Crail. A true believer like Don, I'm sure, would find this all reasonable and credulous (and I can't wait to get off the phone to tell him what I've learned). But I'm not one of those true believers. I'm imprisoned in the shackles of reason.

"What happened when you finally visited Crail?" I ask Michael Murphy.

"I didn't meet anyone. I didn't introduce myself or anything. I just walked around and felt the place, with my feet and my skin. And I felt that, yes, I had been there before, though I couldn't recall when in this lifetime."

I ask him if anything momentous happened—spirits and such.

"I'm afraid my trip was so brief, I'd have to go back to drink it all in. I just recall it was a very special place. Very haunted in a way."

He mentions something about a sect of Indian gurus with which I am not familiar. I don't tell Michael Murphy this. Nor do I tell him that I don't understand this "true gravity" concept, or being one with the ball, or any of it. I just know that Don Naifeh does, and it makes him happy.

Before ringing off, I tell Michael Murphy that we will be on the lookout for "the occult and magic" on the golf course. Don, at least, is always doing that.

"Would you call me if anything happens?" Murphy asks. "I'd love to hear about it. Give me a buzz after your round if there are any stories you think I should know."

I tell him, yes, sure, of course we will, and I thank him for his time and kindness.

"So?" Don asks, wide-eyed.

I repeat my conversation with Michael Murphy verbatim. Don doesn't think what I've just told him is strange or fishy or possibly spurious, the elegant fiction of an accomplished writer. He thinks it's "cool."

"Very nice guy," I say, wondering when a seagull is going to alight upon *my* consciousness, when I'm going to feel the magic and occult in my life. I look at my pal Don, crumpled and worn like an oft-used paper sack, beaten and wrecked after a spectacular day hobbling around the oldest golf course known to man. I see his fatigue. I sense the pain in his feet and his knees and his hips, the stiffness in his wrists and elbows and neck. And he glows.

"Let's get some rest, buddy," I say, heading for the stairs. "Tomorrow morning you're playing Burningbush."

In Search of
Burningbush

In addition to his usual arsenal of golf balls, knee braces, disposable cameras, and cigarettes, today Don Naifeh brings with him to the golf course a first edition copy (hardback) of *Golf in the Kingdom*, signed by the author. He's like a Jehovah's Witness going door-to-door, with the gospel tucked under his arm and an evangelical fire in his belly.

"You're not going to bring that on the links, are you?" I ask during the brief drive from our hotel to the Crail Golfing Society.

"I was thinking about it. You know, reading key passages before I played certain holes."

I look at him as if I ate something sour.

"All right. I'll leave it in the car!" he says, laughing that big hacking smoker's laugh of his.

"Leave it right on top of your crutch," I suggest. "Huh? How's that for symbolism? You haven't used the damn thing all trip, not once. Instead, you've leaned on the Gospel According to Murphy. Huh?"

"It's amazing, really," Don replies. "I mean, not once. Not even close. I'm glad I brought it, for emergencies, if, you know, something happened. But, man, I am so pleased I haven't had to use that crutch. It's like going through an entire round without once having to use your sand wedge to get out of a bunker."

We travel to the end of the road, as it turns toward the beach. There, set above the sea on a magisterial bluff, is the Crail clubhouse. And below it, all around it, are the links that have been calling to Don Naifeh for the past twenty years.

I park and hop out of the car, eager to unpack and putt and meet the caddies and play golf. Don stays in his seat.

"You all right?" I ask.

"Yeah. I just need a moment," he says.

I leave him to his meditations—or whatever he's doing—and walk around to the back of the car to start unloading our equipment from the hatchback. Through the rear window, I peek at Don hunched over his book, reading silently and bowing slightly, like an observant Jew with his Talmud. I squelch the impulse to say something funny, to reduce the ethereal to the here and now, realizing that it is my discomfort with this kind of devotion that is strange, not Don's piety. The truth is, I don't know what he's doing, or what he's thinking, or what he's dreaming. I just know that it has something to do with far more than slapping a ball around a sheep pasture.

So, instead of being a wiseass, I quietly set up his bag and remove his shoes and wait for him to emerge. When he does a minute or two later, I merely say, "Welcome."

He hugs me then and says, "Thanks."

The first at the Balcomie Links is a little par-4 of 328 yards, playing straight downhill from the clubhouse to the valley below. Beside the green, there's an old boathouse formerly used by Crail's life-saving crew. It's a lovely sight this view is, pleasing to the eye and cheering to the heart. All you see is desolation and openness—and then, there, in the distance, a stolid, roughly hewn building and a fluttering flag, reminding you that you are not quite as alone as you previously imagined, not walking the ground in solitude. The hand of man is evident, but gently and in moderation, letting Nature, the true star of this show, have her rightful place in the spotlight. I think I would feel very lonely to play the Balcomie Links by myself. I am glad to have Don Naifeh by my side.

Feeling very centered, I address my golf ball at the first tee. (Don, of course, is not quite ready to play.) The opening-tee-shot jitters that we all experience at one time or another have somehow flown away during this voyage to Scotland; I feel no angst, no fears, only grace and power. Once again, as I've done during every round of our pilgrimage, I make my best true, pure, authentic swing to commence my journey out and back, away and home. (The trick I've yet to master is to make this swing on my second, third, and thirty-third attempts.) The ball flies off my driver like small artillery fire, getting from here to the distant out there in a blink, flying, climbing, sailing, momentarily exempt from the laws of true gravity, whatever they may be.

"Mmmm," I murmur appreciatively, delighted by what I have authored with my funny red driver, my metallic lollipop.

Anyone who has ever seen what happens to a golf ball when it lands on the fairway of a links golf course knows that my drive ought to bounce hard and run and run all the way up and onto the green, leaving me a tasty eagle putt to commence my round. That's what "should" happen.

But my ball hits a deep green soft spot, where last night's rain has collected, and stops forty yards short of the putting surface.

"Great drive, Michael!" Don says. "The streak continues."

"Should've been on the green," I mutter. "Didja see that? Thing just stuck. The one soft spot on the whole course, the only one, and I manage to find it."

I am having an out-of-body experience. I can hear myself whining like a petulant brat. I can see myself losing sight of what today's round of golf is really and truly about. I see this all from a safe remove, as though I were dead and my ghost has returned to watch my body go through its motions. But I'm helpless to stop myself from behaving like a complete asshole.

And I hate it. I hate that I'm focusing on what didn't happen instead of what *is* happening and what *will* happen. I hate that I am capable of interpreting this unfortunate result as some sort of grave injustice. I hate that on this day, Don's day, I am losing track of the lessons my friendship with him has taught me.

Distracted by irrelevancies, I almost miss the seals moaning comically, as though they've had too much whisky, on the rocks in the sea behind the second green. I almost miss the cattle grazing on the hillside, arranged just so, as in a bucolic landscape painted by that Dutch bovine specialist Aelbert Cuyp. I almost miss the signs, real and imagined, that Burningbush is all around us.

And so I pay my penance. I play angry and make bad scores. Don Naifeh, limping over each of Balcomie's 5,922 yards as though each divine inch of ground were made of goose down and marshmallows, plays happy and makes good scores. He hits the first four fairways, the first four greens, and shoots even par for the first four holes. He is in heaven. I am in a hell of my own making.

Which makes the fifth such a treat: it's a 459-yard par-4 that bends around the sea, like the letter *F* missing the short middle line in the center, and it's the number one handicap test at Balcomie Links. They call it "Hell's Hole."

I laugh. I have to laugh. These damned connections won't stop grabbing me by the shoulders, won't stop shaking me wide awake.

My caddie, Jerry, a local fireman and a member of Crail, hears my guffaw. "Aye, s'all ye can do a' this hool," he comments, handing me my driver.

When we get to our tee-shots, resting at the bottom of a steep hillside, with the sea on the right and farmland behind the green, our caddies direct our gaze toward a herd of cattle grazing contentedly behind the putting surface. "Ye see tha big block one? Aim fer him!"

Don and I trade smiles. "You hear, Don? The black one! Not the white one with brown spots. Hey!" I shout at the cows. "Stand still! You're supposed to be my target."

"You gotta love it," Don says. "Scotland. What more can I say?"

Suddenly Hell doesn't seem like such a bad place. Indeed, once I pull myself out of my self-inflicted I'm-the-unluckiest-golfer-in-the-world miasma, I'm able to see once more what a charming place Crail is. With the exception of Hell's Hole, there aren't too many places on the course where a player feels beat-up or overextended. The Balcomie Links coddles you, teases you, tickles you—it doesn't bludgeon you with big-shouldered brutishness. It's seductive.

"I'm in love," Don tells me, resting on the seventh tee. "I'm completely in love with this place."

I make some lame joke about how easily he gives his heart to any course that allows him 37s on the front nine. But I know what he means. To Don Naifeh, a place like Balcomie Links—or Burningbush, or whatever you want to call it—is home, a comforting, reassuring oasis that makes both body and soul feel protected from the aches and sorrows of quotidian life. Gimpy Don, whose physical appearance would seem to suggest a man better suited to the padded confines of a convalescent community, seems to have found his home on a Scottish golf links. I'd like to find such a place, too, on or off a playing field.

As we play the ninth, tenth, and eleventh holes—the last of which is a par-5 evocatively called "Lang Whang"—my anticipation for the thirteenth grows voraciously, so much so that I rush through the preceding ones like a child at an amusement park, bypassing the Tilt-A-Whirls and carousels so he can be first in line at his favorite roller coaster. (This is unlike me; while I generally play with alacrity, when I'm in Scotland—especially when it's sunny—I want the day to never end, for each hole to go on forever, for the sensual pleasures of a rugged links to linger in my nose and ears and hands until the night takes it all away.) Don is 6-up in our match; I've already conceded him the victory (and another thirty or forty pounds) in my head. What I'm playing for now is the possibility of epiphanies.

Don has made little comment about Burningbush vibes as we've toured the Balcomie Links. He's smartly realized that the sweetest reward of playing this lovable golf course is the *playing*—not the interpreting, not the detecting, not the untangling of dense hermeneutics. The playing. Messages from the land, or Michael Murphy, or the spirit of Shivas Irons can be heard clearly, Don seems to understand, only when one isn't listening too hard.

The only indication I get that Don is even subconsciously aware that we are approaching Lucifer's Rug is when he makes a sloppy bogey on number twelve, a relatively easy par-5. He's neither rushing nor paralyzed, it seems to me, just infinitesimally distracted, as though he knew he were being watched by a pretty girl. Or an all-seeing guru.

As we make the short stroll from the twelfth green to the thirteenth tee, I quietly ask my caddie if he's read *Golf in the Kingdom*, wondering if he'll give me and Don a well-rehearsed speech about the significance of the upcoming hole.

Jerry confesses he's heard talk of this *Kingdom* book, but he's never actually read it himself. Some of the other Crail members, he thinks, might have skimmed it. But no one really talks much about it as far as he can remember.

"So, this hole," I say, nodding at the thirteenth tee, "it doesn't have any significance or anything?"

"Bloody difficult," Jerry allows. "Ye might wanna hit driver t'day."

I look to Don for signs of a revelation, hints of a visitation. Something. Anything. He only says, "Nice par, Michael. It's your honor."

I tee my ball high and waggle my driver, finding my center as I shift weight from foot to foot. When I am perfectly balanced and ready to swing—a three-quarters-ish swing it's got to be, since the distance is a wee bit too short for a full driver and too long today uphill and into the wind for a 3 wood—I stand over my ball and wait. Maybe something will happen.

I wait a few seconds longer. I can see the individual dimples on my ball, the grass cut short and prickly beside it. I can hear the ocean and human breathing, possibly my own. I can smell salt and freshly mown grass, taking me back to summer afternoons biking around Fox Point, Wisconsin, wondering if places like Scotland and Treasure Island and Burningbush really existed. I'm alive and receptive. Ready, really ready, to receive.

Nothing.

No bolts of energy. No magnetic halos. No ghosts.

Just a damned difficult golf hole waiting for me to make my best try.

Oh, well. I make a halfhearted pass at the ball, sort of a disappointed and disillusioned golf swing, without much conviction behind it. The results are predictably unappealing: The ball flies high and weak, on the approximate trajectory of a 6 iron, and lands with a disheartening thud in the jungle of gorse fronting the green.

I shrug. "Lucifer's Rug," I say to no one in particular. "I wanted to play this hole better. Alas."

Then I almost drop my club from shock.

Don emits a full-throated scream that nearly stops my heart, not to mention everyone else's on every corner of the golf course. It's a yell that's part fire alarm, part torture victim, part joyful noise.

It's very loud.

I look around to make sure Don hasn't witnessed someone being murdered on the hole behind us. As far as I can tell, nothing looks out of the ordinary on the Balcomie Links, except, of course, for the startled and quizzical looks on the faces of all the other foursomes enjoying an otherwise placid day on the links.

Our caddies are wide-eyed, like one of those tropical fish species with bulbous headlights for eyes. Screaming on a golf course?

I smile uncomfortably. No one says anything, including Don, whose poker face—developed over years of practice at card tables around America—betrays nothing. He's not explaining.

The tee at the thirteenth is so silent I can almost hear the echoes of my friend's primal cry bouncing back to my ears off the distant sea boulders. For a moment, everything has stopped at the Crail Golfing Society's golfing grounds.

With heads down and feet absentmindedly pawing at the turf, like a trio of bashful schoolboys forced to watch an educational film about human reproduction, the caddies and I start to giggle nervously.

I look up from the ground, glance at the loopers, and shake my head in amazement. "I don't know," I say quietly. "I have no idea."

"Gavema feckin heart-attuck!" Jerry says, shaking his head and grinning. We all laugh, including Don.

With the ice broken, the unbearable tension released, like gas out of a balloon, I say to Don, "Well, you want to explain that little . . . whatever it was?"

"Not really," Don says mysteriously, teeing his ball low.

"Scarin' awee thu demons," Don's caddie, Andrew, offers. "At's all."

"Something like that," Don says, extracting his 3 wood from his bag.

"Ye might want driver t'day," Andrew reminds him.

"Nah. This is the club," Don replies, settling himself over his ball.

It's not—not with the wind and the uphill and the nefarious vegetation awaiting anything hit short, it's not. I know this, and so do the caddies, but we're helpless to warn Don. No matter how badly they or I or he wants him to play Lucifer's Rug well and wonderfully, we can't do it for him. He must learn for himself, as we all must.

The cracking sound of Don's golf club meeting his ball is nearly as loud as the piercing yell that preceded it. I follow the flight of his shot as it climbs and soars: in the distance I see the green, waiting patiently; in the middle I see Don's ball hovering over the thorny danger; in the foreground I see the author of this 219-yard journey frozen in place, with his hands beside his left ear, classically posed like Ben Hogan with a prosthetic boot.

Because it is set on a hilltop, the putting surface of number thirteen at the Balcomie Links is difficult to see from the teeing ground. I see Don's ball disappear over the cliff's crest, but I don't see it land. At least it got over the trouble—that I know.

When we finally arrive at the green—after I've extricated my ball from its spiky prison—Andrew locates Don's tee-shot. It's just off the green to the right, almost exactly pin high.

"Well, it was the right club," Don says, surveying the situation, still winded from the climb up the hill.

"Nice shot, Mr. Screamer," I say to him. "You ought to do that more often. Well, actually, you'd better not. I don't want to go to prison."

Then, standing between two bunkers, Don chips toward the hole. His ball takes a peek at the flagstick as it rolls past, catching a slice of the cup. It stops less than a foot from nirvana.

"Wow," I say, genuinely impressed.

Don taps in for par. And as he extracts his ball from the cup, he asks me, "Now, Michael, if that chip would have gone in would that have proved to you that there's such a thing as magic?"

"Hey, I'm just happy we haven't been ejected from the golf course!" I joke. The truth is, if Don would have made birdie here after screaming like a coyote caught in an ankle trap, I would probably have been too stunned to continue. Too scared.

As our group walks to the fourteenth tee, I ask Andrew about his "demons" theory. What's that all about?

He tells me that Don's yelling was probably meant to scare away the devil or anyone else hanging around the hole ready to do mischief. Jerry nods. Makes sense to him.

I repeat Andrew's "interpretation" to the source of our inquisitiveness, inscrutable Don.

"Don't you remember, Michael?" he asks me. "Right there, on Lucifer's Rug, 'First he stood on one leg, then the other, once with his eyes and once with his eyes closed. Then he cupped his hands and cried out to the heavens, something between a yodel and a wail for the dead.' That's exactly what Shivas did."

"Right. And he also played the hole with a wooden cane in the middle of the night," I reply.

"Well, you got any plans tonight?" Don says, chortling.

"You really are intent on getting us incarcerated before we leave this town, aren't you?"

"Connections, brother." He looks back to the thirteenth green. "Me and Shivas."

We're standing now on the fourteenth tee, which looks down toward the green, 150 yards away. To the left I can see the first green, with the lifeboat shed beside it, and on the right the sea laps up against the boundaries of the golf course. "You want connections, Donnie? I gotta tell you what's sitting right below this tee. I mean, literally below our feet."

"A gravesite?" he inquires, almost hopefully.

"Maybe. I don't know about that. But what I'm certain about is that directly below us is a cave. Right here, in this very hillside. In fact, look at your scorecard. Number fourteen is called 'the Cave.' No kidding."

"Seamus MacDuff! " Don says, pronouncing the first name like "seem-us," as would anyone who's read *Golf in the Kingdom* a hundred times but never heard the name used in conversation. "Shivas's teacher. He lived in a cave on the golf course."

"Thought you might like that," I say, feeling like a dad who has just presented his son with a new bicycle.

"Wow," Don says reverently, utterly liberated from the bounds of reason. He doesn't need convincing of anything. He knows where he is now. "Guys," he announces to the group, "I'd like to take a moment to hit a sea ball, in honor of some special people."

Instead of explaining to Andrew and Jerry yet another of Don's eccentricities—they seem to understand him well enough on their own—I feel a strange and unstoppable impulse. Am I inspired or merely worn down? Caught up in momentary madness or touched by true gravity? I don't know. And I don't care.

"Wait, Don," I say. "I want to do something."

I reach into my bag and pull out an old ball. I walk past my friend Don Naifeh to the right edge of the box, facing the sea. And I put my ball on a tee.

Don says nothing. He smiles contentedly and nods.

The North Sea waves lap languidly against the sea rocks, like so many kittens nuzzling against their mother. Far beyond, on a distant shore, I can make out Carnoustie and the rest of the eastern coast of Scotland slithering away to the gray horizon in an indistinct blur. Out there is eternity, the true meaning of forever.

I say a silent prayer. "May all my troubles cling to this ball and fly far away, never to be retrieved." I think of the wife I have lost, and the lover who is gone, and all the joys and sorrows I've had on golf courses speckled around the world. I see my pains, both real and imagined, ignored and enlarged, attached to the golf ball, rent from the darkest reaches of my soul and made manifest and plain, ready to be released, if not forgotten. "Good-bye," I say to them, and to myself. "Good-bye."

I swing my authentic true magic swing, the one of my imagination. I drive the ball as far as humanly possible, to the place where time begins anew. It goes and goes, beautiful and lonely there above the icy waters. And it goes and goes.

I don't believe in god—not the god that's worshipped by the world's competing religions. Not the one that is invoked as a handy excuse for wars and cruelty and subjugating the heretical Others. But I know in that moment, standing upon Seamus MacDuff's cave at the Balcomie Links, only steps away from where Shivas Irons made his midnight ace, I've been saved.

Don watches my ball sail into the unknown, and he puts his hand upon my shoulder. "Beautiful," is all he says.

By now, our caddies have seen about all the mystical hoodoo they can handle. I can vaguely hear them whispering between themselves while we play the fourteenth. Words like *demons* and *spirits* and *feckin daft* seem to be a central part of this conversation, and I don't blame the fellows. They arrived at the golf course today expecting to tote our bags and give us some yardages and maybe a story or two—and in the bargain they've been made to participate in maniacal yelling, intentional ball losing, and impromptu literature lessons. All in the name of golf.

Neither Jerry nor Andrew can seem to stand it any longer: They want to know what all this nonsense is about. They're not angry—not at all. They're just bloody confused.

As we walk from the green to the fifteenth tee, pausing to look into Seamus MacDuff's cave—which has the distinctly inglorious odor of spilled beer and urine wafting from it—Andrew asks about the sea ball ritual. He's not condemning it or anything; he wants to make that clear. But, well . . . why?!

Limping noticeably toward our next hole, "Mill Dam," a wee, drivable par-4 of only 270 yards with the sea running along the entire left side, Don inhales deeply and sighs. "Well, I'll tell you a story," he says.

Several years ago Don was in Reno, Nevada, playing in a poker tournament there. While sitting in a high-stakes game, with money and chips blanketing the table, he got word over the phone that his mother, Maxine, back in Tulsa, Oklahoma, was not well. Don's brother, Larry, advised him that he ought to get home as quickly as possible, so dire was their mom's prognosis. Don immediately cashed in his chips, jumped in his car, and started the long drive through the night, hoping to get home in time to see his mother one last time. Speeding across the desert, drinking Diet Cokes and slapping himself in the face to stay awake, Don figured he could make it to Oklahoma in twelve to fourteen hours, stopping only for gas.

While refueling outside the small town of Pahrump, Nevada, he learned that his mother had passed on.

"I stopped near the side of the road at the Cottontail Ranch, a whorehouse," Don recalls, stepping onto Crail's fifteenth tee. "I got my driver out of the trunk and an orange golf ball, back when they still made those. And I said good-bye to my mother then and just absolutely crushed it, as good as I've ever hit one."

His eyes are misty, but he doesn't look sad.

"And you know what?" Don says, nodding. "That ball I hit may *still* be in the air."

The caddies nod reverently. I tee my ball. Don looks out to sea.

I don't tell him at the moment, but I suspect the ball I hit from Seamus MacDuff's cave might still be flying, too. I envision Don's orange memorial to his mother and my white testimonial to all my past wounds circling the globe like two tiny satellites, occasionally passing each other on their peripatetic odyssey, saying a wordless "hello" in the language of golf balls as they intersect. The thought makes me happy.

Setting myself on the tee at the fifteenth, I get a strange feeling, a bout of precognition, that in five seconds or so the ball I am now hovering over will find itself at the bottom of the cup out there in the not entirely inconceivable distance. I've never had a hole in one in my life, and I certainly wouldn't dare to dream my first could come on a par-4. But, strangely, I just somehow *know*.

I make my prettiest, most elegantly powerful golf swing—and *bam*! I crush it like a defenseless grape during harvesting season in Napa Valley.

Directly into the gorse.

About twenty yards from the tee.

This very well may be the shortest drive I have hit in the past five years and definitely the shortest tee-shot I've ever made in Scotland or in the presence of Don Naifeh.

"What happened there?" my partner asks me innocently.

"I don't know," I say. "I was pretty sure I was going to make a hole in one."

Over lunch in the Crail clubhouse, overlooking the roiling land we have just spent the past four hours or so traversing, I pay Don Naifeh the seventy-six pounds he won in our match. "Here you are, bandit," I say, handing him the colorful notes. "Don't you feel a little guilty coming out here and shooting a 74—and telling me with a straight face you've never played the golf course before."

"I had a good caddie," Don says, complimenting Andrew, who, along with Jerry, has joined us for a sandwich before returning to the links. "And, besides, Michael, you know I *have* played this golf course before. Probably a hundred times. I just never got my tired old body here before, that's all."

The caddies look at Don curiously. Unlike the typical round, in which their clients ask all the questions, today Andrew and Jerry feel compelled to ask some of their own. "Pleed here b'foor?" Andrew inquires.

"In a way," Don says cryptically.

I explain to the local fellows my gimpy friend's obsession with this book we've been talking about, this *Golf in the Kingdom*—how he's a member of the Shivas Irons Society and a certified believer in "true gravity" and other concepts that are too lofty for my limited comprehension. And I tell the caddies that their golf course—the one they walk almost every day of the week; the one they conduct their club matches upon—is quite possibly the inspiration for the golf course in the book, whether the author actually knew it or not.

They look at me puzzled. I've succeeded in confusing them even more.

Don asks me for the car keys and excuses himself for a moment. As I watch him shuffle away, a "Crail Golfing Society, 1786" sweat-shirt rakishly tied around his hunched shoulders, I tell Andrew and Jerry that all the yelling (the demon chasing) at the thirteenth was, as far as I can tell, Don's weird reprise of something his hero Shivas did in the book.

They nod thoughtfully. And Andrew says, "Daft bugger."

"Feckin' daft," Jerry agrees.

We all laugh. But still. The man *did* show up at this faraway golf course he's never seen before, walk every yard of its hills and valleys on his own two atrophied legs, and shoot 74. Fourteen shots better than me—me with my muscular thighs and L.A. Marathon–running feet. "He beats me every day," I confess to them. "Shoots in the 70s every day. I mean, look at him. You saw for yourself."

"Aye," they say. And that's all that need be said.

Don returns to the table clutching his copy of *Golf in the Kingdom* in both hands, like an offering plate. "Gentlemen," he says to Andrew and Jerry, "this is a first edition copy of Michael Murphy's *Golf in the Kingdom*, signed by the author." He strokes the cover affectionately. "I want you two to have it."

The caddies tell him how awfully nice that is, and is he sure?, and all that. But I can tell they're thrilled to have the source of the day's peculiarities available for investigation.

"Please read it," Don requests, "and pass it around the club. Make sure people here know what they've got."

The caddies promise they will.

Then Don produces from his pants pocket his pink Sharpie pen, the same one he's been using to inscribe names on golf balls before hitting them into the ocean. On the inside cover of the book, just below Michael Murphy's signature, he adds his name, the date, his score (in parentheses), and this inscription: "To Andrew and Jerry and all the members of the Crail Golfing Society, Thanks for letting me play the magical Balcomie Links, also known as Burningbush."

12

History

"I've always associated the golf course with romance," Don tells me, limping up the fifth fairway at Cruden Bay Golf Club, one of the most naturally dramatic linkslands in all of Scotland, and one of my favorite places in all the world to make wind-influenced bogeys. We've come here to what seems like the ends of the earth—it's actually the northeast corner of Scotland, but same difference—after Don's odyssey at Royal Aberdeen, where he endured his first (and we both hope *only*) round without the assistance of a caddie. That journey nearly killed him, he swears. I suspect, as the old chestnut goes, it only made him stronger.

Instead of rambling on about memorial balls and unseen forces, today Don is fixated on that one abiding topic of male fascination that doesn't involve televised sports: women.

According to the scorecard, the fifth at Cruden Bay is a par-4 of 454 yards. But we're playing through the cavernous dunes today as though it were a par-5. There's a demoralizing gale in our faces, taunting us. (Well, me at least.) On his second shot, Don, exhibiting both physical and mental control, hits a perfectly placed 3 iron to within pitching distance of the green. I, exhibiting neither quality, use a badly chosen driver off the fairway to send my innocent and unsuspecting ball into rough tall and thick enough to hide a rhinoceros. Farewell, sweet prince . . . I hardly knew ye. I start to talk about the quality (or lack thereof) of our respective golf shots; Don's mind is elsewhere.

"I wonder how Kristy plays this hole. It's gotta be a par-5 for her. Gotta be!" Don muses.

He's mooning over the hostess at our B&B, Kristy Middleton, daughter of Alan Middleton, Cruden Bay's former club secretary. Kristy, Don discovered shortly after checking into our course-side accommodations, is a former Scottish Ladies Amateur finalist and Cruden Bay Club Champion, not to mention president of the club's ladies section. Never mind that she's tall, physically fit, and terribly sweet—her golf resume is enough to send Don into paroxysms of ardor. Usually, after our typical breakfast of porridge and pig entrails, Don can't wait to rush off to the golf course, where every pro-shop proprietor in the country eagerly awaits him and his credit cards. Today, although I have spoken glowingly about the spectacular golf course at Cruden Bay, regaling my pal with rapturous accounts of the otherworldly dunes and peculiar hole designs (number fifteen is actually a dogleg par-3), he tarried over his empty plate, chatting up Kristy about her curriculum vitae. A Gershwin melody played in my head—"I've got a crush on you . . ."—and an Elizabethan revenge drama involving well-deserved retribution pulsed in my heart. How I'd like to see my friend Don Naifeh with a delightful lassie like Kristy Middleton instead of J, the bitter hag he's presently allowing to torture him.

We're playing the sixth, the evocatively named "Bluidy Burn," when Don realizes something encouraging. "You know, Michael, when I review my history, the results are pretty good with me and women and golf. Actually, let's see," he says, counting in his head.

"Let's see. Yeah. Seven. Seven first dates that took place on a golf course that led to romance."

"Extraordinary," I say, having difficulty conceiving how that would all work.

"Isn't it?"

"I don't think I've ever had a date, first or otherwise, on a golf course," I tell him. "Sex on a golf course a few times. But never a proper date."

"Well, then we've definitely got different histories," Don remarks, surveying the distance to his next layup spot.

"That's true," I say, ruminating on what an understatement Don has just spoken. It's a gulf so huge I'm not sure either of us could ever cross it.

Our caddies today, Frasier and Ray, are two lovely guys, middle-aged members of Cruden Bay Golf Club, who, I soon discover, have between them a huge gulf in green-reading ability. My man, naturally, is the weaker of the two in this regard. But the tales he tells! While I bumble my way around the links, he keeps me entertained with yarns of ancient battles and rivers running red and abandoned castles that may or may not have been the inspiration for Bram Stoker's *Dracula*. Apocryphal or not, Frasier has me convinced that Cruden Bay isn't merely a beautiful place to play a memorable round of golf; it's a book waiting to be read.

Speaking of which . . . as a courtesy to Don, who, since our day at the Balcomie Links, seems to be conducting an informal poll of every Scotsman he meets, I ask my caddie if he's ever heard of a wee volume called *Golf in the Kingdom*.

Nope. What's that? Nay.

Almost everyone we've met here in Scotland, the land of Shivas, hasn't read, seen, or in many cases heard of the sacred tome. All this mysticism stuff we visiting Americans like to blabber on about seems to them somehow silly and fatuous, I suspect. Isn't golf just a game, a simple game chiefly about taking a walk beside the sea and getting a little white ball into a hole?

Well, yes, it is. And my partner and chief competition seems to have gotten that last bit down quite well. Despite playing a personal record seven rounds in a row—all on foot—Don continues to make birdies and shoot in the 70s and astonish everyone who witnesses him drag his broken body around the links, one limp at a time. Frankly, I'm getting tired of paying him thirty to forty pounds a day for the privilege.

But I'm learning golf is about other things, too.

We're playing the outward corner of Cruden Bay, holes ten through fourteen, which occupy a sunlit meadow exposed to the sea. It feels just now like a perfect representation of heaven, if only that intangible place had golf holes so lovely. We've already made four birdies between us on the outward nine, and while I'm tickled to see nice scores on the card, thanks to Don my thoughts are elsewhere.

Women. History. A time before we walked these grounds and a time when we no longer can. Where we've been and where we are going.

"You've never told me," I say to Don.

"What?"

"History. I mean, yeah, I know about how much romance the game has given you. How you've fallen in love with women after playing golf with them. But, Donnie, I don't think you've ever told me how you fell in love with golf."

We walk together in the warm afternoon light. We chase our shots together, heading toward home. And Don Naifeh tells me his love story.

It goes like this:

Thirty-five years ago, little Donald Naifeh, ten years old, was recovering from a fractured femur and a shattered hip. He suffered these two latest injuries after the quintessentially childish and playful act of jumping off a picnic table. These broken bones weren't anything new to the young lad: he had already had a dozen fractures before the age of ten. Indeed, the simple act of walking—of learning to walk—would frequently result in broken bones. So he often got himself around on crutches and sometimes a wheelchair.

Two years earlier, on a family trip to Florida, Donnie watched Shell's "Wonderful World of Golf" on the television with his father, Jack. Don's dad played some, and his neighbor friend David had a dad who played some too at the local country club, the descriptively named Rolling Hills. One day Donnie's friend invited him to come swimming at the country club. At one point in the afternoon, between splashing around in the water with his pal, Don Naifeh watched a man, a stranger, hit golf balls on the club's practice range.

That summer, Don's boyhood friend Steve Sherrill got a set of golf clubs for his birthday. Don spent many summer evenings lolling on a lawn chair, watching Stevie conduct a systematic excavation of his lawn's crabgrass using a 7 iron. When his legs were feeling strong enough, Don would get up and whack a few tennis balls with one of the metal sticks.

In January of 1964, he discovered something peculiar and, to his mind, remarkable about the game of golf. On another family trip to Florida, Don learned that the object of the game of golf was to make the *lowest* score possible. Since he was often recovering from one annoying injury or another, little Don Naifeh spent many hours—too many hours, more than he really wished to—playing the lonely card game of solitaire. The object in that game was to finish with zero cards in your hand. And even when that wasn't possible, the fewer cards you had the better. This tiny realization—that his favorite card game and this strange sport of golf shared the same scoring principle—awakened in him a peculiar curiosity. He couldn't play golf—he couldn't play much of anything, for that matter—but he was fascinated by what he thought of as the solitaire concept. And golf became one of his favorite things to watch on television during those endless afternoons when his brittle and mending bones wouldn't allow him to be out playing football and basketball with the other neighborhood children.

That Christmas, Jack Naifeh got his invalid son a set of golf clubs. He knew the kid probably wouldn't ever use them on a giant golf course like Rolling Hills Country Club, but, what the hell, he figured Don could slap around plastic whiffle balls while he watched Arnie and Jack doing the real thing on television.

Don loved his sticks—Voit irons and three persimmon woods, back when woods were made of wood. Though fractures frequently put him on the bench and the clubs in the garage, whenever he was well enough Don would imagine he was one of those heroic guys on television as he pelted his mom's furniture with indoor drives. Whenever he thought he might never get well—or didn't feel like enduring the arduous therapy that would make him well—Don remembered his golf clubs, shiny and polished, so lithe and graceful, and he felt like he had some incentive to recover.

The next summer, after several months of unusually good health, a time during which he managed to avoid a single bone fracture, his older brother Larry and some of the neighborhood kids invited Don to join them at the local pitch-and-putt a mile away from their street. Don rode his bike there with his crutches and golf clubs balanced across the handlebars of his bike, and he ended up using his bicycle as a kind of makeshift "cart," toting himself and his equipment from hole to hole. He wasn't very good—in fact, he probably took 10 or 15 strokes on every hole—but then and there he made a decision: he was tired of pretending he was "normal" enough to play touch football, only to come home crying to his parents when he had snapped another bone merely from falling down the wrong way. Golf would be Don Naifeh's game.

This was a sport, he believed, that allowed him the most pleasure with least amount of physical risk. For a boy who had to worry that one ill-timed trip upon a basketball court or one too-hard slide on a baseball diamond might render him convalescent for six months, golf seemed something like a savior, a nonthreatening frivolity that, nonetheless, affirmed his blossoming boyhood. It was something he could *play*. With other children. With his brother. Maybe even with Big Jack.

One balmy afternoon that year, the neighborhood kids invited Donnie to join them at La Fortune Park, an all-par-3 municipal course. No one seemed to care that he was presently confined to a wheelchair, thanks to another broken leg suffered in a bike crash. Even if you only watch, they urged him, come along for the ride. Don was going to do just that—being with Steve and Dave and Larry was way more fun than sitting around the house playing solitaire—but at the last moment, before they piled into mom's car, he grabbed a few of his clubs. Just in case.

Somehow he knew he was ready to play golf. Maybe not physically. But he was in every other way *ready*.

Don "played" the first six holes at La Fortune that day, wheeling himself from tee to rough to fairway to green. You would have to be using the word *play* very loosely to describe what happened during Don Naifeh's first visit to a "real" golf course, since there was nothing fun to him about advancing the ball five or six feet with every feeble wave of his freshly polished clubs. He'd wheel himself to his ball, park the chair, press himself up off the seat, make a frail swing that often missed everything completely, sit down, and start the whole process again. The management of La Fortune seemed supportive enough of his experiment: so long as Don kept his chair off the greens they didn't care if some cripple kid rolled around the golf course with his pals.

By the seventh hole, though, Don Naifeh had seen enough. Close to tears, frustrated with the game and his body and the general unfairness of everything his young mind understood, he left his clubs with his brother and wheeled himself to the parking lot to wait for mom to come pick him up. He was done with golf.

At least he thought he was.

His neighbor Steve Duren—another Steve—one of his best friends and playmates, got Don to enter a prestigious local tournament Steve called the Fifty-fourth Street Open. It was a very limited field, this event: only Steve and Don could enter. The idea in the Open was to hit plastic balls from water meter to water meter, from one end of Fifty-fourth Street to the other. Cars and porches and the front window of the grouchy guy on the corner were major hazards, and dogs and mothers with strollers were the appreciative gallery. The winner got the cherished prize of getting to go first on the way back down the street.

A year later, Don Naifeh could stand again. He was well—or as well as he had been in many months—and his dad thought now would be a fine time to take some lessons at the park, where the city was offering a weeklong "camp" for aspiring golfers. Dad was right. Don wasn't any sort of prodigy, not by any means. He didn't display any sort of innate talent for the game in his group lessons at summer camp. But he did master the rudiments of golf: how to grip the club, and how to stand, and that sort of thing. He felt like the precious secrets of Arnie and Jack and those other immortals he watched on television had somehow been revealed to him, despite his handicaps.

With his son passably aware of how to hit a golf ball without injuring himself or others, Jack Naifeh would often take the boy to the range after work at his law office. Sometimes one of the neighbor dads would, too. Everyone on the street knew that if they were going to hit golf balls, they should bring little Donnie with them. Because even if no one could identify in him a molecule of talent for the game, they could clearly identify something more important: the kid really loved golf.

And it was true. The game, young Don realized, had a lot to offer a special boy like him. He could play it, he figured, for the rest of his life without fear of injury. He could be with his dad and his brother and his friends outside, where youngsters preferred to be on warm Oklahoma afternoons. And best of all, he figured he could learn to get better. And wasn't that the whole point of being alive, the whole reason for being put on this planet? To learn?

Certain of this last part, even in puberty, Don Naifeh worked at becoming the best little golfer his disabled body would let him be. As he stood over one jumbo bucket of balls after another during his daily visits to his sacred grass temple known as the range, he heard whispers from older, bigger players about the championship course just over the hill. He came to know it as the "Big Course." Perhaps one day, he imagined, he might get to play that Big Course, where, it was rumored, some of the holes took able-bodied grown men three—and sometimes more!—shots to get from the tee to the green.

Hitting balls seven days a week, Don Naifeh grew up to become a pretty decent ball striker. (By the time he was in his midtwenties, after years of toil and countless other physical setbacks, he was a legitimate single-digit handicap.) But walking, the simple act we almost all take for granted, was an enormous deterrent from playing golf competitively. Don considered entering tournaments and, in his most secret fantasies, playing professionally, just like the dashing heroes he watched on television while his broken legs healed. Once he even entered a local U.S. Open qualifier, but Don dropped out after twenty-nine of thirty-six holes. He just couldn't make it, no matter how badly he wanted to hear his ball drop into the cup on the final hole. His legs wouldn't let him.

So Don turned his energies to making money, to being a "success," whatever that was. He graduated in the top 20 percent of his training class at Merrill Lynch, where he was being groomed to be a big-time stockbroker with a $1 million portfolio and all the glittering accoutrements to show for it.

Then he tore his Achilles tendon, met a catalytic woman named Hippie Beth during his physical therapy, became metaphysical, and, almost overnight, reversed the course of his existence. Instead of collecting corporate equities, Don Naifeh devoted himself to the humble task of discovering the meaning of life.

It was around this time that Don Naifeh first read a book called *Golf in the Kingdom*. His hippie friend, Beth Field, a beautiful spiritualist with a fondness for meditation and yoga and incense, introduced him to the book (as well Richard Bach's *Illusions*) saying that if Don truly loved the game of golf, he ought to read the strange and wonderful tale of a Scottish shaman named Shivas Irons.

He was twenty-eight, just finished with broker training, and slightly confused but exhilarated by infinite possibilities. Everything seemed possible, for him and for the world.

One summer, on a brief trip home to visit his family, Don felt like visiting some of his old haunts—including La Fortune Park, where his childhood par-3 course still stood, welcoming players of all abilities. He grabbed a few old clubs from the basement (they may have even been from his first set) and a ball or two and drove to the golf course, his head swirling with memories. It had been nearly eighteen years since the first day he had visited La Fortune, more than half his life ago when he first wheeled himself around (and off) the golf course.

Something nice happened that afternoon: using a pitching wedge, he sent his ball 109 yards through the humid air directly at the flagstick. Though he couldn't see the lower half of the pin, Don knew this pretty shot was going to be awfully close to the hole. When he limped up the hill to the green, he found his yellow Titleist 6 grinning at him from the bottom of the cup. "Hole in one!" he yelled to no one in particular. "My first hole in one!"

Then it hit him. He was standing on La Fortune Park's seventh green—the same one he had walked off from eighteen years previous, certain he was through with golf, through with trying to be like all the other boys playing in the afternoon sunlight.

He realized then that golf was a game meant for him. Someone or something was trying to speak to him from another realm, a spiritual one, perhaps. And the message was this: the game of golf was put here on earth for Don Naifeh to play.

The sixteenth at Cruden Bay is a 182-yard par-3, with a green surrounded by several pernicious bunkers that, I assume, give the hole its name: "Coffins." I could be wrong. There might actually be graves beneath the putting surface. Don finishes his history lesson here at this hole, telling me, "I was dead for a short time there, Michael. And golf brought me back to life."

He makes birdie at Coffins, and I get a little shiver.

"Sometimes," Don tells me, limping to the seventeenth, a hole where, local legend has it, hundreds of dead warriors were once buried, "I feel like it was created just for me, that all the rest—Nicklaus and Woods, smoking and not walking, Shivas Irons—is just part of my consciousness. Sometimes I feel like it's all a dream that I made up to bring me peace, or some sort of comfort. Reality is all perception, right? Well, Michael, when I had that epiphany, that message delivered in the form of a hole in one, I knew that I had been here, in this realm, on earth, on a golf course, before. And so I've always thought I'd find the meaning of life on a golf course."

He shrugs. "So that's why I play the game."

I neither believe nor disbelieve my friend's tale. It may be a sober report told with the dispassionate eye of a skeptical newspaperman or a fantastic fiction created in the mind of a magical realist. Either way, I know it's true.

The seventeenth at Cruden Bay is called "Bilin' Wallie" ("boiling well"), named for a natural spring that flows to the left of the tee box. As we're passing this old watering spot, I motion to Don to join me for a drink. He looks apprehensive. "Are you sure that water is drinkable? It looks like there's a lot of—what is that? Algae?"

"I drank from it the last time I was here, a few years ago," I tell him. "And I'm still here, so to speak."

"Aye, s'fine," Frasier assures Don. The caddie bends down and scoops up a handful of water to demonstrate.

I follow. Then, reluctantly, so does Don.

I wipe my mouth with the back of my hand. "Ah! Connections! To the land, to those who drank here before us, to history!"

He thinks I'm joking, of course. He thinks I'm poking gentle fun, hiding behind sarcasm and humor to mask my uncertainties.

But this time I'm not. I *have* been here before, on this very spot, albeit three years ago, not three lifetimes ago. I was happy then, entwined with a lover who made everything beautiful and exciting in this world seem possible and probable. I was in love and alive, traveling through this blissful place with my goddess, not caring particularly one way or the other what kind of score I made on the golf course, just so long as the good long walk led me back to her, back to happiness. Back to home.

Suffused with fresh water boiling up out of timeless ground, energized perhaps by its alchemical powers, I make birdie on the seventeenth. On the eighteenth, with our match on the line, Don chips in from fifteen feet off the green, for a birdie 3—his fifth of the day, a personal record.

We shake hands all around. "Thanks," I say to Don, who has soundly beat me yet again. I catch his eye in the dying light, so he knows I'm serious. "That's a round I'll never forget."

"Me either," Don says. "I set all kinds of records for myself today. Birdies, and rounds in the 70s, and rounds under my own power— if that's even a statistical category!"

"I think we made some history today, my friend," I say.

He looks back toward the golf course. "That's the funny thing about it, I guess. We make it every day, whether we're trying or not."

13

Seeing Things

"Getting there is half the fun," they say—they being those lucky souls who sincerely like the act of moving, of being in transit, of going. Such people remind me of male friends of mine who aren't so much interested in the consummation of sexual desire but the pursuit of it. Anticipation is what thrills them; arriving at their destination is what finally kills that feeling of eagerness and robs them of their real pleasure. Having spent many years as a magazine travel writer, canvassing the globe in pursuit of adventure and beauty and the ineffable otherness of faraway places, my tolerance for the getting there part has weakened over time. I suppose my desire to skip the planes, trains, and motorcycles segment of the journey and just simply be where I want to go is another example of favoring results over process. As Don says, the only way to be happy on the golf course is to focus on how you're playing, not on how you're scoring, since the latter will inevitably send you into fits of despair. Same thing with travel. If you get caught up in the delays and indignities and wastefulness (of time and money) involved in getting from where you are to where you want to be, you'll surely drive yourself to annoyance, if not madness.

I'm thinking such things while Don and I wait beside the A98 coast road for a nice fellow from the Automobile Association ("AA"; they have one fewer "A" in their rescue-service initials over here) to arrive with a few liters of petrol for our very thirsty chariot. On the way from Cruden Bay to Nairn, we've run out of gas.

While I fume over the lack of fumes in the tank—a faulty gauge is to blame—Don, incorrigible, chips golf balls on the shoulder of the freeway, using the yellow emergency call box as his target, as though the Fifty-fourth Street Open were being conducted on a barely inhabited stretch of northern Scotland. As tends to happen when Surlyn meets asphalt, one of his balls skips madly sidewise, across the thoroughfare, and into high brush on the other side. Like any self-respecting child competing in the Fifty-fourth Street Open would, he takes off in search of his missing toy, seemingly oblivious to the (light) traffic that roars past from both directions.

I start to call out to him, "Be careful!" or, less charitably, "Are you insane?" But I know whatever I say won't make any difference. He's undeterrable, like a hound on the scent of a small mammal.

Until this moment, I've progressively worried less and less about Don's physical well-being on our journey together. He's demonstrated to me—and, more important, to himself—that the physical challenges of playing golf without a motor buggy will neither stop him nor injure him. He consumes painkillers and anti-inflammatories about as prodigiously as he does Diet Cokes and Marlboros, but he gets by. Somehow he does. My instinct to protect him, to shield him from danger, has been, I realize, innocent and pure, like a mother's toward her children. I'm finding out, though, that being unshielded is exactly what Don Naifeh wants most. He wants to either triumph or fail on his own terms, on his own two unsteady legs, as it were. And I've got to let him. Even if it means watching him get plowed into the gorse by a speeding lorry while he looks for a wayward Titleist.

The evening before, at an Italian joint called Casa Salvatore, in the charming little riverside village of Elon, I gave Don a small taste of the "worrying about your friend" medicine by standing up in the packed restaurant and singing an aria from *La Traviata* while a roomful of Scotsmen and their lassies looked at (and listened to) the crazy Yankee who had somehow stumbled into their world, lungs blaring. The trattoria's owner—the eponymous Sal—an Italian signor married to a Scottish woman, likes to entertain his diners with impromptu melodies, and he offered me a free dessert if I would do the same. (I had told him I was a big opera fan and sang a wee bit myself.) So I did, much to Don's anxiety. From the moment I sang the words "*Un di felice*" until I warbled the final "*d'amor!*" Don had upon his face the kind of pained grin one normally sees on the deeply embarrassed or inconsolably worried. For just a minute or two, I felt as though we had switched roles.

When I returned to our table (amid pleasant applause and bravos), Don told me, "Now I've seen it all. I thought you were kidding when you said you were gonna sing. Wow." He lit a cigarette. "This trip is getting very surreal."

I'm thinking something along those lines as I watch Don pitching golf balls across the motorway, narrowly missing oncoming cars with his lob wedge. Here I am in a remote corner of Scotland, accompanied by a Rigoletto-like companion who, even in a travel debacle moment, insists on staying "connected" with his savior sport. I start wailing "*La donna e mobile*," and the scene is complete.

Don returns to safety without hurting himself or unsuspecting motorists, but he's slightly perturbed. "Couldn't find that one," he reports. "I *hate* losing golf balls. That's only the second one this whole trip."

"You've lost only one ball in eight rounds of golf in Scotland?" I ask rhetorically. "That's gotta be some kind of record."

"And one on the damn motorway," Don says, nodding.

"Well, one day some road maintenance worker will be cutting back the brush from the highway, and he'll find your ball. And even though he won't have any idea how a golf ball could have been hit so far off a golf course, in this spot, you two will be connected somehow, by golf," I say, attempting to be appropriately profound.

"Damn!" Don exclaims, ignoring me. "Running out of gas cost me a golf ball."

"Well, actually, having a chipping practice section on a highway is what did it. But, anyway . . ."

Just then the AA man comes with a plastic jug of fuel, and we're on our way to Nairn.

Seeing an endless chain of impossibly charming seaside fishing villages—I mean, so pretty and innocent and unhurried I just want to cry, if not fire off three or four rolls of snapshots—the concept of getting there being half the fun suddenly doesn't seem so ridiculous. I'm eager for Don to see the Nairn Golf Club, where, only weeks before, the Great Britain and Ireland squad proved to be most inhospitable to the American Walker Cuppers, giving the visitors a bracing lesson in how to play links golf. But if our car were to break down another few times I wouldn't be terribly dismayed. The scenery hardly gets more lovely than this anywhere I can recall, and I've been to a couple of pretty places. For instance, we visit Penan, a one-street-on-the-beach town made famous as the location for the movie *Local Hero*. Though the time-zone differences are all screwed up, I insist on calling my friend Josh back in Minneapolis from Penan's red phone box (outside the Penan Inn), since he once called me from the very same spot. The connections concept is starting to grow on me.

On the same principle, we stop at the wee town of MacDuff, so Don can get a photo of himself posed beneath the village's welcome sign. His fellow cult members, he's sure, will be thrilled to see one of their own perched beneath Old Seamus's name. Arranging himself for the portrait, Don nearly tumbles headfirst into a barley field. We talk at some length about the metaphorical ramifications of our trip together nearly coming to a shattered-fibula conclusion at Mac-Duff—Don seems to think there would have been something poetic about it—before moving on toward Nairn.

"It's funny, Michael," Don remarks as we buckle ourselves into the car. "So much of my life has been concentrated on just *not falling down*. You might be surprised at how that tends to condense everything into slow motion. It can be a pain in the ass—like when I'm trying to keep up with you on a golf course. But, on the other hand, I get to see certain things a little more closely."

Me? I go fast. I'm rapacious. Impatient. I can't wait for anything. Maybe a fear of falling down would do me good.

In hot pursuit of our afternoon tee time down the road, we pass a number of great-looking golf courses, including Tarlair, a wind-whipped one set on a brutally exposed hilltop plateau in MacDuff. Each time we don't stop to play a golf course—and in this part of Scotland nearly every village seems to have its own links—pain shoots across Don's brow as though someone has kicked him in the shin. He reminds me of my brother and me on childhood car rides with my parents. Every other weekend we'd visit our grandparents in Chicago. About halfway there, outside of Gurnee, Illinois, we would pass a gigantic amusement park called Great America. My brother and I would crane our necks as dad sped past the object of our desire, taking in as many images of cascading roller coasters and spinning Ferris wheels as possible until the cruel highway took them away from our mesmerized eyes. Don's like that with golf courses.

"You see that!?" he'll exclaim. "I mean, Michael, *look* at that. I swear, that could be Seamus MacDuff's training center," he'll say, referring, of course, to *Kingdom* or its sequel. No golf course is merely a golf course to Don. It's a symbol. A precursor. An artifact. And like Willy Loman, Don believes such a thing is not to be ignored—attention must be paid.

I share some of his longing. Just as a promiscuous Neanderthal wishes to sow his seeds with as many potential childbearers as he can manage to drag by the hair into his cave, I want to play every golf course I see—and not because some mystical dude (a *fictional character*, mind you) supposedly practiced all manner of golf shots on land much like this or that. Nor is my desire merely a severe case of the common golfer's malady of "been there, played that," which manifests itself most comically in the commemorative tags that hang from golf bags like so many keys on a chain. I've long since lost interest in checking courses off a mythical top-100 list. What I'm looking for, I guess, is that rare golf course that gives me that feeling, that certain *mmmm* of deliciousness, when site and air and light and ground conspire to produce a sense of wonder and awe, of everything being right with the world. Every golf course we eschew on our journey is, in a small way, a missed chance to rediscover that state of grace.

Still, we motor on, pausing only to take photos of black-faced sheep and shaggy-banged longhorns, of endless vistas overlooking the blue-as-berries sea, of wee main streets we could imagine ourselves shopping at in our later years. The day is a succession of glorious postcards, all of which prove that, yes, maybe it's true after all, the getting there can be as good as the there you seek.

Thanks to some driving worthy of Jackie Stewart, himself a tidy little Scottish golfer, we arrive in Nairn an hour before our late-afternoon reservation. This allows us time for a brief accommodations search, which has become one of the more jovial habits of our pilgrimage. Our usual MO is to stake out the golf course (so we know where we have to go in the morning) and backtrack from there, looking for B&Bs or inns within walking distance of restaurants and shops. Don has quickly learned what to ask for when he rings the bell as I wait in the car: "two single en suite rooms, one smoking, one non, full breakfast in the morning." Though most places prefer to let their rooms to couples, without a single reservation the entire time we've been in Scotland, we've managed every night to find inns willing to let us have double rooms at a single rate, typically around thirty pounds a man, including all the morning hog meat you can handle.

The first place we see after tracking down the Nairn Golf Club is the Golf View Hotel, an imposing stone and wood castle that towers over the coastline. Joints like this typically have trouser presses and miniature soaps in the rooms and, therefore, cost twice as much as a B&B that has only a regular iron and full-size bathing bars. But Don says he's got a feeling they might be willing to give us a bargain since it's midweek and the parking lot doesn't look too full. And besides, he says, he'd love to have a phone in his room for once.

"You need to make some calls?" I ask, curious.

"Yeah, I'd like to, you know, touch base back home," he replies evasively.

"All right," I say, with an involuntarily raised eyebrow. "You can try them. But I bet they're going to want, I don't know, fifty or sixty pounds."

"Hell, I'll pay it. I win that much off of you every day on the golf course anyway."

I wince exaggeratedly and watch my buddy lumber into the lobby, where, I imagine, he'll have a brief conversation filled with mutual misunderstanding of the other guy's accent. And then we'll move on to a little B&B down the street.

Don comes out a minute later, looking very proud. "Say hello to your new home," he says through my open window.

"Two singles?" I ask.

"Yep. Forty pounds."

"Including breakfast?"

"But of course," Don says. "Come on, let's get checked in. We can make a few calls before we hit the links."

When we get to our adjoining rooms on the third floor, Don sounds like a child on Christmas morning. "Television! Big old bathroom! Clock radio!"

"Trouser press," I remind him, hanging some of my rain gear from the appliance. Seeing Don's naked joy at the modest comforts of a full-service hotel reminds me that no matter how much unspoiled nature one looks at on their peripatetic wanderings, a little dose of civilization at the end of the day is sometimes the prettiest sight of all.

Of course, the rugged charms of a hundred-year-old links has its appeal, too. The Nairn Golf Club is one of those rare golf courses where the description "seaside" doesn't accurately portray how intimate a player's proximity to the churning water truly is. On five of the outward holes, the beach on the right is easily in play for those who slice, fade, push, or otherwise fly a wee bit to the reactionary side of their intended target. At high tide such shots translate into lost balls; low tide means you're playing in a very large sandbox. The layout eventually turns inland, taking advantage of some unusually varied topography (for linksland, that is), combining some of the best elements of heathland golf with the primal attractions of sea-level dunes. I love the place.

Despite the magnificent surroundings, excellent local caddies, another preposterously sunny afternoon sky, and thousands of seabirds in the water and on the ground to enliven the game, Don seems grim, distracted, angry. Nairn boasts what are generally considered the finest putting surfaces in Scotland, but Don doesn't appear to be having much joy on them, even when sinking the occasional spectacular putt over a hillock, off a slope, and into the bottom of the cup. Considering the grandness of the day and the location, I'm sad that Don isn't more fun to play with. Do I get like this, I wonder? (Yes, I know I do, and I don't like it.) Note to self: don't let whatever's bugging you affect innocent bystanders; as we've learned from Frank Loesser via Frank Sinatra's voice: like a lady who leaves her escort, it isn't fair, and it's not nice.

Jack, Don's caddie today, notices his man's low spirits and attempts to cheer him with a lascivious compliment, the kind that seems to spring forth from a Scottish caddie as readily as impossible arpeggios from the piano of Oscar Peterson. Don rips his drive on the tenth, a par-5 called "Cawdor," of *Macbeth* fame. "Aye, 'atsa blundie!" Jack exclaims.

"A blondie?" Don asks, perplexed.

"Aye, sir. A fair crack doon the muddle!"

I'm inspired to repeat my semifunny golf joke involving buttercups and pussy willows. Don smiles glumly and stares straight ahead.

The rough at Nairn Golf Club is particularly pernicious since, upon initial consideration, it looks harmless. Consisting mostly of tall wisps of grass as elegant as a field of Giacometti sculptures, the rough appears frail, almost effete. It's not. No matter what you hit—wedge, mid-iron, "rescue" wood—the grass swallows the shaft of the club as though it preferred steel and graphite instead of sunshine and water. A visit to the overgrown areas off the fairways quickly turns easy pars into double bogeys.

Don has reminded me several times throughout our pilgrimage that one of his favorite things in all of golf is to 1-putt for double bogey. We get to do that a lot today—though it doesn't seem to cheer him much. He makes a brilliant birdie on number fourteen, a 219-yard par-3 playing directly into a swirling wind coming off the North Sea, hitting the green with a cut 3 wood and dropping the subsequent twelve-foot snake. But on sixteen, Don makes an ugly triple on Nairn's version of the Road Hole, going from bad to gorse. Throughout all the windblown theatrics, I hear from him much swearing and whining and other unpleasantries. This is not the Don Naifeh I love to play golf with.

On the eighteenth, "Home," a par-5 with the wind blessedly at our back, Don makes a 10, the first time I think I've ever seen him shoot in double figures on a single hole. His inflated score comes from several futile swipes in the hay, which advance his ball one, two, and zero feet. On the seventh of his flails, he whiffs completely, extracting with his wedge enough vegetation to design a lovely floral centerpiece. He looks at the bushel of grass clinging to his stick, like an Afro wig on a pole, and he laughs, loudly and sincerely. He laughs because, really, what else is there to do at this funny old game. Or, for that matter, this funny old life.

He whiffs and he laughs. *That's* the Don I like to play with.

After I tap in for my par, finally managing to escape the golf course without having to dig into my wallet, Don tells me he has a confession to make: twenty minutes before our tee time, while I was availing myself of Nairn's slick practice green, he was on the phone in the clubhouse with J, getting his heart torn out.

"You wanna win a golf match from me, partner?" he jokes. "Make sure I talk to her before we play. It's the surest way to get me off my game."

I make some reassuring noises about not needing that mean old hag, about fish in the sea, and all that. But Don just shakes his head.

"You don't get it, Michael," he explains. "Or maybe you don't notice."

"What?" I wonder.

"Well, like, today, getting from Cruden Bay to here. We stop in all these pretty villages and such. And you're looking around taking photos and admiring the architecture and what have you. And I'm noticing all these cute Scottish schoolgirls. And they're all staring at my shoe."

"I'm sure they've never seen anything like it before," I say, watching the sun drop into the sea over Don's shoulder. "People are fascinated and maybe a little scared by what they don't know."

"True. Yeah, that's right," he says, looking down at his right foot. "But they don't look at me the way they look at you, or any other man. I'm a joke to them."

"That's not true," I say.

"And I meet a woman who looks beyond all that, and, well, I don't know. I guess I'm willing to let a lot of shit slide that I know I shouldn't."

"Come on," I say, guiding him to the parking lot. "We need to talk."

I take Don to an Indian restaurant I remember from my previous visit to Nairn, with my ex-wife. He's never had this kind of food before, spicy and strange, and, it turns out, he's never had the kind of pep talk I try to give him over plates of chicken tikka and chutney-coated papadums.

Though it takes me appetizers, main courses, and desserts to impart what I hope will be an inspirational message to my downtrodden friend, the basic theme of my encouraging words is this: "It's awful to feel lonely; it's even worse to be abused." Sensitive to Don's way of looking at the world, I pepper my sermon with as many golf metaphors as I can manage ("Sometimes it's better to pitch out sideways and take a bogey instead of bringing a big number into play by trying to force a shot beyond your capabilities"), but he's nearly inconsolable.

"Don't you understand, Michael?" he pleads. "I don't want to be alone."

"I know," I tell him. "Nobody does."

And I really do know. I've confronted the bleak emptiness of a house devoid of loved ones and pets and, yes, even furniture. I've seen the blackness left behind when love walks away. I know.

I look at Don Naifeh, sitting across the table from me, a cigarette in his hand and a plate of half-eaten curry at his elbow, and suddenly I'm gripped with a profound sense of *missing*. I miss my lost wife. I miss my lost lover. I miss my dog. And only Ella, the canine, will be waiting for me upon my return from this trip to the Kingdom of Golf. The others are gone. They were here, in this country, in this village, at the nearby golf course even. But they're gone now, taking with them parts of me that will never be retrieved. When Don and I finish our journey, our quest for what exactly I'm still not sure, he'll go back to his little apartment in Phoenix, I'll go back to my little house in Los Angeles, and nothing except my faithful hound and lonesome memories will be waiting for our return.

The sitar music, previously exotic, is now merely depressing. The signed photos on the wall of the restaurant's owner with his arm around unrecognizable local celebrities (if there can be such a thing in a town of fewer than 5,000 souls) were formerly cute. Now they're a reminder of how far from home we've come. And how far we've still got to go.

"You're going to be fine," I reassure Don, who has taken temporary solace in his nightly examination of the day's scorecard.

"Yeah. I know I will be," he says, alternately nodding and shaking his head. "I'm just not there yet."

"Maybe not," I tell him, thinking of our eventful circuit from Cruden Bay to Nairn, from the first tee to the last green, from home to the great distant out there and back to home. "But you know what they say?" I remind my friend. "Getting there is half the fun."

14

Lowdown

Playing Royal Dornoch, ancestral home of Donald Ross, the former greenkeeper whose much-loved course architecture continues to thrill players of every generation, was supposed to be the highlight of my trip to Scotland. For years I've dreamed of coming to this spectacular links, at the height of the Highlands on Scotland's northern tip, with my golf buddy Don Naifeh. From the time I first saw the place, ablaze with yellow gorse blossoms outlining the tumbling fairways, I wanted to come here with a special friend who I knew would love the land—and the experience—as much as I. My ex-wife had visited with me, many years ago, and found Royal Dornoch a lovely place to take photographs; as for the golf—well, weren't all these sheep pastures pretty much the same? Don Naifeh, I knew, would be able to tell the difference. He could discern paradise when it was spread out before him, like a sumptuous buffet or an inviting woman.

This was supposed to be the day when I discovered that everything was indeed right with the world, just as I had secretly suspected all along. Reports to the contrary, accompanied by niggling bouts of the blues if not full-blown depressions, had been, like reports of Mark Twain's death, greatly exaggerated. Life really *was* too perfect for words. And what better way to underline that inspiring fact than with a salutary walk on one of the greatest golf courses on the planet? With a friend? Particularly one with super x-ray vision, the kind that helps a guy see through all the irrelevancies and distractions of everyday existence and get right to the essential core of what really matters in this funny journey through time.

That's what was supposed to happen—because I had imagined it all and scripted it all and wanted it all.

Alas.

It's the kind of gray, moody sky that Don has been forcefully pining for, as though he feared he might be cheated out of his fair share of drizzle during his fortnight in bonnie Scotland. Though Dornoch is at the approximate latitude of Anchorage, Alaska, some sort of weird wind current—the gulf stream, I think—keeps this near-Arctic playground temperate. Still, the rain, which seems this day not to fall but to *materialize*, as though it were the product of an unseen mist machine hidden off stage right, is sufficiently nippy as to make the day better suited to otters than golfers. Naturally, Don's cheered by the prospects of battling the elements, if not his saturated partner, who has already resigned himself to an afternoon of grip-it-and-slip-it. Perhaps it's some strange measure of my character, the atmosphere's way of spotlighting a sort of deficiency in my constitution, but I realize all over again that I don't like playing in the rain. It's a control issue: on a clear and sunny day I have less control over the places my golf ball goes than I would like; when it rains, I have even less control than I normally do.

Happy golf, I've noticed, happens when a player follows the motto espoused by Alcoholics Anonymous and has the grace to know the difference between what he can and cannot control. Angry golf, conversely, occurs when a player tries to hold dominion over everything that obstinately refuses to be changed. I resolve to play the happy variety today, resigning myself to the whims of weather. Don, I can tell, has made no such vow.

We're paired with a father and son from Tampa, Florida, who, I must report with more than a little envy, have an overseas membership at the Royal Dornoch Golf Club. I had the opportunity to get one of these about seven years ago, back when considerably less had been written about the club, and when it cost something like— I'm not kidding about this—$300 to join! Stupidly, like an over-cautious investor who wants to wait and see how this little start-up company called "Microsoft" is going to do after its IPO, I hesitated and equivocated and vacillated for lame reasons I can no longer recall. Now there's a long waiting list.

The dad, John, is a surgeon; though he is clean-shaven and bespectacled, I can't help thinking of him as "Dr. John," despite the utter lack of resemblance between him and the gravel-voiced, organ-tickling singer from Nawlins. As we walk off the green of the par-3 second—where I have managed to take five strokes despite missing the putting surface by two feet with my tee-shot—I ask the doctor to tell me about being an American member of an esteemed Scottish club. John says it's great fun and that the locals are quite nice, but occasionally he's ashamed to admit he's from the United States. He relates a horrifying story about another American member, an orthodontist from California, who, though able-bodied, insists on using a motor buggy, and, to Dr. John's embarrassment, consistently cheats during club matches. "I think he's been asked to leave," Dr. John tells me. "And I sure hope it's true."

I can't figure out Dr. John. He walks the links with a tidy little shoulder bag, and the usual height of his golf shots seldom exceeds the hairline on an NBA power forward—a sure sign of someone who has played a lot of golf in Scotland and learned how to deal with the raging wind. And he's got the cheerful attitude of one who subscribes to the notion that happy golf is the best golf, no matter what your damn score happens to be. On the other hand, Dr. John eschews a caddie and instead uses one of those laser range-finder thingies that the USGA frowns upon in competition (but certifies for practice rounds). He strikes me as a purist with a keen sense of history and tradition who, nonetheless, likes to fiddle with the latest and best equipment because, hey, you never know, it might make this difficult game a little easier to bear.

Just as Dr. John is mortified to be associated with the cheating orthodontist, I'm finding that on today's tour of Royal Dornoch I'm feeling slightly ashamed to be the guy who introduced Don Naifeh into the proceedings. He's playing even slower than usual this day—partially, I suspect, because Dornoch has more severe elevation changes than most links courses—and, to make matters worse, he seems frighteningly obsessed with winning the day's match. (Yesterday's rare loss at Nairn seems to have irked him badly.) His glacial pace of play is annoying; his refusal to concede eighteen-inch putts (all of which I routinely make) is downright ludicrous. Everyone—me, the caddies, our playing partners—looks at Don with the silent question, "What's wrong with *him*?"

Again, as at Nairn, Don seems filled not with joy but with anger. His glee at playing one of the greatest courses on the planet has been supplanted with fury at J—who I later discover has used their recent phone conversations to taunt Don with declarations of her sexual infidelities in his absence—and at me, and the weather, and the world. He's sullen, unresponsive, and *sloooooowwwww*.

Where is the spirit of Shivas Irons when you need him?

By the twelfth hole, a 557-yard par-5 that stretches beside the sea like a yawning cat, I find myself apologizing to the group for both Don's demeanor and his refusal to pick up his pace, despite the gentle imploring of a course marshal, not to mention his buddy Mike. I tell Dr. John about Don's OI, certain a medicine man will understand how debilitating such a disease can be to both a man's bones and his golf game.

"He'd be a lot better off, and he'd play a lot faster, if he quit chain-smoking," Dr. John replies. "And that's coming from a former two-pack-a-day man."

I agree wholeheartedly. But as we continue on to the fourteenth, "Foxy," a brutal par-4 of 445 yards that typically plays into the breeze, I remember Don's startling insistence that rather than trying to play golf in pain, he's better off "medicated" with nicotine, which Don considers something of a wonder drug. "Nicotine isn't bad," he's often told me. "It's the delivery system, the smoke, that's no good." To this I always tell him he therefore ought to get himself some of those patches or the gum. He tells me it isn't the same, and, besides, he tried that stuff once and it almost gave him a heart attack.

I have no way of knowing at that moment, searching with him for our drives in the absurdly ferocious left rough, that Don will indeed have a heart attack shortly after we return from Scotland, that the smoking and the stress and the horrible diet will finally take its toll. He'll survive the attack—indeed, it will be mild enough that he'll be able to drive himself to the hospital, since J will refuse to do so. But, at age forty-five, he'll finally realize that all the "medication" he's been consuming in the form of unfiltered cigarettes is doing him far less good than he's previously believed.

But now, trudging through the overgrowth on Foxy, cursing ourselves for getting greedy with our drives, for missing the fairway when there was, upon further consideration, so much of it to hit over there on the right, we're just two hackers trying to escape the clutches of a very difficult golf hole. And at the moment, maladies like heart attacks and broken bones and broken hearts seem a continent away.

Our match today is very close, thanks mostly to my deadly putting, which comes and goes as capriciously as the weather in the

Scottish Highlands. When it—my putting, I mean—decides to stick around for a round or two, I'm invincible, as invincible as a mediocre ball striker can be. Today is one of those days. I see the line, I know the speed, and the ball goes where I think it ought to. Don, meanwhile, has 3-putted four times already, which, for him, is as unusual as a morning without three Diet Cokes. His stroke looks bad. If putting strokes can be distracted, his is, as if it's thinking of distant loves gone wrong. I can tell he's expecting this day to miss everything he looks at. Rather than confront this sorry state of affairs with grace and humor, he's calling himself "a joke" and the "worst player to ever pick up a club" more than Tiger Woods does during his semiregular bouts of self-flagellating petulance.

Twice in the past four holes, Don has hit drives that skirted the fairway and landed on the fine borderline between a difficult second shot and an unplayable lie in the gorse. Both times I have wandered away from my eminently playable ball and helped locate his seemingly lost ball. Neither time did he thank me. He just shook his head disconsolately and grunted. When it happens again on the seventeenth, I start to deliver a homiletic lecture, but I catch myself. I learned something a couple of hours ago, when I was searching (in vain) for a wicked hook: often a really bad shot on this golf course sends you directly into great stands of raspberry bushes, whose sweet fruit bursts forth from hundreds and thousands and millions of branches, as though the land were offering a tasty honorarium in exchange for the golf ball you have given it. I want Don to see for himself that poor golf shots, even ones that produce lost balls, sometimes create delicious rewards.

At the moment, though, standing on the tee of the eighteenth at Royal Dornoch, all the highfalutin spiritual sermonizing I'm accustomed to hearing from Don Naifeh seems terribly phony. For a minute I'm transported back to my adolescence, when, like most confused lads emerging from puberty, I passionately identified with

Holden Caulfield and his crusade against all things fake. Right now, to my dismay, gimpy Don Naifeh seems like the Wizard of Oz, his frailties exposed. Sure, he's wet and tired and disgusted with the frequency of poor golf swings he's producing. But we're at Royal Dornoch. Together. Where I've always imagined I wanted to be more than anywhere else.

And it's all lost on him.

I have a putt for par on the last to win our match. It looks like it might break a little toward the water on the left. Or maybe it might try to leak right off a little bump behind the hole. Or maybe it's straight. I crouch behind my ball to assess the eight feet between me and victory at Dornoch. Then I start to get up and look at the putt from the other side of the cup. But I stop. What's the difference? I don't care anymore if this putt goes in or not, and the pass I make at the ball proves it. I just want to be done so I can find someplace alone and quiet to have a cry for all my regrets. They were supposed to have magically attached themselves to my sea ball at Crail. So why am I sadder than ever?

"Nice match," Don says perfunctorily, extending his hand.

"Yeah. Thanks." I can barely look him in the eye.

Every conceivable place between Dornoch and Fort Augustus (more than 100 miles south) to shower, unpack, and stew in our respective bilious juices is sold-out. The reason, we're made to understand by dozens of apologetic innkeepers, is that it's the "high season."

I want to tell them, "Hey, can't you see I'm suffering an emotional crisis? This is like the end of a love affair for me!" But instead I sigh deeply and motor on into the night.

We spend an hour driving aimlessly around a charmless section of Inverness, the biggest city in the north, where it seems every third private home has been converted into a B&B. Nonetheless, no vacancies anywhere. Onward, to the loch!

That would be Ness, famed for containing the brontosaurus-like "monster" that has spawned countless television documentaries and even more cottage industries trafficking in Nessie-related dreck. Like many of the lakes in the Highlands, Loch Ness is ineffably beautiful, its still waters framed on both sides by steep hillsides, upon which deer graze and baronial mansions sit, all oblivious, it seems, to the perennial tabloid subject lurking in the black water below. But aside from its obvious prettiness, Loch Ness also has about it a mysticism that has little to do with quickly glimpsed, camera-shy apparitions. I don't know what it is, but I can feel it. There's something alternately spooky and timeless about Loch Ness, placid and turbulent, as though something, some things, are going on there when no one is looking.

When we arrive at the loch's northern shores, around 8:00 at night, the sun has almost completely set, but a penumbra of light still frosts the water. As the temperature rapidly cools, a thick white mist, the consistency of smoke, floats off the lake's surface, as though a master Vegas illusionist had cranked up his dry-ice fog machine to cover the trapdoor in the stage floor. Melodies from *Brigadoon* instantly pop into my head—and so do a few strong ideas.

I pull over our faithful silver Peugeot, set the parking brake, and without any explanation given to my puzzled companion, leave the car.

"What are you doing?" Don asks, as I pop open the hatch.

"Something I did a long time ago."

"What?"

"You could say I'm closing a circle," I reply, grabbing my driver and a couple of balls. I walk down a shallow slope toward the water's edge, my heart pounding.

Seven years earlier, I journeyed to Scotland with my wife. We traveled through the middle of the country on a hotel barge, floating on the Caledonian Canal and Loch Lochy and, most memorably, here on Loch Ness. One sunny afternoon, our barge pulled ashore so that the tourists onboard could clamber out to take photos and buy Nessie-related memorabilia. While the other passengers pawed through T-shirts and key chains and little laughing lizard dolls wearing tam-o'-shanters, I hijacked my camera-toting wife and asked her to join me on the banks of the loch.

And while she snapped photos, I drove golf balls into the middle of Loch Ness.

I don't know why I did it back then. I don't recall attaching any spiritual significance to the act. I suppose I just thought it would be a fun and silly and inexplicable thing to do.

And it was. The balls made a satisfying splash and a distinct *ker-plop* when they fell in the water, and I remember thinking something like, "Wow, I'm hitting golf balls into Loch Ness, here in the Land of Golf. Cool." And I recall my wife, my beautiful wife, smiling at me, her dazzling eyes telling me she hadn't the slightest idea what we were doing here, bombarding Nessie with Top-Flites and Maxflis, but she wouldn't want to be any place else.

As the sun dims and the moon rises, I find a semiflat spot above the lake and drive my golf ball into the nothingness. Later, much later, after what seems like a minute or a lifetime, or maybe longer, I hear the splash, like a trout jumping after a mayfly.

I can feel her smile.

Don appears at my shoulder. "Whatcha doin'?" he asks, grinning.

"Um. Well." I look out at the mist, thickening and rising, like a cloud with wings. "I'm not sure. Saying hello or saying good-bye. Maybe both."

"To Loch Ness?" Don asks quietly.

I feel a small tear, an involuntary solitary lonely tear, sliding down my cheek, like a raindrop on a window. "I don't know. To my past and to my future. Sometimes I wish I could go back. Like *Our Town*, or something. A do-over. A mulligan. Maybe I'm taking one right now."

"Go ahead," Don says encouragingly. "Do it."

I hit another one into the watery void, which buzzes with the electric hum of insects and air and life. When the clubhead meets the ball I feel a slight shock run up from my fingers, through my shoulders, and into my chest. Is it the collision of past and present I feel, the warping of dimensions I'm unable to comprehend? Is it the force of truth I feel, coursing through me? Or is the jolt and shiver just the cool night air wracking my still-damp body?

I don't know. And I couldn't be more content to never find out.

"You really connected on that one, Michael," Don says.

"Yes. You could say that."

We stand there on the shore of Loch Ness, gazing into the murk, never wanting to leave until everything becomes clear or invisible, either one. We review and we plan. We remember and we dream. We get lost and find our way back.

Then the Scottish lake midges—a lethal combination of gnat, mosquito, and flea—attack us with a vengeance historically reserved for invading Englishmen, and we're forced to dash to the sanctuary of our car, slapping ourselves like two of the Three Stooges. I'm no longer irked at Don Naifeh. I know what happens to a man when he can't let things go, let them slip away into the deep dark water, all the way to the silty bottom, where who knows what lurks. Way down low.

15

Sheep

We drove most of the night in search of a place to sleep. Don voted repeatedly for the car, having spent, he told me, many restful evenings in some unnamed desert reclined behind the wheel of his jalopy. I voted repeatedly for a hot shower and a cup of tea. Finally, after much quick braking and ringing of doorbells and offers of one bed and one floor, we found a guest house at the very southern tip of Loch Ness with a couple of vacancies. Beginning at Dornoch and ending at the town of Fort Augustus, we traversed in that one long day nearly half the length of Scotland and suffered only several hundred midge bites for our troubles.

The point is, I tell myself over breakfast, that somehow we got here instead of someplace else. Strange but, yes, true. We're *here*.

I don't believe in fate—or Fate—or the concept of "it was meant to be," since the notion that something is preordained suggests that there had to be someone or something interested enough in the minutia of a billion interconnected stories to bother writing in the incredible plot twists that we individually find so mesmerizingly unbelievable but, when examined rationally, turn out to be the coincidental collisions of pure randomness. Who or what, I wonder, decreed that every possible place to sleep on our Dornoch day should be unavailable, so that Don and I would be compelled to be in Fort Augustus in the early morning hours of this fine August day? Who or what author had a warped enough sense of humor to find me wandering near the elevation locks that intersect the town at the exact moment that a certain and particular boat was being lifted from Loch Ness on a mattress of water, soon to be deposited on the other side of the heavy metal gates into the Caledonian Canal? What writer, mortal or otherwise, could dream this stuff up?

While Don is shopping for tourist junk for his beloved J in the shops that line the locks, I watch the watercrafts enter and rise and leave, enter and rise and leave, like a procession of bread loaves on a bakery assembly line. I see the water and the boats and the big swinging gates, and I think that it was not very long ago that I was on one of those pretty barges standing on the deck with my arm around my beloved wife, waving and smiling at all the onlookers snapping photos and gazing wistfully at the rising water—people standing almost exactly where I am standing this fine morning, seven years later.

I review my life from as far back as I can remember—back to the time when I was almost two and our schnauzer gave birth to a litter of puppies on my bed, depositing all these warm wet wriggling creatures on the soft wool blanket—through my adulthood and up to this very moment, standing beside the Fort Augustus locks, watching boats coming and going, carrying people to and from Loch Ness, to and from their fantasies of travel and romance and Scotland. And I realize all this—life, I mean—goes fast. Too fast.

I chuckle to myself, amused by my ability to manufacture ersatz profundity, to get so sentimental over what, in the end, is the natural course of things in this universe: enter, rise, and leave.

Just then I turn to my left, as if drawn magnetically. Floating into view, next in line at the lock, I see the most lovely boat in the world, big and sturdy and dependable, with potted plants decorating the foredeck and patterned curtains guarding the long rows of windows. The large group of people congregated at its guardrails tells me this vessel is a hotel barge, just like the one I and my dear wife lived on for two weeks seven years ago—or maybe it was yesterday, so vividly do I recall our joy. The height and girth and general grandness of this barge is just like the one we traveled upon back then. Indeed, the captain, Mr. Jones, told us proudly (and often) that our ambulatory Scottish home was, in fact, the biggest vessel on the canal and would always own that honor since anything larger wouldn't fit in the locks. My eyes widening at the approaching barge, I'm reminded of the looks I observed on the onshore faces— was it awe? astonishment?—when they saw the M. V. *Vertrouwen* sail into their town. She was the queen of the lochs, and we were the prince and princess on our royal steed. Since the barge passed through Fort Augustus maybe once a week, coming and going, tarrying for thirty minutes or so as it ascended or descended the aquatic steps, locals would sometimes find a longueur in their day to watch the biggest of them all make its weekly visit. You wouldn't call the arrival and departure of the *Vertrouwen* an event, but its presence did not go unnoticed in a village where the absence of incidence is a way of life.

"Vertrouwen," I learned somewhere along the way, means "the faithful one" in Flemish. My wife was Vertrouwen. Always.

I was not. And so we parted.

But for some very happy days, days of golf and stags, salmon and lingonberries, lake monsters and bravehearts, we were together in Scotland, uncertain how life could be any better.

The barge floats into the lock. Onlookers snap photographs. A husband and wife on deck wave enthusiastically to the audience while their sullen teenage daughter stares at a book, refusing to acknowledge the silly tourist people gawking at this hulking vessel, which, after all, is just some old industrial boat painted up all pretty and bright. The crew tosses ropes, thick as a weight lifter's arm, to personnel on the banks. A dog emerges from the living quarters below to see what all the fuss is about.

I am experiencing what I believe is known in psychology circles as "cognitive dissonance," which is a fancy way of describing a situation that you know (or believe) to be unimpeachably real, yet you also know (or believe) to be unimpeachably impossible.

Standing there in Fort Augustus, watching the present crash into the past, I am certain that this big beautiful barge in the lock is, in fact, the very same big beautiful barge I and my (petite) beautiful wife lived upon when last we were in Scotland. It's painted a different color now, and the crew has changed. But, yes, no, I'm sure . . . this boat is giving off a vibration—a signal?—that she is here, back to say hello, or maybe a final good-bye. It's the barge, *our* barge. I know it is.

I make my way through the crowd, walking toward the boat as though I were being pulled in by a winch, oblivious of the municipal "Warning" signs and rushing water and creaking gates. Hand painted, on the side of the barge, in tidy blue letters, I see the name: *VERTROUWEN*.

She comes through Fort Augustus for half an hour about once a week. I come through Fort Augustus for half an hour about once every five years. We're here at this moment together. Or at least I think that's what's happening.

I reach down and touch the boat, just to assure myself it's as real as I suspect. Then I run off, looking for Don, looking for someone who will believe me.

I can't find him immediately. He's in one of several stores, purchasing love bribes for his woman in Arizona, but I'm not sure into which one he's disappeared. I turn back to the boat. She's still there, rising gracefully.

I see a phone box. My instinct is to call my lost wife, to tell her where I am and what I'm seeing—to tell her I still love her, and to tell her she's never gone away. The boat, *our* boat, has come to greet me at Loch Ness, the boat with our bedroom, our pillows, our sweetness. The faithful one. Maybe it never left.

But I don't know where she is. I know she is *somewhere* in this world, reachable with a phone call or a plaintive cry. I used to know everything about her, all the delicious secrets and transcendent truths. And now—well, I know she is alive someplace, and I don't know where that place is.

I miss her. I miss her so much I can almost make myself believe that she will magically emerge from the sleeping quarters of the barge, a camera around her neck and a smile on her face. And she'll turn to me standing here on the banks and ask me where I've been all these years. She'll tell me she's been waiting for me.

The lock gates begin to swing open. The *Vertrouwen* is leaving.

Suddenly I see on the other side of the water the familiar silhouette of my friend Don, slipping into another junk shop, his arms laden with wrapped presents. I run across a footbridge to him on my two good legs, pumping the air with my fists as though I were kicking toward the finish line in a desperate race.

"Don! Don!" I call out to him, oblivious to the quizzical stares all around me.

He stops and turns to look at me. He appears slightly frightened, worried perhaps that I'm rushing to take away his credit card before he can waste more of his earnings on someone who despises him.

"Don, look!" I say, panting at his shoulder. "That's the boat!"

As the *Vertrouwen* pulls out of the lock and motors toward the open water, I explain to him my history with the barge, frequently interjecting the phrase "what are the odds of that?!" as I outline the coincidences and, yes, connections, such a meeting between man and barge requires.

Don says nothing for a few seconds, watching the boat slide away, taking with it a story I now know can never be retold.

Then he nods. "Yep," he says, still nodding. "This is a very mystical land."

"Mm-hmm," I mumble.

He nods some more. "Michael? Let's go hit some golf balls."

Seven years ago, while the *Vertrouwen* was moored for an evening in Fort Augustus, my wife and I explored the surroundings on a couple of beat-up old bicycles kept onboard the barge. We said hello to cows and *baa*-ed at sheep and generally behaved like two kids on summer vacation, free of school and homework and early morning alarms, free to play and play until darkness came. Cruising down what seemed like the main road, I saw a sign for the Fort Augustus golf course and pedaled off in search of its sylvan blessings while my wife reminded me that I had already devoted myself to eighteen holes that day. I told her I didn't plan on playing; I just wanted to see the layout. She raised an eyebrow, knowing there was at least a 50 percent chance I would keep my word.

When we arrived at the course, situated at the end of an unkempt corridor of prickly bushes, the sun was starting to set. There was no one around—except sheep. Hundreds of sheep. They looked up briefly from the serious business of grazing on the fairway grass, acknowledged us with a bored bleat, and returned to chewing. "Are they supposed to be loose on the golf course?" my wife wondered. I told her I thought they might be the official grounds crew.

We leaned our bikes against a flimsy fence and let ourselves in the gate. Near the first tee I found an honor box, into which players were supposed to place their green fees of a few pounds, which covered admission for nine holes and a replay. The modest yellow scorecard said that the par-33, 2,706-yard course had several peculiar local rules, my favorite of which was: "A ball lying on sheeps [*sic*] wool or on or made dirty by sheep droppings may be lifted and cleaned without penalty . . . and all loose impediments may be moved before the ball is replaced."

"Look at them all!" my wife exclaimed, observing a herd of black-faced lawn mowers trotting across the first fairway. "How do you play golf without hitting them?"

"I don't know," I replied. "But I'd love to find out. Maybe I could run back to the boat and get a few clubs," I proposed halfheartedly, knowing the idea would be subject to a certain and rapid veto.

"I thought we were just going to take a bike ride," she said. And that was the end of that. I never did get to play the Fort Augustus Golf Club and Sheep Pasture.

Until today.

After a few wrong turns and missed signs, Don and I eventually find the course, hidden behind overgrown shrubbery. It's more or less as I remember it, only a bit more decrepit than in my time-burnished recollections. As we change our shoes in the gravel parking lot, I'm struck by the chasm between American golf and Scottish golf. And it's not the style of bunkers I'm thinking about. It's, as politicians like to say while casting aspersions at their opponent, a "character issue."

Augusta National has its Magnolia Lane; Fort Augustus has a corridor of raspberry bushes. Augusta National has manicured fairways and polished greens so perfectly coifed you might mistake them for someone's living room carpet, where the word *crabgrass* strikes fear into the heart of the army of caretakers charged with keeping everything just so; Fort Augustus has pocked and scruffy playing surfaces maintained by a motley band of walking sweaters, whose greatest fear is the phrase "mint jelly." Augusta National is pretty, right down to the azaleas in bloom; Fort Augustus is not, right down to the dandelion weeds poking through the rough.

But there's one other big difference between the two golf clubs: Augusta National does its damnedest to keep out interlopers; Fort Augustus welcomes the world.

Stupid and silly and disingenuous as it might sound, I'd rather play at Fort Augustus. The place has *sheep*.

For the first time since Royal Aberdeen, Don and I tote our own bags and make up our own yardages, since, among other niceties like irrigation sprinklers and commemorative pewter bag tags, Fort Augustus Golf Club lacks Kirby Markers, GPS systems, or color-coded stakes running alongside the fairways. (They do have numerous red-and-white poles planted in the middle of the gorse, so unlucky duffers will have a frame of reference when they search for lost balls in the prickers.) Despite the absence of almost anything that recalls golf as we know it, Don and I shoot decent enough scores on this primal wonderland. And more important, we manage to scamper around the course without "dirtying" our golf balls or murdering any innocent bystanders. Just having them around— the minstrel show blackfaced ones; the sad-eyed white ones; the absurdly cute little lambs—gladdens our hearts. To them we are merely a couple of two-legged bothers who represent an unwanted interruption in their eternal lunch. To us, though, the sheep are confirmation that no matter how many space-age instruments of destruction we wield, no matter how modern and advanced and gussied up we get, the game of golf remains, at its essence, a pleasant journey through a livestock pasture.

At the seventh hole, a 233-yard par-3 called "Croft," the green is perched on the crest of a hill. Between us and our target there's a sea of sheep, contentedly eating and bleating and creating natural hazards for the badly struck golf shot. I tell Don, "This may be the toughest par-3 we've seen in Scotland since Lucifer's Rug."

"Lucifer's Herd!" Don replies, and then emits another of his startlingly loud ululations, which frightens the twosome departing the green slightly more than it does the animals.

"Don, do you have to do that?" I ask, cringing.

He tells me it helps. What it helps I'll never know. But I *am* certain Don Naifeh plays like a major champion when he scares away the devil (or the sheep) or whatever it is he's doing when he does the yelling business. He hits a high drawing 3 wood, just like the pros, that easily carries the sheep hazard and settles three feet from the pin.

Before I tee my ball, Don invites me to try having a scream. "It clears your lungs."

I politely decline; naturally, I make double-bogey from a clump of greenside heather. I couldn't be happier.

By the time we reach the finishing hole, a tricky little par-3 called "Wee Drappie" (which I think means "small drop"), we've managed between us a slew of pars, more than a few bogeys, and not a single birdie—despite playing on a course whose meager length would earn haughty laughs from the High-End Daily Fee crowd back in the States. Of course, a day spent cavorting through a splendid park isn't about making scores, anyway. It's about communing with a friend and the air and the ground and, yes, a whole bunch of furry creatures who care even less about scores on a card than you do.

We repair to the "clubhouse," a one-room garage of a building where the members store their sticks. Over a repast of candy bars and crisps, we explain to a couple of bewildered elderly local fellows how it came to be that we should stumble onto their humble golf club. I tell the gents I had been here before, seven years earlier, actually, and I wanted to come back.

Misunderstanding me, one of the old boys cocks his head and says, "Ye meen ta tull me ye came ta Scotlan' jes ta play ore gowf carse?"

I chuckle and start to tell him no, no. But I see the sheep stampeding over the ninth green and the mist rising off of the canal and the ghost of my wife smiling on me and saying everything is finally all right. And I tell him, "Yes, sir. You could say that."

16

Try, Traigh, Try

Our journey together is coming to an end, as all journeys eventually must. I know this, and so does Don; but neither of us relishes a return to the banal indignities of real life, not when a sublime wonderland like *this*, this Scotland, allows us to play and learn and grow in the company of ghosts and gurus. We're convinced that whether we stay for another two days (per our schedule) or for two more years (per our fantasies) we'll enjoy more epiphanies, more magic, more connections. Like a burbling spring issuing forth from the earth, we suspect Scotland will always be able to quench our psychic thirsts.

Driving west out of Fort Augustus, heading toward the Atlantic Coast, I peer through the rain-spotted windscreen, half expecting (and maybe half hoping) that another talisman of my past will jump out of the mist to say hello. The highway route that begins in the center of the country and concludes at the ocean looks more or less straight on a map. But I discover the road is actually an interminable series of hairpin curves worthy of a Grand Prix circuit. Thanks to the rain and the fog and the comical narrowness of the pavement,

I feel a powerful precognitive sense of impending doom, as though something is getting ready to carry me away from the life I know. Will it be a regal Scottish stag that dashes out of the bushes? A grizzled man walking with a wooden stick and spouting epigrams about the game of golf? Or my ex-wife, thin as a wraith and clothed in her wedding gown, clutching a list of all my misdeeds in her skeletal fingers?

I'm not certain I'm ready to go. Not from Scotland, not from life.

But if I had to—well, a more serene place to rest my soul I couldn't imagine. We motor past vestigial lochs, epic waterfalls, great green glens. To call the countryside here "beautiful" is woefully inadequate. The land is too good for this world—and maybe for heaven, too.

For the briefest of moments, a fleeting synapse of delirium, I no longer care about something so prosaic as golf. But it passes. And I'm restored to my usual state of eagerness, my can't-wait-to-get-there-and-see-it-all desire. (This rapaciousness manifests itself, I'm afraid, in a leaden foot upon the accelerator. After missing several chances to find out what heaven really is like, I rein in our skidding chariot to a semireasonable twenty mph over the posted limit.) Today we are headed for Traigh, a wee nine-hole course I hadn't heard of until Don and his cult brought it to my attention. According to my Shivas-loving partner, Traigh is the kind of course upon which we might discover Mr. Irons having an impromptu game: rugged, natural, true.

Sometimes all these adjectives strike me as left over from an overproduced automotive commercial featuring affluent suburbanites "roughing it" in their $40,000 leather-trimmed SUV. But when we finally do get to land's end—without a single crash involving silver Peugeots or past regrets—I can tell Traigh is the real thing.

"Is that it?" I wonder, peering through the precipitation. "That's got to be it." I see something that looks vaguely like a golf course. But it could just be a recently mown field.

"Well, yeah, it looks sort of like a golf course," Don agrees.

"There's a flag," I say, spotting a yellow banner on the top of a hill, whipping in the wind. "It's definitely a golf course. Is this Traigh? I don't remember seeing a 'Welcome to town' sign. You know, one of those, 'Traigh: Sister city of Bumbleville, Nebraska.' Did you?"

"No. But this has got to be it," Don opines. "Looks like the pictures on the Internet. Sort of."

I park across the road from a miniature, one-room "clubhouse," which doesn't appear to have anyone inside. As I'm setting the parking brake, a bundled woman toting an umbrella emerges from the building, a stern look on her face. "Ye canna park there," she insists. "Fer gowfers oonly."

"We're golfers," I assure her. "We want to play. I mean, if this is Traigh. Is this Traigh?"

"Aye," she says, not entirely convinced that we really do want to play in the typhoon presently engulfing her links. "Nine holes," she reminds us, half suspecting that Americans wouldn't want to waste their time on anything that wasn't eighteen holes and 7,000 yards of water hazards.

"Great," I say, introducing myself and Don. "Can you squeeze us in?"

The lady, Edna—at least I think that's what she calls herself: her accent combined with the storm have affected my comprehension—invites us inside to change and have a cup of hot tea. She says there's no one else on the course at the moment so we're welcome to play whenever we're ready.

That Traigh is presently abandoned does not surprise me. The rain is now beating down violently, with a force that seems powered by more than mere gravity. It's like someone is *throwing* the drops from the sky, whizzing fastballs toward the earth. It is not, in my wimpy opinion, a very nice day to play golf. But Don, I can tell, feels as though he may have stumbled upon his own personal Burningbush, a tangible version of his fictional salvation. Traigh is so far removed from modern civilization—if your idea of Fort Augustus, Scotland, is modern civilization—and set so precariously against the raging elements blowing in from the neighboring Atlantic, that it feels a little like a lost city, a remnant from some ancient shipwreck. Traigh is golf flotsam that has washed up onshore. With reduced visibility exacerbating the conditions, it isn't hard to imagine that you are cut off from the world as we know it, that you might indeed be the first crazy human to have ever played the game of golf on this crazy swatch of land teetering against the ocean. Point yourself in the right direction and your next stop would be Greenland; face the other way and you are confronted with a golf course that doesn't seem to care very much if mortal men pay a visit or not. It's going to be here, absorbing the fury of nature, long after we coddled tourists have returned to our sunny fairways and asphalt cart paths.

"Looks amazing!" Don says, lugging his gear into the clubhouse. "Do you get a lot of play here?" he asks Edna, who seems unashamedly fascinated with Mr. Naifeh's physique.

"Mmm. Aye." She's not sure what Don's question means. I can almost hear her unspoken thoughts. *Well, sure, people play golf here. But only a few hundred people live within 100 miles, so a lad like you from some big city probably wouldn't think it's very much.* "We had an American here jes the other dee."

"Really?!" Don says, mildly shocked that anyone other than he and his friend managed somehow to find Traigh.

"Oh, aye. We did," Edna confirms. "From Colliefoornia."

The words "small world" slip out of my mouth before the automatic anti-cliché mechanism in my brain engages fully. Speaking in Walt Disney platitudes seems especially silly now, considering that the piece of the world Don and I are currently inhabiting doesn't feel much like any world with which I'm familiar. Indeed, as the wind howls around the wee Traigh clubhouse and the rain blows sideways, I'm feeling very far away from home, wherever that may be.

Looking out across the stony bay, I see three stout islands offshore. Those would be Eig, Rum, and Muck, Edna assures me. I don't think she's kidding.

Yes, we are very far from home.

Though the day is better suited to heroic yachtsmen than inveterate hackers, Don and I trudge off to the first tee, dragging along with us two local lads Edna has rounded up on the telephone. The boys, Ross and Donald, don't seem to mind the rain; in fact, the older of the two, Ross, thirteen, dispenses with a hat despite my motherly protestations that he'll surely catch cold. Donald, twelve, a freckle-faced cutie, is about the same size as my bag; but, without a word of complaint, he positions it on his shoulder with a satisfied smile.

"Ready?" I ask Don, uttering perhaps the most rhetorical question ever posed.

"I've been ready all my life," he tells me, grinning like a cartoon mental patient.

I don't use this description lightly or with any offense toward the mentally ill. There *is* something vaguely insane—not to mention surreal—about what Don and I are doing. Here we are at the end of the earth, two otherwise sensible adults, standing in a monsoon with a couple of pubescent boys whose idea of America comes from reruns of *Baywatch*. We really should be someplace warm and dry, someplace kind and pretty, where the cosseting comforts of real American life—the life that does not include surgically enhanced lifeguards flouncing in the sand—make all the travails of traveling far far away instantly disappear, like a golf ball in the heather.

The first hole at Traigh is a tiny par-3, 130 yards straight up a hill. I mean, almost vertical. Even from the close distance, you can't see the putting surface, only a willowy flag being tortured by the elements. I look at Don and his prosthetic shoe, his spindly legs, his hunched shoulders, and I'm certain he won't make it through this torrential round of golf. I'll be surprised if he makes it through the first hole. With the turf as slippery as an incumbent politician, I don't see how he'll be able to climb this first steep slope, unless I and the two caddies carry him.

"Go ahead, Michael," he urges cheerfully. "Lead the way."

Normally I would hit a little 9 iron at this green. But faced with a wind that's thick enough to chew, I do the safe thing and select a 5 iron. "This all right?" I ask my little looper.

He shrugs.

"Right." I squint through the rain long enough to see my ball between my feet. And after I wallop it, I squint through the rain long enough to see that it has come to rest twenty yards short of the green, staunchly embedded in the hairy grass bearding the hillside. Turning to Don, I say, "Not enough club."

He somehow gets a 6 iron to fly through the gale and stop on the green. I know this because I slip and slide up the slope and see for myself. Don, for the time being, has to take my word for it. The boys are showing him a back way around the hole with a slightly less brutal ascent. When he arrives, five minutes later, I've already availed myself of four putts and a 2-stroke penalty for not removing the flag from the cup, barely keeping my score on this diminutive hole out of double figures.

For nine holes, I'll go on to shoot about 55. (It may be more, but at the end of the round my scorecard is the approximate consistency of oatmeal.) Let me put that score in perspective: The entire Traigh layout is 2,456 yards.

But I can explain.

Bad shots on this day get blown 100 yards off line. Seriously. Like an entire football field off line. Good shots, on the other hand, are an abiding mystery: even the caddies, who have toured Traigh several dozen times, haven't the faintest idea where purely struck shots will end up. This is because seven of Traigh's nine holes demand some kind of blind shot. (The two that don't seem in comparison ridiculously boringly *normal*.) The condition of the greens is easily the worst I've ever seen, worse even than the ones at Fort Augustus maintained by sheep. They are slow as a sloth, bumpy as a cobblestone street, and hirsute as an Orthodox Jew. When I remark on the general shagginess and clover-infested quality of the putting surfaces, my caddie Donald winningly reminds me that the greenkeeper pays a visit to Traigh about once every other week. He may even be coming in the next day or two if the rain ever stops.

Despite all this—the bone-soaking weather, the ragged conditions, the randomness of the golf shots—I actually find myself *liking* the experience. Just as professional pugilists often embrace each other after beating the other guy senseless for twelve rounds, I feel a kinship with Traigh and the weather and Gimpy Don. We're all in this together—even if I'm not sure what *this* is, other than a preposterously efficient way to give oneself pneumonia. Meanwhile, Don, he of the atrophied legs and brittle bones, splashes on, hitting one cleverly conceived golf shot after another, toying and teasing the wind and rain to do his bidding. I'm in a hurry to get it all over with, to say, "I've done it"; Don wants only to say, "I'm doing it."

To the boys' great amusement—and, I must admit, mine also—Don does his yelling thing a couple of times, yodeling into the teeth of the gale. This time it's not possible to scare away whatever it is he's trying to chase, mostly because the unseen whatever couldn't hear his ferocious roar with a stethoscope. The wind, an impenetrable wall of granite, brings his voice back to him, like a popped-up drive, as if nature were reminding us never to forget our helplessness, our *smallness* in the face of her epic exaltations. Alone on this lonely golf course, with neither machines nor man-made edifices to keep us company, with only each other, we get the message.

After the sixth hole, "McEachen's Leap," named, one may safely assume, for a disconsolate Scotsman who jumped to his death after finding the hilltop green unmowed after six weeks, great bolts of lightning rip through the sky, theatrically illuminating the seawater with a skein of white and blue electricity. The boys quickly lead us to a wooden shelter meant specifically for such occasions. (Ah, the hand of man after all!) We stand inside it, shivering and joking, cursing like a pack of heathens, feeling very vulnerable beneath the angry sky.

Don lights a cigarette. On cue, I remind him he's killing himself. Without missing a beat he asks me, "Did I ever tell you how I want to die?"

"With a sexy blonde wrapped around you, begging for it harder and faster?" I ask, amusing the lads immensely.

He shakes his head. "On a golf course. By lightning."

We all laugh. "Well, today's the perfect day," I say, a bit too obviously.

"That's what I was thinking," he says. He's a got a look in his eyes that tells me he is not presently on the little nine-hole golf course at Traigh, Scotland; he's gone to a place I'll probably never understand. "Struck by lightning on a golf course. It's perfect: for a second you've got all the energy in the universe in your brain, and then you just sink into the golf course." Don begins to fiddle with the head cover of his titanium driver, as though it were the holster on a loaded pistol.

"You're too young to go," I remind him, half wondering how I'm going to be able to carry Don's extinguished body down off this hilltop. "Plus, you're having a good round!"

Don looks longingly at the sky, rent open by sizzling streaks of yellow and orange, followed by thunderclaps like a thousand timpani, the kind of booms that shake your sternum and vibrate in your belly. "I want to try," he says flatly, as though he might be putting us all on—or as if he isn't.

"Don't," I say. "Don't be foolish. Just wait. This storm is going to pass soon. Right, guys?" I ask hopefully.

The caddies nod and murmur noncommittally. "Meat. Meat not."

"I don't want to wait, Michael," Don says. "I'd rather play through than wait. I'd really rather play. Do you get what I'm saying? Do you know what I mean? You know, golf, love, whatever—I'd rather play."

I start to say, "But the lightning!" or "Come on, be reasonable!" But I don't. I feel a great wave of resignation run through me, starting in my throat and spreading to my fingers. He's right: It really is much better to play instead of wait.

"Come on, lads," I say, perhaps a bit too loudly and heroically, trying a mite too hard to convince myself that going on, no matter the slings and arrows sent down from the heavens, is the right and good thing to do. "Let's play."

The caddies look at each other, afraid to disobey their employers, particularly of the big-tipping American variety. But I know they're frightened. They've seen the neon skies before, and they know why wooden huts get built at places like McEachen's Leap. "You guys can wait here if you want," I tell them reassuringly. "It's fine. Just catch up whenever you want."

They look at each other imploringly, but neither speaks. Finally, Donald looks up at the weather, shrugs his wee shoulders, and hoists my bag on his back. As he steps toward the golf course, which has taken on the consistency of a Florida mangrove swamp,

I'm gripped with remorse. Why should an innocent lad be caught up in our adult trials, our foolish, wise, yearning explorations of undiscovered landscapes and never-visited dreams? He'll find those spots eventually himself. Or maybe he won't. But this is not a journey he needs to make. Not yet, and maybe not ever.

I take my bag from young Donald. "Stay here," I tell him. "Wait until it's safe."

"It's fine," he replies, as though end-of-humanity maelstroms were a daily occurrence in his life.

"Come on, laddie. Just wait until it stops lightning. And you," I say to big Don, "come with me. Let's play some golf."

We step out of the sanctuary of the shed and into the torrents. And we play.

I cannot say how I get from the tee to the green on the par-5 seventh. I cannot say how many horribly ineffectual stabs I make at my ball with a golf club I cannot grip. I cannot say if I made birdie or quadruple bogey (though I would confidently bet it's the latter). I just know that all the energy in the universe decides (forgets?) to converge upon two lonely golfers lost in their memories and lost in their future but very much found in their present.

We stand together, Don and I, on the seventh green, where Don may or may not have made birdie—and I'd like to think he did, though no one will be able to recall or care after this day—and we look toward the sky. The rain continues, washing our faces, but the lightning, the danger, moves away over the Atlantic, in search of worried sailors and mesmerized islanders. I'm neither relieved nor disappointed. Just wet.

The boys, I see, are jogging up the fairway, laughing and braying like newborn colts discovering their legs. Suddenly I feel that way too. My only wish is that Don might, as well. I recall summer afternoons from my childhood, playing with David Hanson and Kevin Zarem and all the other ruffians, jumping and running and flying, doing a dance we didn't know then would ever come to an end. I don't think Don Naifeh ever got to do such a dance. But I'd like to think that when he's on a golf course and he gets himself from the tee to the green, sending his golf ball where he wishes it to go, he feels those youthful rhythms pulsing through his frozen bones.

"The storm's over," Donald announces breathlessly, as though he needed permission to rejoin the game.

"I see that," I say, handing him my putter. "It's turned into a beautiful day."

The rain never stops. Nor does the wind. Saturated, we finish our round, our high-tech prophylactics made a mockery by the Scottish downpour. There is not an inch of clothing on me that isn't wet. I'm carrying an extra forty pounds or so of water weight on my tired body, but inside I feel strangely buoyant, as though I might float away on a pillow of possibility.

"I need a picture," I tell Don and the boys. "Come on, gather up." They all pose, forcing lopsided smiles. But the background is no good. There's nothing grand or timeless about it. Nothing that suggests where we've been for the past two hours. "No," I say, waving them away. "Nah. It's not Traigh. I need a better view. Eig! Rum! Muck! You know: a *vista*."

"Michael, I don't think I can walk another inch," Don says. "I'm finished."

"Aw, come on! A photo!"

"Man, you should have taken one before, back at that—what hole was that?—the one with the bench. Now that was a view."

"The bench has m' neem on it," Donald announces. "Esnah me. But it's m' neem."

"Damn! I missed it. Well. OK. That's it. I'm going back. Gotta have the picture," I explain. "Where?"

"Back on—what hole is that?" Don asks the caddies.

"The Bridge," Ross tells us. "The par-3."

"That's the fourth? The fifth maybe? Oh, man, that's like as far away as possible," I complain.

"You gotta suffer for your art," Don says before I begin the long wet trek to the best spot of all.

When I get there, muttering and cursing, all the time with a grin on my face, I find the bench the lads had recommended. It faces out toward the ocean, peering magisterially over the golf course and out and over the waves all the way to the eastern shore of the United States. And then over and beyond the whole country, past the Mississippi River and the Rocky Mountains, all the way beyond the Mojave Desert to my little house in Los Angeles. I sit upon the bench, there in the rain, and I sigh.

There's a small plaque, just as wee Donald had promised. It says, "In memory of Donald MacDonald: he enjoyed this place."

I feel the water running down my face, and I'm not sure if it's rain or tears.

17

Numbers Don't Lie

Don's on the telephone, back to the States. I'm attempting (mostly in vain) to solve the eternal mysteries of the trouser press. We're five feet apart, so it's not like I'm trying to eavesdrop; I'd have to stick a finger in each ear and hum the "Anvil Chorus" at hazardous decibel levels to avoid hearing his conversation with J.

"All I'm saying is: pick the shot that if executed properly will give you the most satisfaction. That's all I'm saying," Don tells her.

This is the fourth time he's implored her to make him her chosen "shot."

My suspicion is when a guy is reduced to salvaging a romance with golf metaphors, the relationship is probably in serious trouble—plugged in the face of a bunker, if you like. But what do I know? The last time I was here at this grand hotel I was madly in love, sipping champagne and holding hands, and horrible lies and misjudged putts were the furthest thing from my mind.

We're at Gleneagles, in the voluptuous Perthshire hills, the last stop on our pilgrimage around Scotland. I figured after two weeks of bare-bones B&Bs, the immodest charms of one of the world's most luxurious resorts would be a delicious treat, like sending a freshly released convict to a brothel with a stack of hundreds in his pocket. Ensconced in a giant suite with a bathroom the size of my home's living room, we're like two kids who've just discovered how to work the remote control. "This is a pretty incredible room for a Tulsa boy," Don reports to J, shortly before repeating his "pick the shot" advice. He seems particularly fascinated with the terry cloth robes and the white marble bidet, not to mention the abundance of furniture over which he can drape a fortnight's worth of laundry.

Don sighs hotly. "No. Now look. All I'm saying . . ." He lowers his voice. "All I'm saying is . . ."

I can only imagine what's happening on the other end of the line; it's not a pretty picture.

He hangs up, shaking his head disconsolately. "Why do I do this?" he asks me, now laughing at himself. "What am I thinking?"

I suggest, "It's like when you're on a par-5 and you've got 230 yards over water to the green, and you know you should just plop a little 7 iron up there for position, but you feel your hand reaching for the 3 wood anyway."

"Right. But, see, even though you're gonna make a bunch of double bogeys with that play, every now and then you're gonna make eagle. And once, maybe once in a lifetime, you're gonna make double eagle. You're gonna hole it, and that crazy shot you tried over the water is gonna feel like the smartest thing you've ever done."

"Donnie," I tell him, as kindly as I can, "this woman isn't that shot."

He inhales deeply—as deeply as his smoke-damaged lungs will allow—and starts to speak. But then he just shakes his head and shrugs.

"Come on," I say. "Let's play some golf."

"What about dinner?" Don asks. "Didn't you say we have a reservation at 7:00? It's like 4:30 now."

"If it takes us more than an hour or two to play this layout, we might have to think about giving up the game. I'm taking you to the Wee Course. Nine holes. All par-3s."

"A pitch-and-putt?" Don inquires.

"Not exactly, pal. You'll probably need every stick in your bag."

The Wee isn't really wee at all. It's designer James Braid (the author of three of the Gleneagles courses) at his finest. Some holes require a pitching wedge. Some a 2 iron. And if the wind is up sufficiently—which happens every now and then in this country—you might even have to use a driver to get to some of the greens.

The Wee is an exceptionally hilly course, and Don, toting his own bag for only the third time all trip, struggles with both the ascents and descents. From the tee at the third, he can see across the road to Jack Nicklaus's Monarch's Course, one of the few tracks in Scotland that provides players with carts. Looking longingly at the buggies, he says sardonically, "You see that, Michael? That's what separates man from the apes."

"Well, yeah, that and a fondness for tobacco."

And then, right there, on the spot, Don vows that tomorrow, our last day together in bonnie Scotland, he is going to play all thirty-six holes—we've scheduled back-to-back rounds on the theory that there's no use leaving any fuel in the tank—without a single cigarette.

We walk toward the third tee. "That's a fine goal," I say, encouragingly. "I'm so impressed, this time I *will* carry you in if need be. Of course," I say, wincing, "I might need Charlie to help me."

"He gives yardages *and* piggyback rides?" Don jokes.

"The man does it all!"

I'm referring to Mr. Charles Winton, a longtime caddie at Gleneagles whom, not long ago, I described in print as "the world's best caddie." My judgment was highly unscientific: I just thought the man was brilliant. He knows every inch of the Gleneagles courses, including some prickly regions that one prays to avoid, and dispenses advice and wisdom and encouragement in a plain-spoken, kind-hearted style that endears him to all who have the pleasure and privilege of his company for an afternoon out in the park. Knowing we would be concluding our journey at Gleneagles, where my own Scottish odyssey began seven years previous, I requested of the Gleneagles management that arrangements be made so that Mr. Winton would be by my side for a return engagement. With a tee time looming in the morning, I'm eager to play the famous King's and Queen's courses in his sage company; I'm even more eager to introduce the world's greatest caddie to the world's best golfing buddy.

With our match on the Wee all square after nine, Don and I decide on a four-hole play-off consisting of the opening quartet of holes, the ones with the least amount of walking among them. Unfortunately, after completing the first and hitting a wayward tee-shot at the second, Don concedes the match and, more important, the frailty of his physical well-being. "Michael," he calls out to me as I start to climb the hill leading to the second green, "I gotta stop."

"You all right?" I ask, alarmed.

"I think so. But I don't want to ruin my chances for tomorrow by doing something stupid today. So, I'm gonna call it a day. All right?"

"Sure. Of course," I say, slightly stunned. I've never seen Don Naifeh quit in the middle of a round of golf. Even at Royal Aberdeen, with all its moraines, he soldiered on, tapping into unseen reserves of will. Today, it seems, those reserves have been depleted. I hope, I fervently hope, he doesn't have to spend his last day in Scotland sitting in a hotel room (even one with a nice bidet), looking longingly out the window at the emerald playing fields like a dog waiting for his master to return home from work. I want him to depart Scotland in triumph, like a football coach being escorted from the field on the shoulders of his jubilant players.

I want him to *win*—even if I'm not sure what contest he's playing.

"A nice steak, good bottle of wine, some great stories—that'll fix you," I say encouragingly. "Come on, let's go back to our palace."

"Sorry, Michael," Don says, glumly.

"Hey," I say, stopping to look Don in the eyes. "I'm proud of you."

He forces a smile and walks back to the clubhouse, his limping gait more noticeable than ever.

I spread our scorecards on the carpet of our hotel room and do the math.

"Ready?" I ask Don, who has emerged from the bathroom freshly scrubbed and swathed in oversized towels.

"What are you doing?" he asks, seeing me crawl around the floor like I'm looking for a lost contact lens.

"I figured on the night before our last rounds of golf in Scotland we should have a retrospective. Like, you know, a recap of the highlights and statistics. I think it'll lift your spirits. And, besides, I need to figure out exactly how much money you've robbed me for this trip. Maybe I could get a tax write-off for charity."

"Let's make tonight a celebration dinner," Don declares, settling himself into a plush chair. "A celebration of everything that went right with this journey. And, what the hell, all the things that maybe didn't."

I tell Don I like his idea, particularly since our host, James Kidd (generally known to all but governmental record keepers as Jimmie the Kidd), is master of the celebratory arts. His official title at Gleneagles is director of turfgrass management. But Jimmie is better known in golf writer circles as a raconteur, bon vivant, and all-around super gent with whom to raise a glass or seven. "I'm sure the Kidd will like hearing what you have to say about his country. You do have nice things to say, don't you?"

"I'm only gonna do everything in my power to move here!" Don retorts.

"Good. Just make sure you've got guest privileges at whatever club you join. Because I'd like to come over every now and then and visit my money. Now, look, we've got some serious business here," I say, gesturing at the mélange of scorecards. "It's time to crunch the numbers. Ready?"

"Give it to me straight," Don says. "I can take it."

Scanning the rows of figures, the scribbled notations in the margins, the hieroglyphic symbols denoting triumphs and failures, I realize Don Naifeh and I have played an awful lot of golf together— more than a dozen rounds, hundreds of holes. And there he is, plopped in a chair, all in one piece, more or less.

I share the results of my detailed analysis (with editorial commentary) in an official-sounding baritone, as though I were announcing the first-tee pairings at the U.S. Open. With each stentorian pronouncement, Don nods solemnly, like a lawyer at his client's felony arraignment.

Rounds in the 70s. Don: 4. Mike: 0.

EDITORIAL COMMENT: *I've got a friend in Vegas who says that since he moved there and started playing guys for a little something, he's kept track of how many people have had "career-best" rounds on the very day they happened to be gambling with him. He's now up to 137.*

Rounds without a double bogey. Don: 1. Mike: 0.

EDITORIAL COMMENT: *Very impressive to be free of any such blemishes, even if it's only once. I don't think I've ever had a double-bogey-free round in hundreds of tries on this side of the Atlantic. If you would have made me this bet instead of your "lost ball" bet, I would have been certain you were crazy, not just suspicious.*

Holes under par. Don: 16. Mike: 11.
EDITORIAL COMMENT: *The guy just hasn't learned to shoot away from some pins. Watch me enough and you'll get the idea. I shoot away from pins on almost every hole.*

Eagles. Don: 0. Mike: 2.
EDITORIAL COMMENT: *The fact that both of these came on par-4s should tell you something.*

The dreaded "others." Don: 6. Mike: 5.
EDITORIAL COMMENT: *That we collectively kept this total under a dozen is a testament to our tremendous skill, upstanding character, and ungodly luckiness.*

Three-putts. Don: 17. Mike: 12.
EDITORIAL COMMENT: *Three words for you. World. Putting. Championship.*

Amount lost by M.K. to D.N. in eighteen-hole matches, Nassaus, and deranged proposition bets. Too high to calculate.
EDITORIAL COMMENT: *I'd say, "You're buying tonight." But knowing Jimmie, that won't be possible.*

"Can I see those, Michael?" Don asks, when I'm finished with my presentation.

I scoop up the cards, talismanic mementos as colorful as a New England autumn, adorned with pastoral scenes from the links on the front cover and simple maps on the back. "Sure. Just make sure

I get them back for my scrapbook. Or IRS audit, whichever comes first."

Don holds the scorecards in his gnarled hands, making a little paper cake of them, pressing them together and releasing, as though they were a miniature accordion. These cards are his past; they tell his story. They contain within their worn folds a record of all his shining moments and fiery failures, his joys and his woes. By this point in our pilgrimage together, I half expect the cards to begin emanating a purple-orange-pink glow and for Don's arthritic hands to discover a suppleness they've never known, healed by the power of good memories. I've come to expect miracles from the game of golf.

Don squeezes the cards one last time and hands them back to me. He says, "It's been a great journey."

The Straithearn dining room at Gleneagles is one of those grand ballrooms of a restaurant that recalls a tony 1930s nightclub, where platoons of tuxedoed servers wait on the rich and beautiful, carving prime rib and igniting flambés tableside while a string quartet unobtrusively assays the popular classics from a distant corner. Fred Astaire would have been comfortable sipping a martini here. (And for all I know, he probably once did.) The ladies look like ladies at this restaurant, and the gentlemen—particularly those who have done something more than throw a jacket over their golf shirt— look like gentlemen. It's a fine place to propose a toast.

I look around the table: three of my favorite men in all of golf surround me. To my right, Jimmie the Kidd, ruddy-cheeked and smiling, his blue eyes constantly suggesting he's got a secret or a story you'd probably like to know. Across from me, Don Naifeh, dressed as I've never seen him, in blazer and tie, his bald crown uncovered by a floppy hat and his lined cheeks cleanly shaven, looking pleasingly distinguished. And on my left, Mr. Charles Winton, who, per Jimmie's surprise invitation, has joined us for dinner. Clad in a handsome three-piece suit, his thinning hair combed smartly to the side, Charlie looks adorable, like a youngster attending his first wedding. His omnipresent smile tells me he's as glad to be here at this moment with these three fellows at this nice place as we are to share a table with him. I'm as happy as can be expected of a man bombarded by ironic memories, by images of the last time he dined at the Straithearn, in love and oblivious to the possibility of heartache.

We four represent something like a perfect cross section of generations: I'm thirty-five, Don's forty-five, Jimmie's fifty-five, and Charlie's sixty-five. We possess a disparate compendium of experiences and narratives, of loves and losses. But golf—a silly old game meant to keep the shepherds temporarily amused—has brought us together, and it allows us to talk with an honesty that men often find difficult. We probably would feel funny declaring our passionate devotion to the Bach cantatas or the essays of Lewis Lapham; we would probably be embarrassed to repeat the sonnet we wrote for our lover or the Louis Armstrong imitation we do for her amusement. But declare our undying affection for the course architecture of James Braid or the cavernous dunes at Cruden Bay? Well, then we are merely speaking the self-evident truths that all decent men would defend with their dying breath. Golf, without trying, makes us better, more communicative souls—not merely skirt-chasing, sports-obsessed baboons with a graphite stick in our hands.

Golf lets us be true.

Sitting anxiously, with his hands folded in his lap, Charlie tells me quietly that though he's worked at Gleneagles for nearly thirty years, he's never once stepped foot in this restaurant. "I meat be th' furst caddie ta doo it," he reports gleefully. "All tha boys wanna heer aboot it."

A former schoolteacher from Perth, Charlie isn't too proud to admit he doesn't recognize many of the items on the restaurant's encyclopedic menu. (I suspect my boy from Tulsa doesn't either, but I keep it to myself.) Jimmie graciously recommends several house specialties that he reckons Charlie might enjoy, and when the phrase "steak of Angus beef" comes up, I see a wave of relief pass over Charlie's face.

Which all gets me to thinking. What does culture and sophistication and refinement get a man? What's it worth to know the good vintages in Bordeaux and the best way to prepare foie gras and the perfect accompaniment to a chocolate soufflé if you can't attend to the simple things in life? Charlie Winton, I'm pretty sure, hasn't tasted sweetbreads (and I'm even more sure he couldn't tell you that "sweetbreads" is just a nice term for "thymus glands"); though he's a Scotsman, he probably hasn't read the slickly produced lifestyle magazines explaining the difference between Lagavulin and Laphroaig; and the musky mysteries of black truffles would, I suspect, strike him as much ado about a wild fungus.

But Charlie Winton is *happy*. And I don't mean in an ignorant, naive way—a Candide-in-his-garden kind of way. I mean he's happy to be healthy and helpful, able to walk the good Gleneagles land once or twice a day, sharing his knowledge with people who are truly grateful to receive it. He treasures good company and successful collaboration and naturally occurring beauty more than rare casks of port and 320-thread-count tablecloths. Luxury is fine for those who have nothing better to spend their money on, but rare goods and deferential service can never replace a man like Charlie, who works hard, gives freely of his spirit, and reaps the admiration and respect of those he helps. I'm honored to know him.

When the wine comes—a bottle of Chateau LaLagune, ordered on connections (to the past) grounds—I propose three separate toasts. The first is to Charlie, whom I praise for his sweetness, both on and off the links. The second is to Jimmie the Kidd, whom I praise for his congeniality and smartness. And the last is to Don.

"To my friend Don Naifeh, who proved to me, to strangers, and most of all to himself that seemingly insurmountable obstacles are no match for bravery and determination. He went searching for Burningbush, the mystical golf course of his imagination, and he found something even more profound: a love of the game and of the land, the kind of love that carries all who discover it far away from their earthly cares to a realm of peacefulness and contentment. I am very proud of all that Don Naifeh has accomplished on this pilgrimage to Scotland. And I'm even more proud to be his friend."

We clink glasses and nice things are said all around, but I have trouble hearing them, so intent am I on keeping the tears welling in my eyes from splashing down the front of my trouser-pressed blazer.

Jimmie wants to hear all about our journey through Scotland—what we've seen, where we've played, what we've thought. Over plates of smoked salmon, Don and I recount our golfborne adventures, our search for the world according to the gospels of Shivas.

Don nods thoughtfully and says, "Well, my highlights are obviously the golf courses. I mean all of them—the famous ones and the unexpected pleasures. Great courses with great history. Scenic. Challenging. Playable. There seem to be more choices on every hole. You're always thinking here. Plus, the weather is always a factor. I don't know that I've ever hit so many 180-yard 9 irons and so many 100-yard 5s. It's fun to figure out those shots."

He looks at his wineglass, and his eyes glisten. "But as good as the golf has been, my strongest memories will be of the people I've met. Rick MacKenzie and my wonderful caddie, Colin, and having lunch at the St. Andrews Club. The Middletons from Cruden Bay. A member of the Royal & Ancient at the Golf House at Elie. A fellow Shivas Irons Society member at the first tee of the Old Course. And, of course, you two gentlemen, here at Gleneagles. I'll never forget."

He nods affirmatively. "But my strongest memory, my top golf highlight, was maybe seeing my friend here, Michael, joining me to hit balls into the water—and finding out he likes it!"

"The Shivas Irons Society?" Jimmie interjects.

"You've heard of it?" Don asks hopefully.

"I'm probably one of the first members!" Jimmie exclaims.

While the two fellow travelers trade anecdotes and gossip about the subculture of *Kingdom* lovers, I lean over to Charlie and explain what all the fuss is about. He confesses that he might have once heard of this particular book, but, no, he's never read it.

"I don't get it, Jimmie," I hear Don saying. "Everywhere I've gone in Scotland, from Edinburgh to Dornoch, and everywhere in between—almost none of the Scotsmen I've met have read about Shivas. I just don't get it."

Besides the fact that the second half of the book seems to be written by someone "on drugs," Jimmie thinks the reason *Golf in the Kingdom* is more popular in the United States than in Scotland is because Americans need a scripture to outline their faith in the game. To the Scots, golf is part of the fabric of life. It comes naturally.

Then he tells us about something strange that happened to him once, several years ago. He was playing the Balcomie Links with his son David, a golf course architect best known for his work at Bandon Dunes in Oregon, when they came upon the thirteenth hole. "I started developing shivers," Jimmie recalls. "And I said to my son, 'There's something about this hole. Something haunted.'" Jimmie tells us his son experienced the same sense of déjà vu meets psilocybin-laced mushrooms. "We were both touched by something there. And I have no idea what it was," Jimmie admits. "But it was something."

My eyes meet Don's. He's nodding maniacally, like a parishioner who's got the spirit in him. "Exactly!" he says. "Exactly!"

I take another long sip of wine. I look around the table, around the room, around my life. At the moment I miss the love I once had more than I ever thought possible. But the emptiness that was left behind is getting filled with something else. I have no idea what it is. But it's something.

Soaked with cabernet sauvignon and whisky, massaged by tall tales and large laughs, filled with fine food and finer fellowship, I awake to the kind of morning that is too perfect, too sublime for anywhere but Eden. The sun streams across the grassy Gleneagles fields, a whisper of a warm breeze tickles the trees, and a symphony of birds and insects rises out of the forest. Maybe this is Eden.

I don't want to say good-bye to all this. I want to play on and on forever.

On my first trip to Scotland, while traversing the Caledonian Canal, I met a kind old man named Charles, who loved golf nearly as much as he loved his wife of fifty years. Charles liked to rise early to see the world being reborn with the dawn. One morning, I joined him on a bench overlooking an empty golf course, a playground not yet inhabited by enthusiastic duffers. Charles looked and listened and inhaled. And he said, "It's a beautiful world, Michael. And I'm going to miss it terribly when I'm gone. Oh, how I'm going to miss it."

I think of Charles as Don and I step upon the first tee at the Queen's Course. We're the first twosome of the day. All this gloriousness is spread out before us, ready for us to have, to embrace, to enjoy. And, yes, I will miss it when I'm gone.

Nothing matters anymore. The scores. The swings. The putts. None of it. All that matters is we're here for now, for one more day. Together. And then . . . and then we will miss it terribly.

Don's opening nine requires of him 58 strokes, including a 14 on number six. It's the highest score he's shot since age ten. He would have liked to have played better for Charlie Winton and for me and for his caddie, Chris, a former lightweight boxer with a nose to prove it. But . . . the missing has already begun.

Chris keeps us supplied with a steady flow of unfamiliar off-color terminology involving women, as well as numerous recommendations for debauchery in and around Glasgow. Charlie faithfully supplies yardages and suggestions for shapes of golf shots, trying nobly not to notice how poorly his man (and his man's buddy) is playing. Don recounts the time in Arizona he once shot 55 with *one hand*. And I get a chronic bout of the shanks, which earns me many complimentary portions of fresh raspberries.

And I will miss it all terribly when I'm gone.

I recall the photo I have in my scrapbook of me and my ex-wife kneeling before the tee marker of the Queen's sixteenth hole, called "Lovers' Gait." We look very young. And very happy. According to the official Gleneagles yardage book, before the Queen's Course was built, the ground upon which the sixteenth sits was said to have been a favorite spot for courting couples, who would stroll together in these sylvan hills. Charlie Winton says he thinks the hole's name derives from the slopes on either side of the fairway, which seem to merge together like two lovers, arm in arm. I dread playing this hole, fearful that the morning peacefulness might be shattered by an avalanche of regretful memories. But nothing cataclysmic happens. I make par at Lovers' Gait. And birdie at "Hinny Mune," the seventeenth. And par on "Queen's Hame," the last. And the earth does not open up and swallow me whole; nor do demons leap from the woods (or my subconscious) and drag me into an inferno of longing. Shivas Irons does not invite me to join him for lunch. Don does not break his fibula. Charlie Winton does not teach me how to say, "It's a beautiful world, and I will miss it terribly when I'm gone" in Gaelic. No drama. No illusions. No miracles.

And I will miss it all.

Don snaps pictures every hundred yards or so. The ravishing gorgeousness of this golf course has nothing to do with expertly installed waterfalls or assiduously pruned flower beds. It's all about the land—muscular and stolid, swaying like a dancer in thrall to a silent beat. He doesn't say so out loud, but I know it's true: He will miss it, too.

We pause for lunch before our afternoon tour of the King's Course, our last eighteen in Scotland. Don smokes a cigarette—his no-smoking pledge vanished on the tenth tee, shortly after he discovered he had shot nearly 60 for the first nine. To my dismay, his score improved by 16 strokes on the inward half, thereby proving again to him the beneficence of nicotine in his blood. I want badly for Don to honor me—and his overworked heart—with a renewal of his abstinence, but his addiction is stronger, it seems, than the pull of fraternal bonding.

In fact, damn all this spiritualism nonsense, Don seems to be telling me. He wants our final round together to contain all sorts of weird bets—that he'll break 80, that he'll break 40 for either of the nines, that he won't lose a ball—all of which, he explains, will inspire him to get his beaten body "to the finish line."

I tell him, "Man, if James Braid and the Perthshire hills aren't inspiration enough!"

"Do we have a bet, Michael?" he asks me sharply.

"Yeah. Sure," I say, startled. I know he's bound to lose all these wagers (primarily since the King's is one of the tougher courses in

Scotland from the tips), and I know he'll be steamed that he squandered his last journey out and back worrying about silly concerns like scores on a card. But these are his choices—just as the phone calls to J and the cigarettes and all the other self-destructive influences are his choices. Yet, I wonder: what happened to the spirit of Shivas? Where's the joy in merely being on your own feet upon sacred ground? What about all that?

Strange, I think. That switching thing has happened again, that transference. Don's acting like me. And I'm . . . well, I'm placid as a yogi. He's angry about something (J and her aspersions, I suspect); I'm free from all my cares. He's anxious and determined; I'm languid and passive.

It's true: I don't ever want to leave. Not ever. I could play 54 or 72 today, or 10,000. I'm on a golf course I love with a caddie I adore, playing with my very best golf buddy. Where else would I rather be?

Our tour of the King's goes too fast for me. I hit some of the best golf shots of my life, including a drive that finds the green on the short par-4 fourteenth and a downwind mid-iron second shot on the par-5 eighteenth that gets all the way to the putting surface. For Don, I fear, the round seems interminable. He loses golf balls (and control of his temperament) while I follow hawks making lazy circles in the sky; he takes frequent rest breaks, sitting on the edge of a bunker, while I look for his wayward shots; he stews in his own juices while I bask in the rare Scottish sun. He's awash in fatigue; I'm soaked with pleasure.

As our round—and our journey—nears its conclusion, I sense Don's relief. He's been determined to walk all thirty-six holes today, to *make it*. And, style points aside, he has.

Don Naifeh is ready for the end. I want to do it all again. All of it. Oh, how I will miss it when I'm gone.

When Don taps in his last putt on the "Home" hole, I put my hand on his shoulder and say, "You did it."

"Yes," he says, "I did."

"You did it!"

"I did it," he repeats. "I'm not sure what I did. But, yeah, I did it."

We turn together to look back at the golf course, sparkling in golden light, and we say our silent farewells. Good-bye to the sheep and the cows and the ponies. Good-bye to the air and the grass and the light. Good-bye to the music of the spoken word. Good-bye, dear Scotland.

We start to walk off the eighteenth green, toward the clubhouse and toward America. Don takes two labored steps and stops, frozen, as though he suddenly realized he'd forgotten something.

He looks at the golf course. He smiles. And he says, "You got any plans tonight?"

"You mean besides packing and getting ready for our flight? No. I mean, I was thinking we'd find someplace right near the airport, since we've got to get up at, like, 4:30. Why? You want to go to one of those places in Glasgow Chris was recommending?"

"No, Michael," Don says, arching an eyebrow at me. "I've got an idea."

18

Possibilities

In the still of the night, with the moon obscured by an impenetrable blanket of clouds, the tee at the top of Seamus MacDuff's cave seems smaller and more precarious than it does during the day. One bad off-balance swing and you could find yourself tumbling off the plateau and down the hill, legs and arms broken into hundreds of pieces, whether you suffer from brittle-bone syndrome or not. So Don Naifeh takes great care as he steadies himself over his golf ball, all but invisible in the darkness, and prepares to send it into the inky void. He breathes in deeply, and then out. And then he swings.

It sounds good. Solid. He turns his right ear toward the fourteenth green, somewhere out there in the night.

Nothing.

After what seems like five seconds, or maybe more, we hear a thunderous *thump*.

"That sounded like green!" I shout.

"Definitely on the ground," he replies, laughing and laughing and laughing. "Come on, Michael. Try one."

I fish a ball out of my pocket and stick it on a tee. When I stand up to assume my stance, I can only trust and believe that I left a ball on the ground in front of me, so dark is this shrouded night. Both Don and I stay very still for a second, letting the vibrations from the ball tell my hands where it is, waiting.

There! I swing—perhaps a bit too enthusiastically.

Chunk.

"That felt a little chubby," I report. Then we hear my ball whistle into the tall grass fronting the tee, hopelessly lost during the midday light, never mind the midnight dark.

"Try another one," Don says encouragingly. "Put your pretty swing on it."

My pretty swing. I'm not aware I have one of those. But I can pretend. *I'm Ernie Els. I'm Freddie Couples. I'm Davis Love. I'm Colin Montgomerie. I'm Steve Elkington.*

It doesn't work. I'm none of those guys. Golf for me is not ballet with a stick.

I'm just me. And for now, standing on the fourteenth tee, on top of Seamus MacDuff's cave on the Balcomie Links, that's enough.

I make *my* swing, my decidedly unpretty, depressingly inelegant slash. And for now, it's the most beautiful motion ever invented.

The clubhead finds the ball. The ball jumps into the sky. We listen.

Thump.

Don Naifeh and I laugh like schoolboys and dash off into the dark.

We walked reluctantly off the eighteenth green of the King's Course, showered at the Gleneagles clubhouse, packed our little car one last time, and sped off in the fading light for the Kingdom of Fife. My first inclination was to get the last plane to France and spend a night in Paris, drinking wine and eating cheese and stumbling along the *rive gauche* with 5 irons in our hands. Maybe we would hit balls into the Seine. Or off the Eiffel Tower.

But there weren't any more flights. So we settled on Don's idea.

Which was this: a plate of haggis at the Golf Hotel in Crail, a glass of whisky at a local pub, and then, our courage pricked by alcohol and cow innards, off to the Balcomie Links, to do as Shivas had done on that fateful moonlit night, when Fate and Gravity and Beauty all conspired to get the shillelagh-toting oracle's wee feathery into the clifftop cup at Lucifer's Rug.

Prosaic real-life concerns—like falling down in the dark and municipal trespassing laws—no longer mattered. We were on a mission.

For what exactly I didn't know. But at the moment it seemed more important than anything we had ever done.

The bandages had come off and the crutches were cast aside. Don and I were ready to dance.

Don uses two golf clubs as canes, one in each hand. I walk in front of him, ready to break his fall should he stumble. We go slowly, feeling our way through the murk, as leery now of unseen bunkers as we might be during the daytime faced with a dicey approach shot to a sand-cloaked green. Normally I'd be fearful that Don might easily break something. One innocent slip is all it would take. But tonight, sneaking around a deserted Burningbush, I know he'll be taken care of—by me or Shivas or whomever. Nothing bad can happen to him now. He's where he's always wanted to be. And nothing bad can happen to any of us when we get to that sacred place.

I feared for an angry night watchman. I feared for a locked gate. I feared for perturbed ghosts. But as with so many of my fears, real and imagined, the truth was far less frightening than I envisioned. We drove up the serpentine lane to the Crail Golfing Society clubhouse, parked our car beside the pro shop, and waited for the last members and kitchen staff to leave for the night. If anyone had asked us what the hell we were doing in their parking lot at nearly midnight, my plan was to say we had left something on the course—a wallet or a billfold—and we were waiting for enough light to conduct a diligent search. Don's plan was to just tell them the truth: it's our last night in Scotland, and we wanted to play Lucifer's Rug in the middle of the night, just as Shivas Irons did.

"I'm sure we're not the first ones to do it," he explained. "They'll understand," he assured me.

And maybe they would. Thankfully, I never had to find out. When the last light went out in the clubhouse and then the last car pulled away, we loaded our pockets with balls, grabbed a few clubs, and scurried onto the golf course.

Now, down near the fourteenth green, we can see a few yards ahead of us, thanks to some ancillary light reflected in the nearby seawater. Both our balls are on the green! Mine is maybe ten paces from the hole, and Don's maybe six. The flags have long since been put away for the night by the maintenance crew, but the cups are still dug into the ground, more or less where they were the day we played. (Walking side by side, as if we're conducting a missing-person search, Don and I find the target in a matter of seconds.) Trying to "read" the putt, I crouch down and survey the short carpet of grass, which, even in the dark, radiates a glimmer of greenness. It's so smooth, so appealing, like the curve of a woman's buttocks. I want to pet it.

We're playing almost blind. Don gives me an idea of where to aim my ball by rattling his putter in the cup.

I listen. I really listen. The sound is drawing a string from my ball to the hole.

Then I hit my ball into the unknown, certain it will find its home. *Click*. It's gone, leaving behind only silence.

"Oh!" Don exclaims. "Oh, man! It went right over the cup, on the edge!"

I giggle and dance and skip all the way to his side. "Your turn, my friend."

Don settles himself over his birdie putt while I indicate the hole with my golf club. Without hesitation, he rolls his ball up the slope, eighteen inches short of the cup. Then he taps in for par.

"Hey, Donnie!" I remind him. "You made four here during the day, remember?"

"And three in the dark. Isn't that something?" Don says, chortling.

"Nice!" I pat him on the shoulder. "You ready?"

He extracts his ball from the hole. "Let's go play Lucifer's Rug!"

I have no idea where the tee is, let alone the green or the hole. But I point myself in the general direction of where I recall the thirteenth tee being situated, somewhere to the left of the fourteenth green. Don follows, with his left hand on my right shoulder. It's the blind leading the bamboozled.

Just then, a faint sliver of moonlight pierces the cloud cover. There's just enough illumination for me to make out a tee marker ahead of us. I tell Don to wait a second, and I rush to see.

"Here it is!" I call out. "Number thirteen. Lucifer's Rug."

Don joins me on the tee, and we laugh. "I got no idea," he says.

"Me neither," I say. "I mean, I know it's *that* way," I acknowledge, pointing back up toward the hilltop. "But that's about it."

"Let's check," Don says, poking around the teeing ground with his golf clubs. "You'd think the markers would have you pointed in the general direction. Maybe we just line ourselves up with the markers and trust that they're pointed straight."

"Sure," I say, giddy with ignorance. Somewhere out there, 210 yards over the gorse and heather and darkness, is a green, smooth and inviting, waiting for our visit. Somewhere. "It's your honor."

Don prepares himself for the shot of his life, identifying the right place for his golf club with everything but his eyes. He begins to rock from one foot to the other, but I interrupt him.

"Donnie. I know you want to do your screaming thing. But, please. I don't want to have to explain this to the police. Just believe me: all the demons are gone. You already scared them off."

He nods. "All right."

Don Naifeh tees his ball low to the ground, fondles his driver and then his 3 wood, and tosses the big stick to the side. There is no wind tonight. There is no sound. There is no light. Just two friends standing together on a golf course, searching for the truth.

Don assumes his stance, finds his center, becomes perfectly still. And then he goes.

I see a spark jump off the soil as Don's clubhead cuts through the silence. His ball has disappeared somewhere into the black. A lifetime later—an eternity—during which neither of us lives nor dies, we hear his ball land in the inscrutable beyond. Somewhere.

"Shot," I say, as though we were playing under the morning sun.

"Thanks," Don says. "Bit of a dropkick. But it should work, assuming the green is where I think it is."

Neither of us, of course, has the vaguest idea what has actually happened to Don's golf ball. But we both realize at this moment that the where doesn't matter. It's the being that counts.

"Your tee, sir," Don says to me, motioning grandly, like a toreador dancing with a bull.

Driver in hand, I get myself pointed toward where I believe the green to be. I locate my ball by smell. And then I smile.

For a few seconds I go away. I don't know where. When I come back, I hear Don saying, "You crushed it! Sounded like green to me."

We giggle and guffaw and giggle some more, and off we go into that bleak black night, searching, searching, searching.

It takes us five minutes to walk up the hill and find the thirteenth green, which we discover only because I nearly tumble into an adjoining bunker. It's larger than we remember it, like a vast canvas upon which a painter might splash great pools of pigment. And it seems deserted, lonely, somehow incomplete without two round dimpled things resting quietly upon it.

I hear Don's effortful breathing at my side. "Any sign?" he wonders aloud.

The world hears him. High above, billions of years away, the moon winks at us, casting down an elegantly circular beam of the sun's reflected brilliance. A shaft of clarity cuts through the shroud enveloping Burningbush. There's a spotlight now upon the Balcomie Links thirteenth green, and the prima donna standing beneath it, drinking in our adulation, is whiter than a pearl and, at the moment, considerably more rare.

We see it simultaneously. "Ball!"

I run to it, right to the spot the moon has directed me. Down on my knees, as in prayer, I put my face into the light. "It's yours, Don!" I shout. "It's your ball!"

"Really?" Don shouts back, wanting desperately to believe me. "Really? On the green?"

"Right here. It's you."

"Wow. That's, that's . . ." He starts to say "unbelievable," but thinks better of it. He limps over to the light. "Damn," Don says softly, reverentially. "That's my ball."

"So where's mine?" I wonder. "I hit it great. I mean, it felt like I did. I didn't see it, of course."

"No, the swing looked good," Don concurs. "It's gotta be up here somewhere. Maybe through the back of the green?"

We search there. Nothing.

"Maybe—did you cut it a little?"

"It's possible," I tell him. "Anything's possible."

We search to right of the green. Nothing.

"You didn't pull it, did you?"

We go to the left of the green, back toward Seamus MacDuff's cave. Nothing.

"Well, Michael, you realize there's only one more place to look."

"The hole," I say, nodding, instantly aware that my ball *can't* be in the hole at Lucifer's Rug. Because that would mean my life, the one I've known for all these years, would be over, and a new one would have to begin right here, right now, on this spot where Shivas Irons proved that dreams are true if you dare to let them be.

I don't bother getting up. Crawling over the mossy ground while Don pokes around the darkness with his putter, I feel connected to the earth and everything it contains. Any second now, or maybe never, I'll bump into the hole. My fingers will curl over the edge, feeling the cool dirt beneath my knuckles. And then my hand will go down, down six inches, and I'll feel something hard and certain, and I'll cry out with joy, and I'll tell Don to join me, and we'll see it there, together, there at the bottom of the cup, the physical manifestation of an idea staring back at us, unblinking, settled and calm, with the unwavering conviction born of truth.

"Over here!" Don calls out.

He's got the handle of his putter stuck in the hole, as though he were plugging a dike, fearful that something gooey and wonderful might spurt forth out of the soil. I leap up and fly over to his side, fifteen feet away.

"Sorry, Michael," he says. "Just the cup. No ball."

I say, "No, of course not. That would be too weird." But inside I'm crushed. I mean, I *couldn't* have made a hole in one in the dark at Lucifer's Rug. The impossible is not possible. Still, in a distant region of my mind, where secrets and fantasies reside, I sort of thought, "Yes!"—yes, I had. The metaphors had already begun to spin in my brain. It was going to be like one of those loaves-into-fishes moments, one of those Red Sea deals, the kind of only-explainable-by-divine-intervention occurrence that converts skeptics into pious acolytes.

Funny thing is, I'm already converted. To *what* I don't know. The sublime? The connected? The ways of Shivas? Maybe. Perhaps. Possibly. Or maybe perhaps possibly not. I am, however, certain of this: I'm not the same man I was two weeks ago.

And I think that's a good thing.

We never do find my ball. Conspiracy theories abound on this matter. My favorite is that the green somehow swallowed my shot, ensuring that a part of me could never leave Burningbush. On the other hand, the elusive orb might well have been hiding just a few feet off the putting surface, or nestled in a clump of shaggy grass, waiting for some happy Scotsman to find it the next morning. The man would be bewildered why someone would leave a perfectly good golf ball lying around for nothing, but the answer to that puzzle would eventually be clear to him, too. The word *connections* might not spring readily to the lucky finder's lips, but the ball in his pocket would gently remind him anyway. It would tell him, "Others have been here before you, and others will come after you've left. So play on. Play on and on!"

Don paces off the distance between the hole and his ball. It's about thirty-five feet—one for every year I've been on this planet. He asks me to "tend" the cup with my putter. And then he "reads" the line—a little left to right, ever so slightly downhill—with his ears. The spotlight of moonbeams has moved on to another corner of the Balcomie Links, having discharged its solemn duty of helping us find Don's ball on the green. I can vaguely make out his hunched figure poised over what I presume to be the most important putt of his brief existence.

In the silence, I hear the distant pulse of the sea, coming and going, coming and going, living and dying. I hear the stars sizzle in the sky. I hear atoms and neutrinos and all the matter of the galaxy whizzing through the night. And then I hear a familiar click—the same one I've been listening to for a fortnight now. He's done it.

I wait forever for Don's ball to depart his domain and enter mine. I peer into the blackness, searching for some sign of movement. But nothing comes.

"What happened?" I ask.

"I was going to ask you that," Don says. "I can't see anything."

"It never got to the cup, Donnie. Did you hit it? You hit it, right?"

"Oh, yes, I did." He limps toward me. I stride toward him.

We both see it: He's left his putt about halfway between him and me. He's got about twenty feet left for par.

"Tough to judge distance in the dark," I say. "It's just astounding that you somehow hit the green on this hole. In the middle of the night!"

"That wasn't my best birdie effort," Don replies, ignoring my let's-look-on-the-bright-side equivocations. "Didn't get it to the hole."

"Pretty tough to judge speed in these conditions."

He's not listening. He's too busy reading the line with his feet—with his broken, misshapen, mismatched feet. The ground is talking to them. And no amount of prosthetic heel lifts or protective padding can stop the message from being heard.

I return to my spot beside the cup and stay quiet. The rest of the world is screaming—the sea, the sky, the land—but I am very still.

Don walks back to his ball. He stands over it for just a second. And then he rocks his shoulders, and then a click, and then it rolls, and then I see it, so round and perfect, like the planet we blessed fools inhabit, coming to me, coming to its home.

When his ball is six feet from the hole, Don Naifeh says something I've never heard him say, not in Scotland, not ever: "Made it."

Six feet later, his ball is in the thirteenth hole of the Burningbush Links.

I shout. I jump. I raise my arms in triumph. "OH, YES! OH, YES!" Don joins me, his arms floating upward on currents of joy. We embrace, with the hole beneath our feet.

"Now tell me you don't believe!" Don says, laughing. "Now tell me!"

We talk of pars in the night, and guiding spirits, and magic happening every second. And then we turn back toward the golf course, the empty links running to the sea, and we say our silent thanks.

I look up at a universe too vast for me to understand, and at my friend standing near my side. I rock from one foot to the other, finding my center. And then I yell like Shivas Irons, not at all afraid that someone might hear me.

Acknowledgments

In Search of Burningbush is in your hands today thanks to the assistance of numerous people, including, among others, James Somerville, John Duncan, Mariana Field-Hoppin, Peter Lederer, A. Sneddon, David Thomson, J. F. Horsfield, Nina Mackie, Rosemary Pettendrigh, Rick MacKenzie, Mickey McLean, Duncan Christy, and Sandrine Pecher. I'm thankful to have had the keen eyes and finely tuned ears of R. Zakaela Othmer attending to the final manuscript copy. Above all, two beautiful advocates were responsible for this book making the leap from writer's dream to published reality: I am eternally grateful that Jennifer Joel and Mark Weinstein had the vision to see what others could not, and I want the world to know that I love them dearly.